THE CUMBERLAND BARD

Robert Anderson of Carlisle 1770-1833

Together with a facsimile copy of the 1828
Ballads in the Cumberland Dialect
by Robert Anderson

Sue Allan

The song beguiles dull Care, at Night's black hour;
Now calls a starting tear from Sorrow's eye;
Then grant me, fate, awhile the soothing pow'r,
To charm the rustic with wild minstrelsy:
If, midst coarse weeds, he find a simple flow'r,
The learned critic's frown I'll proud defy!

(from title page of 'Ballads in the Cumberland Dialect' 1808)

BOOKCASE

Publications by Sue Allan

'Penurious Poets & Ballad Mongers' in *Some Nineteenth Century Ballad Singers & Sellers in Cumberland and Westmorland* (The Ballad Partners, 2019)

'"Staged Authenticity" in folk song performance' in *Old Songs, New Discoveries* (The Ballad Partners, 2019)

'May Day, Morris and more: Morris Dances in Cumbria in the early Twentieth Century', in *The Histories of Morris* (EFDSS/Historical Dance Soc., 2018)

Folk Song in Cumbria: A Distinctive Regional Repertoire? (PhD thesis, 2017, https://lancaster.academia.edu/SAllan)

Greetings from Wigton – A celebration of the town & its people in words and pictures, with foreword by Melvyn Bragg (McMechan, 1999)

Copyright: Sue Allan
First edition 2020
ISBN 978-1-912181-35-3
Published by Bookcase, 19 Castle St., Carlisle, CA3 8SY
01228 544560   bookscumbria@aol.com
Printed by The Amadeus Press.

Contents

*Robert Anderson, The Cumberland Bard: engraving from an
original painting, whose whereabouts are unknown, by George
Sheffield. The portrait was used as a frontispiece in George
Coward's Anderson editions, the first of which appeared in 1866.*

Preface

1770 proved to be a vintage year for poetry in the historic county of Cumberland: it was the year that future Poet Laureate William Wordsworth (1770-1850) was born, but 1770 also saw the birth of Cumbrian vernacular poet Robert Anderson. He was popularly known during his lifetime and ever afterwards as 'the Cumberland Bard'. Although he also wrote in Standard English, the best of Anderson's work is undoubtedly his verse in his native tongue, the dialect of north Cumberland. Inevitably the language restricted the markets he could reach in his own time and possibly even more today. This accounts for Anderson's relative obscurity, especially when compared to his fellow Cumbrian Wordsworth, the touchstone of Romanticism and icon of the Lake District. I hope this book may bring Anderson, the man, the poet and the writer of popular songs, to a wider audience in Cumbria and beyond.

The last edition of his works in print was that of 1904, so the facsimile of the 1828 edition of Anderson's *Cumberland Ballads* incorporated into this volume brings into circulation works which have not been easily available to the reading public for 116 years. Explore them, read them aloud – perhaps consulting the glossary from time to time – and you will soon get your tongue around the words, hear the rhythm of the lines and get a rare glimpse into how Cumbrians lived, loved, worked and played some 200 years ago.

Framed silhouette of Robert Anderson

1. Introduction

The nineteenth century saw a 'multiplication of dialect versifiers' in Cumberland and Westmorland. None were more prolific than Robert Anderson of Carlisle. Despite being born into poverty and with little formal education, he went on to publish a collection of poetry in standard English and popular editions of Cumberland Ballads in dialect. His life and his works give us insights into the working and social life of Carlisle and rural north Cumbria. He left a rich legacy of songs written in both Standard English, for performance at London's Vauxhall Gardens, and of dialect ballads which entered the folk tradition.

Dialect literature has largely lost its significance in regional culture today. It once had a powerful ability to connote ideas of the north, of Cumbria and of a simpler and more stable past, however much of a contrived realism that is. We feel instinctively that working-class dialect is more direct and, like its speaker, perhaps more natural and honest compared with the affectedness of upper-class language.[1] A varied mix of different classes were involved in the production and consumption of dialect verse. Although most of its core writers and audience probably came from the working- and lower-middle classes, it is important to remember that dialect in Cumbria (Cumberland and Westmorland) would have been spoken by many people we might regard as 'middle-class' today. Anderson always also included fulsome dedications to members of the local gentry in his books. Presumably he did this in order to get his work accepted by polite society and through the patronage of notable figures have his books recommended to others in their circle.

Anderson's *Poems on Various Subjects* was published in 1798, the same year as the first edition of William Wordsworth's *Lyrical Ballads*, but whereas Anderson was keen to follow in the footsteps of his hero, Robert Burns, in engaging with and writing about the people around him, most of Wordsworth's verse concerned his first love – nature, and the grand scenery of the Lake District – rather than its inhabitants. In the preface to the second edition in 1800, Wordsworth states that his objective was 'to choose incidents and situations from common life, and to relate or describe them, throughout, as far as was possible in a selection of language really used by men'. However, although *Lyrical Ballads* does feature a few rural characters, nowhere does Wordsworth use the dialect of the people living around him. Neither does he mention what are sometimes called 'peasant and labouring class writers', or 'vernacular poets', who lived and wrote in the county. Nevertheless, both he and Robert Southey are listed as subscribers to Anderson's 1820 *Poetical Works*.

As Michael Baron has noted, if Wordsworth had actually read Anderson's volume of 1805, or any of the dialect poems printed in Carlisle newspapers from 1806, he would have realised that far from being narrowly regional and naïve, many such pieces juxtaposed the local and the national, often mixing verse and prose in sophisticated ways. In fact writers like Burns and Anderson were by no means 'peasant poets'. They both wrote and published works in Standard English as well as dialect, and both poets appeared to delight in what has been termed the 'carnivalesque tradition' of poems about folk festivities which featured a cast of lively characters: 'a swirl of well-dressed farmers, barefoot country lasses, whores, and weaver lads' as well as songs of love and loves lost that had universal appeal.[2]

Cumbria's rich heritage of vernacular literature is as much a part of the region's story as the more exalted writings of the Lake Poets. It is an important expression of regional identity which began to find its voice through the words of poets like Robert Anderson. It can still strike a chord today, as in the final verse of his Cumbrian anthem 'Canny Aul Cummerlan':

Yer buik-larn'd wise gentry, that seen monie counties,
May preach and palaver, and brag as they will
O' mountains, lakes, valleys, woods, watters and meadows,
But canny auld Cummerlan' caps them aw still.

4

2. Dialect literature

Most dictionary definitions of dialect accept that the word describes a variety of language peculiar to a district or class, although there does remain a popular usage which sees the term as implying 'rustic' and 'uneducated'. The situation is, however, rather more nuanced as the idea of any 'spoken standard' form of English only emerged in the eighteenth century after a proliferation of printed materials helped fix London English as a more formal language, with orthographic deviations from the norm branded ideologically abnormal.' Dave Russell, in his book on Northern England, also makes the point that dialects are not debased or incorrect versions of Standard English but 'valid linguistic systems derived from Old English, Norse and Norman roots' possessing their own distinctive accent, vocabulary and grammar. Northern dialects and accents in particular having a central role in reinforcing and constructing a range of ideas about the North.[3]

There was a strong antiquarian interest in dialect in the eighteenth century. As the century progressed there was also a changed cultural perception of the north and its people, as the middle and upper classes came under the influence of Romanticism. The people of the north then became manifestations of the 'noble savage', surrounded in their solitude by a sublime landscape, and speaking an uncorrupted language in harmony with nature. The dialects of central

Cumberland and Westmorland retained many components of their vocabulary and grammar with Old English and the Scandinavian languages, particularly Old Norse, intermingled in the dialects of north Cumberland with elements of Lowland Scots, Scottish English and Northumbrian.[4]

Dialect literature publications of the eighteenth century in Cumberland begin with Josiah Relph of Sebergham (1712-1743), followed by Ewan Clark of Wigton (1734-1811); Charles Graham of Penrith (c.1750-1796); Isaac Ritson of Eamont Bridge (1761-1789); Susanna Blamire (1749-1794) and Catherine Gilpin (1738-1811) from the Carlisle area; Carlisle's Mark Lonsdale (1758-1815), who became a manager at Sadler's Wells theatre in London; blind poet John Stagg (1770-1823) from Burgh by Sands, who ran a library in Wigton for a while well and was also a popular fiddler at country gatherings – and, most prolific of all, Robert Anderson (1770-1833). Far from being 'peasant poets' though, almost all these poets wrote in Standard English as well as Cumberland Dialect – and Scots in the case of Susanna Blamire. The lively and engaging narrative poems about country festivities from the pens of Lonsdale, Stagg and Anderson acquired great popularity and had a longevity throughout the century, while Anderson's songs were performed well into the twentieth century.[5]

Interest in dialects grew as the nineteenth century progressed, developing from earlier Romantic antiquarian roots into the object of study by philologists and linguists. This was not a phenomenon unique to our region, although it did seem to have developed a particularly strong literature of its own. John Russell Smith's 1839 bibliography of 'provincial dialects' lists 64 books from Cumberland and eight from Westmorland. They are mainly of poetry. The earliest was Josiah Relph's

Miscellany of Poems, which was published posthumously in 1747.[6] The influence of Romanticism undoubtedly was a factor in the rise in popularity of these works in dialect, in particular the poetry of Robert Burns whose *Poems, Chiefly in the Scottish Dialect* were published in 1786. Burns was building on a tradition of pastoral writing which goes back much earlier in the eighteenth century to Allan Ramsay. The second wave of nineteenth century dialect 'versifiers' comprised William Dickinson (1798-1882) of Workington, John Rayson (1803-1859) of Carlisle, Whitehaven doctor Alexander Craig Gibson (1813-1874), the St John's in the Vale mason turned school teacher John Richardson (1817-1886), Stanley Martin - 'Gwordie Greenup' (1846-1940s) from Cockermouth and the Denwood family, also of Cockermouth, of whom Jonathan Mawson Denwood (1869-1933) probably has most in common with the earlier writers.

Interestingly, in his preface to *The Folk-Speech of Cumberland and Some Districts Adjacent,* Alexander Craig Gibson makes the sweeping claim that his dialect is a superior 'pure Cumbrian' than the dialect of earlier writers, as 'Miss Blamire, Stagg, Anderson, Rayson and others, have all written their dialect pieces, more or less, in the Scoto-Cumbrian which prevails along the southern side of the west Border'. He also dismisses the dialect of the Furness area as an 'intermixture' of Lake District and Lancashire speech, asserting that his own dialect work, by way of contrast, is the 'unadulterated old Norse-rooted Cumbrian vernacular'. Some 25 years later in the 1893 Coward edition of *Anderson's Cumberland Ballads,* however, despite his reservations on the 'purity' of the language, we find him unstinting in his praise of the poet 'as a portrayer of rustic manners, as a relater of homely incident, as a hander down of ancient customs, and of ways of life fast wearing or worn out, as an exponent of the feelings, tastes, habits, and language of the most interesting class in a most interesting district, and in some other respects, we hold Anderson to be unequalled, not in Cumberland only, but in England.'[7]

By 1907, when Archibald Sparke published his bibliography of dialect literature from the region, he was able to list 158 books wholly or partly in dialect, including thirteen different editions of Robert Anderson's *Cumberland Ballads*.[8] This, Marshall and Walton in their wide-ranging social history of the Lake Counties, refer to as a 'multiplication of Cumbrian dialect versifiers', noting that critical to this flowering of vernacular poetry was of course a literate population able to read it. In fact, literacy levels in the north of England were generally high in the nineteenth century. Cumbria in particular, like Scotland, had an unusually high provision of schools. Anderson's great friend and mentor the schoolmaster and poet Thomas Sanderson remarks in his essay on 'manners and customs' (1820 Anderson edition) that, 'the education of the peasantry has become more general by the erection of new schools; some of which are endowed, and the rest supported by petitionary subscriptions among the inhabitants, or by the quarter-pence of the scholars'. He adds that most 'can read, write, and cast up account.' There were also village reading rooms and most market towns had one or more booksellers by 1829. The growth of the popular press and rise in levels of literacy meant that a literate public which included both rural and urban workers 'celebrated their Cumbrian patriotism by reading, in the printed word, the speech of their forefathers'.[9]

Trying to define dialect production in class terms is

problematic, however, as that while the chief protagonists–
writers, publishers and printers, many of them
auto-didacts–could be described as 'cross-class' or possibly
'artisan class'. In any case, what we might call class strata
were quite flexible and porous in the north Cumberland of
the late eighteenth and early nineteenth century. In a similar
way, the boundary between city and country was less sharply
drawn: 'The urban culture of eighteenth-century England was
more 'rural'… while the rural culture was more rich than we
often suppose.'[10] However, it may be that some of this
regional patriotism appealed to a bucolic past which was
already becoming a memory in parts of the region itself, and
both these poets tend to write retrospectively about a past
viewed through the prism of both nostalgia and Romanticism.
Lonsdale and Anderson were in fact both familiar with
writing for performance in London, as well as for publication,
with Lonsdale a manager at Sadler's Wells and Anderson
writing songs for Vauxhall Gardens.

Most of the writers in the vernacular, the dialect poets of
the eighteenth and nineteenth centuries, celebrate the lives of
Cumbrian 'peasants' and their bucolic festivities, which were
populated by a cast of characters that included dancers,
fiddlers and singers, as, according to Anderson's mentor
Sanderson, music 'generally composes a part of the education
of a Cumbrian peasant'. While it is tempting to think that
lively narrative poems like Anderson's 'Bleckell Murry Neet'
or Lonsdale's 'Th' Upshot' comprise a faithful alternative
social history, describing rural life and times, both poets have
a tendency to write retrospectively about a past viewed
through the prism of nostalgia and Romanticism, and both
framed these works as much for performance as for
publication. It is possible to argue that all dialect is a

performance to some degree, and indeed many so-called 'labouring class poets' or 'peasant poets' found outlets on the stage, especially in Lancashire and Tyneside. As a competent musician and performer, Anderson's real strengths are in his song writing, producing work which continued to be performed into the twentieth century.[11]

Anderson's language is a lightly marked form of dialect, presumably moderated with the intention of reaching as wide an audience as possible, with a view to selling more books.

In much the same way, recent scholarship has illuminated our view of Robert Burns's language, which it is claimed is a form of 'stage Scots' – a hybrid language using linguistic stereotypes like 'lass', 'lad', 'guid', 'auld' and 'lang', which were widely-known and used in eighteenth century 'Scotch songs'. This of course meant that he could reach a wider audience in England. This does beg the question as to why Anderson's songs in modified Cumbrian dialect, apart from the few songs published in *The Universal Songster*, have not achieved national recognition and popularity on the same scale as Burns's songs. The answer may lie in the relative qualities of the two poets' work: Anderson often aims to emulate Burns but does not always succeed. In addition, Burns's oeuvre is deemed a national one, whilst Anderson's is perceived as merely regional, and was, therefore, little published outside the region.

3. 'Memoir of the Life of the Author': Anderson in his own words

It's sweet to reflect on the days o yen's youth,
If rear'd to religion, industry, an truth;
We spworts cud enjoy, but nae harm did to yen,
Sec innocent teymes fwok can scerce see agen!'

The Author on Himself, Anderson's
Cumberland Ballads, 1893

Robert Anderson's memoir of his own life appeared in Volume I of the two-volume 1820 edition of his *Poetical Works*. Thomas Sanderson had originally been asked to provide the biography, along with the notes, glossary and essay on Cumbrian 'character, manners and customs' included in the book, However, he says in an introductory note that he had to write to Anderson for details of his early years, but what the author sent back was 'so copious and interesting a narrative, and is written in a style of such unaffected simplicity and openness, that the reader will not regret to find it supplying the place of my intended Memoir'. Given this illustrious precedent, it would seem appropriate to do the same, so the account of Anderson's life and times here is his own, followed by just a few explanatory notes.

'At six o'clock, on the snowy morning of February 1st, 1770, I beheld the light of this wild world; and first drew breath at the Dam Side, parish of St. Mary, in the suburbs of this antient city; a poor little tender being, scarce worth the trouble of rearing. OLD ISBEL, the midwife, who had assisted at the birth of thousands, entertained many fears that I was only sent to peep around me, shed tears, and leave them. Accordingly, "Ere twelve times I'd seen the light, to the church they hurried me": and I have sometimes had reason to exclaim, Oh! that near my fathers they that day had buried me!

'The youngest of nine children, born of parents getting up in years, whom poverty had with all their kindred kept in bondage, knowing only hard labour and crosses; well do I remember the fond caresses of my beloved mother. Oft did I get the halfpenny to spend, that could ill be spared, besides experiencing indulgences unknown to my brothers and sisters. Mankind ought to condemn this blind prejudice of parents, in favour of any child; especially, as it happens among the wealthy, as well as the industrious poor, that the youngest or the most idle is ofttimes the greatest favourite. On the other hand, harsh treatment ought carefully to be avoided; since we find it drive many to wretchedness, prostitution, and the gallows.

'At an early age, I was placed in a Charity School; supported at that time by the Dean and Chapter of Carlisle, for children only. Blessed be the Institutors and encouragers of such seminaries; who place the offspring of the labouring classes in the true road to knowledge and to happiness in a future state! Still do I remember the neat dress, slow speech, placid countenance, may every feature of good old Mrs. Addison, the teacher; who might probably be related to the immortal author of "Cato," and "The Spectator;" but unlike him who published to the world lessons of wisdom, she only gave instructions in reading and plain sewing: yet as Shenston observes, "Right well she knew each temper to descry."

'Having studied my letters, the see-saw drone of the "Primer," and waded through the "Reading Made Easy," and "Dyche's Spelling Book;" I was now turned over to a long, lean, needy pretender to knowledge; and under him I learned to write. His figure was similar to that of the mad knight of La Mancha; (never have I perused Cervantes' inexhaustible treasury of humour, without having my tutor in view); and under him, "Free from the rod I spent those happy days." Impelled, probably, by necessity, he devoted so much time to angling that his few poor starved-looking beings were shamefully neglected. As for me, learning could not be considered a toil. He always selected me to accompany him up the banks of Eden or Caldew, for a double purpose: First, proud was I to carry for my master the speckled trout, small flounder, or silver fry: and if disappointed, I was employed gathering colt's foot, bittany, ground-ivy, and various herbs, according to his instructions. These he used as substitutes for tea; being forced by poverty, like too many, to what he otherwise would have despised. As he, at all times, shewed a great fondness for me, I am led to suppose, it was during our Summer excursions, that an attachment to rural scenery first stole over my youthful mind. The love of nature, where she seems to say, "Behold me, man, in all my wild attire!" which grew with me from that period to manhood; and the dearest wish of my heart has ever been, to creep into retirement, where, in peace, I might strike the weak strings of my harp, a few years before life's closing scene.

'At this period a circumstance took place which endangered my life. Being detained at school later than my comrades, on crossing a few stones placed in a part of the river Caldew, my foot slipped, and I fell unseen into the deep. Fortunately, an old woman, whose face and figure are still before me; in getting a pail of water, beheld the weak, plunging, or rather sinking victim; and with difficulty I was saved. My mother shed tears over her drenched child, and I was ordered to bed till my clothes were dried: for such was the poverty of the family, I could not reckon more than one suit at a time.

'My parents, who could not only read, but delighted in reading, finding I did not make a progress equal to their sanguine expectations, placed me under Mr. Isaac Ritson, in the Quaker's school: but in a few weeks, that learned and ingenious man left the city for a short time. He was born at Eamont Bridge, near Penrith, in 1761; and such was his progress in learning, that at nine years of age, he had made a great proficiency in the Greek language. As a proof of the acuteness of his ideas, he understood the propositions of Euclid almost on the first perusal. At the age of sixteen, he commenced teaching in Carlisle; and although much esteemed by the inhabitants, he resigned his school about two years afterwards. His poetical attempts discover a wild imagination; but harmony seems not to have engrossed much of his attention: indeed we seldom find a talent for poetry and mathematics in any person. For some time he studied medicine in Edinburgh; and there formed an intimacy with the celebrated Dr. Brown; whose eccentricity of manners bore a strong similarity to his own. He next proceeded to London, where he lived by his literary labours, principally a reviewer in periodical works; and there published a translation of "Homer's Hymn to Venus." In an obscure lodging, at Islington, he departed this life, aged 27 years.

'Among our neighbours was a decent industrious old woman, born in the Highlands of Scotland: proud did I feel to run her errands; and at her fireside I spent many a winter evening, delighted beyond measure, with the wild Scottish ballads which she taught me, while labouring at her wheel. Gilderoy, Johnny Armstrong, Sir James the Ross, Lord Thomas and fair Annette, The Duke of Gordon and his three daughters, Barbary Allan, and Binorie, were my greatest favourites. From this cheerful, kind-hearted, well-informed creature, I imbibed the love of song, which has to the present day so particularly engaged my attention.

'My parents now felt happy in placing me under my last and best tutor, Mr. Walter Scott; a learned and truly respectable character. He was born at Archer Beck Side, Cannobie, Dumfriesshire; and like many, felt anxious in early life, to court the smiles of coy fortune in another country; conscious, no doubt, that virtue when combined with industry, would obtain a just reward. He has now been a teacher in Carlisle, upwards of 54 years; esteemed by all ranks, in the town and neighbourhood... His religious principle, modest demeanor, and strict attention to his numerous pupils, will cause his name to be revered, long after he has sunk to the silent tomb. As a tutor, he will seldom be equalled; and never could this antient city boasts of one-more anxious to check those under his care; when he justly supposed them in pursuit of what might in the end lead to ruin. He was a bitter enemy to noise, sloth, filth, idleness; or whatever might draw the mind from virtue: but always shewed a just partiality to such as paid proper attention to their school duties.

'The death of an amiable wife and daughter naturally caused in this venerable teacher, now in his eighty second year, a depression of spirits; and, without doubt, occasioned numerous infirmities, that have now forced him to give up a profession, which long afforded delight to himself and others. His chief amusement during his leisure hours was reading;

and when the weather permitted, he enjoyed a great pleasure in angling; an exercise that injures the health of too many, in all countries. Under this worthy friend to mankind, I made a considerable progress in arithmetic, though to this necessary branch of education, I always felt a strong aversion, and would much rather have pursued the study of grammar, of which I never attained any exact knowledge: but one of the leading duties of a child, is, to bow to the will of his parents; and that duty, my friends well know, I felt a pleasure in fulfilling. It now affords, on reflection, the most unalloyed happiness I enjoy, or wish for.

'Not long after this, I experienced the greatest loss hitherto known, in the death of an attentive and affectionate mother. "I hear her voice, I see her pale hand wave, To check the errors in a thinking child." She was of a consumptive habit, and reduced to that of a skeleton, by a painful and lingering illness. Her sufferings, even now draw forth many a tear; and my prayer is, that mine may be borne with the same degree of Christian fortitude. This shock greatly affected our numerous family; and although the sound of the earth on a parent's coffin is often soon forgotten by youth, yet a long course of years has not been able to erase the impression from my mind.

I think of eve's long wish'd-for hours,
When joyous home from school I flew,
And with affection's dearest kiss,
My arms around her neck I threw:
Tho' luxury our board ne'er grac'd,
'Midst poverty content was giv'n
And all that wealth or wisdom boast,
Are nought, without this boon of Heav'n?

'About the expiration of my tenth year, it was judged necessary for me to quit the school, and earn a little by hard labour, wherewith to assist a poor father, now become infirm. Although my stock of learning was trifling, yet I felt exceedingly rejoiced at the proposal; for, being of a timid disposition, I always crept to school, trembling, like a culprit going to receive punishment. My first labour was under a brother, a calico printer; and at the end of the week, well do I remember the happiness it afforded to present my wages (one shilling and sixpence) to a beloved father.

'From infancy I was fond of drawing, particularly animals, and to this amusement my evenings were chiefly devoted, "From trifles simple, man's pure pleasures spring." These rude efforts, besides putting a few pence in my pocket, caused me to be looked up to by my companions, as petty artists would to a Gilpin; and also enabled me to procure occasionally from a library the works of Addison, Pope, Fielding, and Smollet; but the perusal of poetry afforded the greatest pleasure. Since arriving at the years of manhood, I have frequently smiled, on beholding in a cottage or farmhouse, many of my juvenile attempts at drawing. Being self-taught, they discover industry; but not the dawnings of genius.

'My next change was, to be bound apprentice to a pattern drawer; and in November, 1783, I cheerfully commenced the study of that business under a truly respectable concern, T. Losh & Co., Denton Holme, near Carlisle; where I enjoyed all the happiness an industrious youth could hope for, being treated with every mark of esteem. At this time I also turned my thoughts to the delightful science of music; and my father purchased me a german flute for which he undoubtedly gave all he could raise. This has soothed my harrassed mind, during

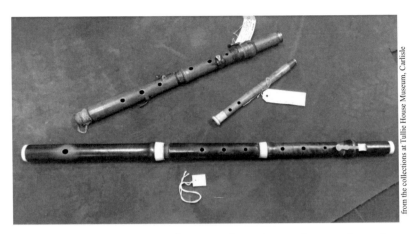

Anderson's instruments: a flute, a tabor pipe and part of another flute. The collection of his instruments also includes a clarinet, which Anderson became interested in after hearing one played in church.

many an hour of sorrow, but my greatest joy was to please a parent, who delighted in old Scottish airs. "Ev'n age itself is cheer'd with music." Such was my fondness for that instrument, I soon made progress sufficient to enable me to amuse my friends, neighbours, and those who enjoyed an evening's walk on the banks of Eden or Caldew.

'From childhood, a love of rural life grew with me; and I let slip few opportunities of spending the sabbath in some village, particularly during the Summer. It was on paying a welcome visit at a friend's house, that I was first smitten with female charms; which then seemed greater to me than I can now describe. Picture to yourself a diffident youth in his sixteenth year, daily pouring out the sighs of a sincere heart, for an artless rosy cottager, somewhat younger than myself. "She was all my thoughts by day, And all my dreams by night; At church, she drew my attention from the preacher, and great was my mortification, if she happened to be absent on my visit to the neighbourhood, On her, "I could have gaz'd my soul away," and such was my passion, I had a thousand times fancied to myself our joining hands at the Hymenical altar. Had my income, which was then barely sufficient to afford the necessities of life, been adequate to my wishes, I would cheerfully have made a tender of my services to her who was more dear to me than wealth is to the miser.

'My leisure hours, during some years, were chiefly devoted to reading and music; pursuits which in youth or age are truly commendable. Companions I sought but few, yet they were virtuous, and worth a friend's remembrance.

'Prior to the expiration of my apprenticeship, I was engaged to serve five years in London; the thought of which was pleasing, as it promised fair to lead to improvement in that profession which to me has now become useless; being unable to gain employment in the united kingdoms. Unfortunately, I had pledged my word to serve a deceitful wretch, whom necessity compelled another as well as myself to arrest for wages, earned by long study and close application. The distress, occasioned by the villainy of my employer, beggars all description. I was for some months confined to a wretched garden from which I seldom durst venture; and but for the kindness shewn by a sister, my life must have been forfeited to want and misery. Fortunately I got employment under but as amiable as the other was wicked: his kindness was like that of a parent; he proved more the companion than a master.

'Whilst residing in the metropolis, my greatest pride was that of visiting Westminster Abbey; and it would afford me equal pleasure, were I now a resident in that proud city. Mr. Addison justly observes, "When we read the dates of the tombs of some that died yesterday, and others six hundred years ago, we cannot help considering that great day, when we shall all of us be contemporaries; and make our appearance before our awful Judge together." To gaze on the works of Roubiliac, or Nollekens, must indeed excite the admiration of every one possessed of common feelings.

'In the year 1794, being at Vauxhall Gardens for the first time, I happened luckily to fall in with a pleasant youth, whose appearance was truly respectable. We felt equally disgusted with many of the songs, written in a mock pastoral Scottish style: and supposing myself capable of producing what might by the public be considered equal, or perhaps superior, on the following day I wrote four, viz. "Lucy Gray of Allendale," "I sigh for the Girl I adore," "The lovely brown Maid," and "Ellen and I." "Lucy Gray" was my first attempt at poetical composition; and was suggested from hearing a Northumbrian rustic relate the story of the unfortunate lovers. She was the toast of the neighbouring villagers; and to use the simple language of my Northumbrian friend, "Monie a smart canny lad wad hae game far efter dark, aye through fire and water, just to get a luik at her." James Walton, a neighbouring farmer's son, from his wonderful agility as a dancer, was the proud hero who won Lucy's affections: but "disease, the canker worm," preyed on her damask cheek; and this blooming bud of innocence died in her seventeenth year. James seldom spoke afterwards; but haunted her grave, or a favourite seat, their place of meeting, in a dell, near a rivulet; and ere long, according to request, he was laid by the side of his Lucy.

'The above mentioned songs, with several others, I offered to my friend, Mr. Hook, a composer of celebrity. They were set to music by him; and my first poetic effusion was sung by Master Phelps, at Vauxhall, in 1794, with great applause, and loudly encored. The others also obtained the flattering approbation of the public; to the great joy of the author. For my services, he granted me free admission to that delightful scene of amusement; visited by the first ranks in London, and the neighbourhood.

'About this time, I frequently attempted to write: on a smaller scale than any other person had done. By candlelight, and without the aid of glasses, I wrote the Lord's Prayer, Creed, Ten Commandments, a short Psalm, and my name, on the size of a sixpence; which was given to a worthy friend, Mr. PALMER, of Drury Lane Theatre. I also wrote the Lord's Prayer, twelve times, on the same size; now in the possession of a lady, whose kindness was beyond all expectation, Mrs. Howard, of Corby Castle. It was then my intention to write the whole of the New Testament, which, with ease, I could have produced on a sheet of paper, twenty two inches square; but finding this would engross the hours of leisure for some years, I declined the undertaking.

'My poor father, whom I had regularly supported, now paid me an unexpected, but pleasing visit. He was then in his seventy-sixth year; but walked from Carlisle to London in six days, a distance of 301 miles. Although tears of joy streamed down the cheeks of each on meeting, yet it was with great difficulty. I prevailed on him to remain a fortnight; for he could not bear the noise and bustle of London: he accordingly returned to Carlisle, in seven days, highly delighted, I feel it impossible to write concerning him without shedding a tear; for the greatest happiness I enjoy, now in life's decline, is the reflection of having fulfilled my duty to him, whom I saw laid in his grave, in Autumn, 1807. Would to God, all who have it in their power would act in a similar manner to a helpless parent!

'During the latter part of the time spent in London, I enjoyed pleasure in the society of both sexes. Until my arrival in the metropolis, I had not seen a play performed; although from my boyish years, the works of our dramatic authors yielded me great delight; the Theatres Royal, particularly Drury Lane, I visited whenever my pocket would permit. A friend, already mentioned, frequently supplied me with orders; but diffidence ofttimes prevented me from requesting that which afforded him pleasure to give.

'In October, 1796, I bade adieu to friends, and the metropolis, merely at the request of an aged parent. His letters stated him to be unhappily situated; and duty, from infancy, still prompted me to obey him. An offer of employment was held out by Lamb, Scott, Foster, & Co. Carlisle; this I accepted. The situation thus obtained in my native place, proved in every sense as agreeable as man could desire. I experienced from friends, who became numerous, every proof of esteem. In 1798, ambition led me, like too many of my brother scribblers, to publish a volume of poems, printed by John Mitchell, and dedicated to J. C. Curwen, Sq. M. P. From this publication I received little more than dear-bought praise; for numerous subscribers yet stand indebted to me.

'Already have I adverted to the pleasures rural life afforded; and my attention to the manners of the Cumbrian peasantry was now greater than ever. My only poetical delight has been the study of nature; and pleased am I, when my Muse appears in her rustic dress. She has occasionally visited my lowly shed, arrayed in the mock trappings of grandeur; but that only called forth a smile, instead of thanks, from the humble Bard. In December,1801, an attempt was made to amuse the reader, by publishing a ballad in the Cumbrian dialect, (BETTY BROWN;) and the praise bestowed by many, but particularly that of a respectable and learned friend, Mr. THOMAS SANDERSON, encouraged me to other attempts in the same species of poetry; till at length a number of these pieces were produced, sufficient to form a volume, which was sent to the press under the title of "Cumberland Ballads," at the urgent request of my above-mentioned friend, who was so kind as to furnish notes to it. This publication did not a tall improve my finances; much of the subscription money was lost; and what was received was barely sufficient to defray the expences attending it. The work, however, becoming somewhat popular, the edition was soon exhausted; and a new impression was sent into the world, from the press of Mr. Hetherton, of Wigton, who purchased the copy-right. In 1808, another, and I am sorry to say, an incorrect edition, was published.

'Prior to the second edition, I departed from Carlisle, March 20th, at the earnest intreaties of a friend; having the promise of a more lucrative situation, at Brookfield, in the neighbourhood of Belfast. On reaching Dumfries, great was my anxiety to pay the tributary tear at the tomb of nature's Bard, ROBERT BURNs; whose fame will increase, whilst literary merit has its admirers. It was this alone which induced me to prefer a journey through Scotland, to a short sail from Maryport. The morning was so tempestuous, that it was with difficulty a friend conducted me to the corner where his remains were deposited. The deep snow hid the narrow mound, and the flat stone laid over it; but the trodden pathway shewed the respect paid by strangers to the Bard's memory. The humble inscription did not certainly do his genius any degree of justice., I read it with disgust; and with a heart-felt sigh, accompanied by a tear, plucked some grass from his grave, which yet remains in my possession. My kind, lamented friend, politely introduced me to Mrs. Burns; who was pleased to place me on the chair where the departed favourite of Scotia sang his "wood note wild." Her situation seemed comfortable; her dress plain, but neat: and I could not help inwardly exclaiming, O that mankind had paid more attention to him by whom future ages will be amused—I wrote a few lines on visiting his tomb; but finding it impossible to do justice to my feelings, the effusion was never shewn. My Muse accompanied me, notwithstanding the inclemency of the season; and during.my pedestrian journey, amid heath-covered hills, clad with snow, "The Mountain Boy," and "The Vale of Elva," were written: the first of which was published immediately on my arrival in Belfast.

'Owing to the times, and a want of spirit in the proprietors of Brookfield, the print-works were closed, in less than two years. During that period I had published much in the Belfast newspaper; which led me to enjoy the society of some literary characters, but too many pretenders to merit. An adieu to Erin was written, and about to be published, when I met with an unexpected engagement, at Carnmoney, six miles from Belfast. My lodging here was at a retired farmhouse, with a peaceable family; but where the scenery of a barren country to a native of Carlisle was extremely unpleasant.

'It is much to be lamented, that no provision whatever is held out by the British Government, to the poor of Ireland. The scenes daily witnessed were to me distressing; yet, while suffering all a human being could bear, I never found them sunk into a state of melancholy. Cheerfulness and hospitality are the characteristics of the country; and may such be the case while the Emerald Isle produces a Shamrock! Duty soon led me to share my income, with the wretched and helpless; which, my friends well know, added no little to the happiness of many, and afforded me true pleasure. Charity balls, as they are termed, were frequently held; and at these I collected considerable sums, which, without doubt, saved numbers from the grave. Subscriptions were liberally attended to at the printworks, whenever they were deemed necessary; not only for the wretched families employed there, but for the helpless throughout the neighbourhood. On these occasions, I was uniformly appointed collector; and I still pray for the happiness of my fellow workmen, whose benevolence will seldom be equalled. Notwithstanding my continual anxiety to serve my brethren in a strange country, I frequently experienced the most base acts of ingratitude; even my life, indeed, has been threatened by those whom I never offended!

'The many narrow escapes I have had, are truly singular: one of them may be stated. About the year 1805, a clergyman, whom I had respected from my childhood, and would have done any thing to serve him, snapped a pistol at my head, across a small table; without the least provocation. This happened in Carlisle, in the presence of several persons. °During the many years spent in the land of cheerefulness, I own, my foibles too often led to misery. Whether prince, peer, prelate, or peasant, every mortal suffers justly for indulging in weaknesses; and these frequently lead to repentance when too late. Calico printing having been on the decline for some years, throughout Ireland, my return to England became necessary: and in the beginning of March, I left Belfast; anxious to see old friends and the place of my nativity. I sailed in the Lion, and landed at Whitehaven, after a speedy and pleasant passage. Such joy it afforded me, to tread on British ground, that I could have kneeled down, and kissed the earth, amidst the multitude assembled on the quay.

'On entering Carlisle, my surprise at the improvements made throughout all parts of this ancient city, was beyond description. Few persons, on returning to the place of their nativity, have experienced more kindness; not only from the companions of youth or manhood, but from rich and poor, to me unknown. In consequence of my return, a dinner was ordered at Mr. Gibson's, the Grey Goat; at which a numerous and respectable party attended. Mr. Henry Pearson, Solicitor, whose humour has amused all classes, was appointed president; and the evening was spent in a festive manner, which afforded a pleasant morning's reflection.

'At that time, without any prospect of happiness, save what St. Mary's workhouse might afford, my friends advised me to publish. Diffidence would have prevented me from making such an attempt, had not necessity forced me to it. A Committee was appointed, who have used every exertion to ensure my happiness in the winter of life; and the same anxiety has been shewn by many throughout various parts of the kingdom. In publishing this simple Memoir of one "unknown to fame, "I consider it my duty to give thanks to MR, ROBERT PERRING, Editor of the Carlisle Patriot, for the activity he has shewn in correcting the work for the press. His kindness can only be forgotten, when memory forsakes me. My only wish is to leave the noise of the town, and in retirement to pillow my head in peace with mankind. Sweet is solitude, where around Nature opens her wide field for contemplation. Thus situated, the heart acquires patience, and the mind becomes accustomed to think; for we there behold the grandeur of the great Creator's works. This harmonizes the soul, leaving an ecstacy of bliss, unknown to the millions who glory in society.'

It might be useful to gloss Anderson's account of his life with some additional observations at this point. It is interesting to note, for example, that both his parents could both read and write and were keen for their youngest son to be educated, and that his teacher at the Quaker School, Isaac Ritson (1761–1789), who wrote *Copy of a letter, written by a young shepherd, to his friend in Borrowdale*, which is held to be the first published prose in Cumberland dialect - although his brief time teaching in Carlisle pre-dates its publication in 1788. His interest in songs and music were evident from a very early age, and he seems to have played the flute throughout his life. His songwriting success at London's Vauxhall Gardens, the foremost pleasure garden in the capital, will be explored in another chapter.

His artistic talents meanwhile stood him in good stead when he went out to work in the local textile industry, drawing patterns for calico printing blocks for Losh & Co. Calico printing began in Carlisle around 1760 with the firm of Scott, Lamb & Co, according to Jollie's 1811 *Cumberland Guide*. By the time Anderson was going out to work there would have been mills and warehouses all along the River Caldew to the south and west of Carlisle. Losh & Co's cotton stampery at Denton Holme in Carlisle was founded by Thomas Losh, whose brothers also traded as calico and cotton printers. A notable Whig family, the Loshes were good friends of the Curwens and the Howards, to whom dedications appear in a number of Anderson's books.

The first edition of *Ballads in the Cumberland Dialect,* in 1805, is dedicated to Colonel Henry Howard of Corby Castle, commander-in-chief of the Loyal Cumberland Rangers, the Right Honourable Thomas Wallace and Major Sir Wilfrid Lawson. The period 1803 to 1815 was the height of the Napoleonic Wars, a time when the threat of invasion by Napoleonic forces was very real. Local militias were set up throughout England, comprising both regular county militias and 'irregular' militias or volunteer forces raised by members of the local gentry, which acted as a kind of Home Guard. Surprisingly, Anderson does not mention his membership of the local militia, in his memoir, although his activities with the Volunteer Band and the Loyal Edenside (later Cumberland) Rangers do feature in the extant pages of his diary 1801-1803. His poem 'The Invasion', written on December 20 1803 and published in his first edition of his *Ballads in the Cumberland Dialect* in 1805 clearly shows the mood of the times:

> How fens te, Dick? There's fearfu' news—
> Udsbreed! the French are comin!
> There's nought at Carel but parades,
> And sec a drum, drum, drummin:
> The volunteers and brigadiers
> Are aw just mad to meet them;
> And England e'en mun hing her head,
> If Britons dunnet beat them.
>
> Then there's the Rangers aw in green,
> Commanded by brave HOWARD—
> Of aw his nowble kin, nit yen
> Was iver caw'd a coward;—
> They'll pop the French off leyke steyfe,
> If e'er they meet, I'll bail them:
> Wi' sec true Britons at their heads,
> True courage cannot fail them.

The period of around ten years when he lived and worked in Northern Ireland, taking the long way round to

Belfast by travelling through south west Scotland, determined to visit the grave in Dumfries of his hero Robert Burns. Burns remained a lifelong influence on him: an illustrious forerunner both as a writer in the vernacular, a song writer par excellence and a celebrated poet in literary circles – all objectives to which Anderson aspired. His first engagement in Northern Ireland was at the linen works at Brookfield in County Antrim, some fifteen miles north-west of Belfast, and after that closed down he moved on to the Carnmoney Cotton Printing Works, slightly closer to Belfast, where he was employed until his employer's death in 1818. He was, by all accounts, a skilled and able workman, producing good wood blocks for printing but becoming aware of the poverty in which some of his fellow workers lived and the lack of support they received, he soon became known and well-liked for his generosity, his campaigning for better conditions and the charitable gatherings he organised.

While living in the province he became friendly with local writers like Andrew Mackenzie and Samuel Thomson and wrote poems which appeared in the *Belfast News-Letter* and *Commercial Chronicle,* as well as in Alexander Mackey's Belfast anthology of *Poems on Various Subjects* in 1810. Some of Anderson's Belfast pieces were also included in his own *Poetical Works* in 1820, including a number dedicated to 'Maria of the Cottage', a certain Mrs Munster, formerly Marrianne Kenley, who was herself a writer: her novel *The Cottage of the Apennines; or, the Castle of Novina: a Romance* was published in Belfast in 1806. Carlisle Library's collection of Anderson manuscripts includes a number of letters he wrote to 'Maria' or 'Marianne', mostly discussing her writings, about which he was enthusiastic. He seems to have attended soirées at her home, which he calls 'the cottage of literature'. On one occasion, bemoaning the fact that a bad leg prevents him from walking over to her house, he says: 'I draw a little, and flute a little, and groan a little, and doctor a little, and eat a little, and talk a little, and read a little and study a little, and scribble a little, and sleep a little, thus pass the hours away.' In recent years these letters were transcribed by Anderson's 5 x great niece Joan Williams. The bound manuscripts appear to be in Anderson's best hand, perhaps intended as a souvenir for himself of a romantic friendship? Although he addresses Maria as 'Dearest of women' on one occasion and signs 'Yours affectionately' sometimes there is, however, no suggestion of any relationship beyond friendship. On the contrary, we often find him writing in the letters about his illnesses, complaining about 'the sting of poverty' and generally seeming to be depressed and full of self-pity – attitudes all evident in his diary of a few years earlier.

attended with the Con Side Rangers; at
the Castle; afterwards in the Bitts where
a concourse of people were assembled to
see the shooting Match for prizes given by
Mr Howard. The first 10 - 6 and a knife
won by R Bonstead. The second 5 won by
Jos Foster. Got tipsey like all the rest
in the evening.

31. Walked to Cummersdale in the morny.
Spent the afternoon in idleness. — Supped
with the Band, and a few friends in the
at Fosters; and played in the new year
wrote to Jack Coulby, and Miss Markyile

Jany 1 - 1802. Began the new year
with working all day. — Called on in
the evening by a smart female, wishing
me to make one of a party. Would to God
she had been acquainted, or ten years
younger; then would this have been a
happy night. — Am sorry for Mrs
Johnston who was ill all day: good
creature I wish sincerely she were well
again for the sake of her small family.
— Spent a pleasant evening with and
drank tea with Miss N—

2. A rambler all day. — Heard of
the ring being lost, with a letter by entrusted
to the care of I loop Esqr; and know not
how to apologise for his negligence in the
extraordinary affair. — Drank tea with M.
and played at — during the
evening settled with Mr Gate behaved
more like a friend than otherwise

*Page of Anderson's diary showing the end of December 1801
and a hopeful start to January 1802 'Began the new year
with working all day…'.*

4. Fragments of diary 1801-1803

At last, aw the play-things of youth thrown aseyde,
Now luive, whope, an ear, still the days did diveyde,
As wi' restless ambition leyfe's troubles began;

The Author on Himself', Cumberland Ballads 1893

Additional light is thrown on both the character of Anderson and his daily life in the extant manuscript of his diary which runs sporadically from October 25 1800 to October 25 1803. Overall, most entries appear to have been written in autumn and winter those years, although whether this was because he was busy with other things at other times, or was ill or depressed we do not know. Nor is it clear that he kept a diary throughout his life, of which these are the only surviving fragments. Interestingly, none of the later commentators in collections of Anderson's work mention the diary, so perhaps it had been kept private by members of Anderson's family for a period after his death. A book plate with the name 'Mrs Purdie' on it, found in the box which houses the Anderson manuscripts at the Jackson Library, backs up this theory, as the Anderson artefacts held at Tullie House Museum were donated by the Purdie family.

The daily life we glimpse in these fragments is not always an edifying spectacle, as we often find him out drinking heavily and suffering the inevitable ill-effects the following day. On February 6 1802, for example, the entry reads simply 'Spent the day in intoxication' and in Sunday November 7 he records he was 'Very ill from the Debauch of last night'. His father, we learn, is quite sick and Anderson, while most willingly to attend to him, often seems to be suffering from depression – not least because of his poverty. On Christmas Day 1800 he writes:

> 'Arose without one coin in my pocket; and doubt this will be the poorest week I have known since I first joined the social pleasures of Christmas; and I had promised myself to spend a week's happiness; hoping for the payment of money due for teaching, to have discharged everything , and rested in peace. But he who trusts tomorrow deserves to go without it if it be in his power to provide today...'

In the diary we also meet his friends and acquaintances, those with whom he socialised at the inn and Harmonic Society gatherings, his fellow members of the (Eden Rangers/Cumberland Rangers) Volunteer Band and the more genteel circle of acquaintances he mixed with at literary soirées and teas - an example of the latter being Miss Catherine Gilpin, a close friend of the late 'Muse of Cumberland', Susanna Blamire. At a party on Tuesday December 8 in 1801 Miss Gilpin 'freely sang me some of her own excellent comic songs', and on the same occasion he also inspected 'Thomson's boasted collection of Scottish songs harmonized by Haydn, Pleyel and Kogeleich', which included songs by Blamire. In September 1801 he spent an evening at Jossie's inn – a regular haunt – 'where singing, dancing and the flute kept all alive'.

Musical activities seem to absorb much of his leisure time, in particular the 'Harmonic' or sometimes 'Philo-Harmonic': the local Harmonic Society, which organised small gatherings of amateur musicians and singers. The meetings could be very jolly, but at other times were evidently no great source of pleasure: on October 24 1803 he 'Met a jovial few at the Harmonic, where the song, dance, tune and jokes went off merrily' but a few months later on February 14 1803, saw the audience participation getting somewhat out of hand late in the evening: 'all were stupid, except when obscenity was started, then, like a pack of dogs in full cry, all gave mouth. Such are Societies in general, where instead of mental improvement, the morals of raw unthinking youth are frequently corrupted...'

The entries for 1802 are the most complete, shedding light on his musical activities with Harmonic and the Volunteer Band, including marches he composed for them. There is general socialising, some work drawing patterns – which he seems to be doing on a freelance basis at home – as well as the usual attempts to write poems and persistent efforts to court publishers and get his work published in the hopes of bringing in some much-needed income:

Jan. 23 Wrote to Soulby [Penrith printer]

Jan. 29 Read the song I have given to Jollie and published in his journal, written by Mrs Dugald Stewart. Quite sick of myself and tired of the world, finding that my expenditure still exceeds my income.

Jan. 30 Called on Crito [Thomas Sanderson] and made some musical arrangements…
Wrote to Mr Howard in London requesting instruments for the Band

Feb. 6 Spent an agreeable hour with Mr Str——g. Received a

letter together with 30s [30/-] for the Edenside Rangers Slow and Quick March from my friend Thompson, who tells me it is the last letter he will be able to write, as he finds himself at Death's door

Feb. 10 Met the Band at Willy Law's where we spent a pleasant evening

Feb. 12 Received twelve copies of "Mary", one of my songs set by Mr Thompson, who likewise sent me some Proposals of an intended Musical Publication by subscription, to consist of six songs, by Burns and myself.

Feb. 20 Composed a March. Called it Col. Howard. Wrote to Penrith with some songs.

Mar. 9 Saw Soulby from Penrith who brought me a Song by Dibdin. Spent a pleasant evening with him at the Har. [Harmonic]. To receive from him a collection of the most popular songs.

May 23 Sunday. Join'd in our party by Mr How, and a Mr Dand, both men of good sense. Went to church, where I heard for the first time a clarinet accompany the vocal but uncultivated melodists, and was not a little pleased with the effect it produced – cannot help thinking two Bassoons and two Clarinets, with the four vocal parts, would be more solemn to my ear… [It seems Anderson was sufficiently impressed with the clarinet to purchase one himself, as there is one in the collection of his instruments – two flutes and a tin whistle, at Tullie House Museum]

May 25 Attended the Har. Boustead Pres. [probably a reference to him being 'President' or chairman for the evening], a pleasant company, but no singers.

Aug. 29 Received a letter from Newcastle with a number of songs and music by Thomson.

Sept. 1 Requested to draw some Patterns for Barrow of

Kendal. Spent the evening at Jossie's, where singing, dancing and the flute kept all alive.

Sept. 13 Attempted a Song, which only served as a lighter to my pipe.

Oct. 16 Rec'd my yearly sum of £10 from my employers which will tend to make me happy by paying off my debts.

Oct. 20 Drank tea at Miss Gilpin's where Dr and Mrs Harrington, Miss Mitchinson, Mrs Mitchell, Miss Pearson, Miss Ward, Miss Addison, Miss Hodson and Mrs P were of the party; experienced more freedom from all than expected, being the only plebeian in company. Sung some of my late Cumberland Songs, which gave great pleasure.

Nov. 7 Very ill from the Debauch of last night

In 1802 Anderson was living in Lowthians Lane, lodging with Mr and Mrs Johnston, former travelling actors who went on to become inn-keepers - until Mr Johnston was imprisoned for debt. This is all documented by Mrs Charlotte Johnston (1768–1859), later Mrs Deans, in her wonderfully detailed and evocative autobiography *Memoirs Of The Life Of Mrs. Charlotte Deans* in 1837.[12] When he was released from debtors' prison in 1802, in order to support their large and growing family, Johnston went to work in Jollie's printing office while Charlotte took in mending and washing. They also took in a lodger, Robert Anderson, who, Charlotte writes, 'proved himself a friend when the hour of distress again overtook me'. The hour of need was the sickness (probably TB) which laid them both low for some weeks with fever and delirium. Charlotte eventually recovered, distraught to learn that her husband had died. As he had been a Mason, she hoped for help from the 'Brothers', but none was

Portrait of Charlotte Deans, also known as Mrs Johnston by unknown artist.

forthcoming, possibly because Johnston had been in prison or perhaps because the couple were touring actors rather than respectable citizens. Friends rallied round and organised a benefit performance for Charlotte and her ten children, to star a well-known actor of the day, Mr Grant, an old friend of the Johnstons. Charlotte writes with gratitude about Anderson's support: the poet not only wrote a prologue for the performance, but also sold tickets for it and acted as doorman for the evening.

This is all documented in Anderson's diary, where on January 7 and 8 he reports on the couple's illnesses, the following day being 'sent for by Dr James, who requested me immediately to seek another lodging; telling me Mr J. was dangerously ill of a fever. His son Henry was yesterday taken ill and is worse this day. Left the house and went to Mr. Gibson's.' On the 10th and 12th Anderson is evidently very worried about the Johnstons, both of whom are said to be worse and on the 13th he sets off for Charlotte's home town of Wigton to 'acquaint their friends'. He learns on the 14th that Johnston has died so heads off again to Wigton with the news and then, it seems, going on to organise the funeral which, he reports, was attended by a number of Masons, the Edenside Rangers and 'a great concourse of people'. The following month we find Anderson registering Johnston's death, settling the funeral accounts and back living in his old rooms in Lowthians Lane, with a heavy heart: 'but what a change do I feel in the loss of Mr J.'

The benefit performance was planned for June and on May 28 Anderson reports receiving 'a polite letter from Mr Grant together with the Bill of fare for the Benefit'. But all was not plain sailing, with one or two individuals proving to be somewhat obstructive, prompting an angry outburst from the poet: 'Provok'd in the evening by the insolence of that nasty sottish-faced superannuated ignoramus Glendinning, who threatened to stop the Performance. Curse on him! May

Lowthians Lane, where Anderson lodged with the Johnston family 1801-1803. The lane leads off English Street, and in Anderson's day would have led right through to Lowther Street.

he be double damned in the next world, not ever taste happiness in this, who would injure the widow and helpless family; but I trust the views of this stupid starveling will be counteracted by a generous public.' This was indeed the case, and the following day Anderson reports 'with pleasure' that the Masons 'have granted leave for the Performance'. On June 7 the performance took place and was a great success: 'I have never seen a room so full of people' writes Anderson, noting that he was 'enraptured' with the singing of Miss

Wolstein, although unable to hear much of the concert as he was prevailed upon to be 'a door-keeper, against my will.' Two days later he was able to pay Mrs Johnston £1 16s in ticket money, but such a small amount could not support Charlotte and her fatherless children, who were soon back on the road with a travelling theatre company.

In 1803 life went on in much the same way as the previous year, although there are fewer diary entries. Those of particular interest include the following:

Feb. 13 Heard Dr Grisdale preach at the Cathedral. Got a glance of Kate's eyes. [This is one of just a few references to Anderson's interest in the opposite sex] Received a long letter from Miss Gilpin about her song "Billy Sutton" and wrote a longer answer. Spent a couple of hours with Mr Lonsdale, and drank his farewell glass, as he is intending to leave Carlisle tomorrow for York. Oh that I had a companion as well informed, as good and agreeable in his manner as Mr. L. [this may just possibly be fellow poet Mark Lonsdale, although he was by this time principally working in London at Sadler's Wells].

Sept. 9 Joined the Cumberland Rangers at the request of my friends. [the second half of that year was height of the fear of Napoleonic invasion]

Sept. 13. Appeared with the Band in full uniform before Lieutenant Colonels Howard and Wallace. Wrote to Mr Thomson.

Oct. 13 Wrote three verses of Cumberland Ballad but burnt it.

Oct. 15 Had two hours conversation with Crito, who advises me to publish my Cum. Ballads.

Oct. 18 Attended Parade and wish this din of arms were over.

Oct. 20 A letter from Soulby.

There are no diary entries beyond the end of October that year, perhaps because Anderson was at this point busy writing Cumberland ballads for publication: in 1804 the Penrith printer Soulby published a songster including a number of Anderson pieces and the following year the first edition of *Anderson's Cumberland Ballads* printed by W. Hodgson of Carlisle, and dedicated to Colonels Henry Howard and Thomas Wallace, Major Sir Wilfrid Lawson and 'the officers of The Loyal Cumberland Rangers.'

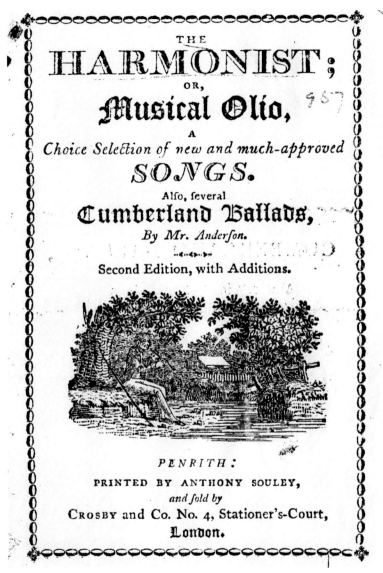

THE

HARMONIST;

OR,

Musical Olio,

A

Choice Selection of new and much-approved

SONGS.

Also, several

Cumberland Ballads,

By Mr. Anderson.

Second Edition, with Additions.

PENRITH:

PRINTED BY ANTHONY SOULEY,

and sold by

CROSBY and Co. No. 4, Stationer's-Court,

London.

Title page of Soulby's The Harmonist or Musical Olio, *published 1804.*

5. 1820 – 1833: poetry and poverty

On Anderson's return to Carlisle in 1819, all at first looked set fair. He was greeted with a dinner in his honour and encouraged by friends to publish again, as a means of supporting himself as the poet notes at the end of his 'Memoir'. (see Chapter 3). Thomas Sanderson had originally agreed to contribute a biography - along with explanatory notes to the poems, a glossary and an 'Essay on the Character, Manners and Customs of the Peasantry of Cumberland' – but felt that Anderson's words in his own memoir were more eloquent. And so the two-volume edition of *The Poetical Works of Robert Anderson* was published in 1820, with the support of 864 subscribers, who are listed in Volume II and include a wide range of people from booksellers to local worthies such as Sir James Graham of Netherby and Mr Curwen of Workington Hall as well as notable literary figures like Thomas Carlyle, Robert Southey and William Wordsworth.

At the end of his 'Essay', Sanderson is fulsome in his praise of Anderson, commending his Cumberland Ballads to readers as being 'the most perfect specimens of pastoral writing that have yet appeared' and wholly accurate 'In delineating the characters of his peasants, he has closely adhered to nature and truth, never raising them above their condition in life by too much refinement, and never depressing them below it by too much vulgarity. He holds them up often to laughter, but never to contempt.' He admits, however, that 'The locality and peculiar phraseology of his Cumberland Ballads must necessarily circumscribe their popularity; but their general merit is such as will always find them admirers among those who are acquainted with the provincial idiom in which they are written, and with the manners and scenes which they delineate.' Given this paeon of praise it is then surprising to find that *The Poetical Works* comprised mainly poems in Standard English with just eighteen Cumberland dialect ballads, none of them Anderson's most popular songs like 'Betty Brown' and 'Barbary Bell', 'Guid Strang Yell' and 'A Peck o' Punch', which had proved so popular in cheap print editions. Or perhaps the fact that they had been published in those humble editions went against them, as it seems clear that the publication aimed to appeal to the genteel sensibilities of its more aristocratic and middle-class subscribers rather than the 'peasantry' Sanderson describes.

The original intention to provide financial support for Anderson in his later years, was not however successful, and questions were raised about possible misappropriation of funds in the local press. On Friday September 12 1823, under the heading 'The Cumberland Bard's Affairs', *The Citizen, or Literary and Scientific Mirror* reported that although it had been hoped to provide Anderson with an annuity from subscriptions, funds did not materialize. The publication's requests for an explanation seem to have been ignored, despite the undertaking being a public one, which should have been reported on. The strong denouncement of the whole enterprise continues: 'There were 1200 copies printed, at 12s. These oughts, with proper management, to have been productive of a round sum; and yet there is now no money in the hands of the Treasurer, nor in the hands of the publisher, nor anywhere else that we can hear of. We know it is said that Mr. Anderson has acted improperly; still we can see no reason in this for withholding the required information. A Committee taking the affair in hand, implied that it would be better under other management than "the bard's." But why did this Committee ever start the business so poorly resolved, as they seem to have been? When they chose to act for 1200 persons, they took upon themselves, in our opinion, a highly responsible charge. Four or five hundred pounds must have passed through their fingers, and it is due to their own honour, as well as to the proper curiosity of the subscribers, to know how this cash has been appropriated.' Despite going on to publish a list of committee members, 'all highly respectable gentlemen', in the hopes of forcing them to disclose the information requested, nothing seems to have come of it.

On February 28 the following year, *The Citizen* published a letter in support of Anderson from John Rayson (1803-1859), a young lad with aspirations to be a poet himself and whose parents had been friends of the 'Bard'. A new edition of *Cumberland Ballads* had just been published by John Jollie of Carlisle, and Rayson was evidently keen to encourage the public to buy copies, especially, he says, 'when it is considered how much the author was disappointed in his hopes of what was to arise from his last publication, and that he has now no income whatever of any kind. I should expect every admirer of talent, every friend of humanity and of depressed genius would come forward upon the present occasion and lend a helping hand.' Evidently keen to get his own verse into print too, his poem 'Lines on the Cumberland Bard' follows, with its doleful opening lines:

Behold our Bard in silent gloom,

> E'en of his peace of mind bereft,
> His looks bid welcome to the tomb,
> He finds few friends in Cumbria left.

Anderson was by now just 54 years of age, but enduring poverty and depression, along with an over-fondness for the bottle probably made him seem, and feel, older than he was. As Robertson puts it in his biography in the 1843 edition of *Cumberland Ballads*, he had become 'soured and distempered', living in poverty and with a morbid fear of the workhouse:

> I long have drunk of pleasure's cup,
> And often have been the son of pain;
> And I have tasted friendly joys,
> That I must never share again:
> For time hath now my forehead bared,
> And cherish's hopes, all, all are fled;
> I cannot soothe another's woes,
> Or dry the tear by sorrow shed!

> Cold Poverty, with haggard look,
> Now threatens sore, in life's decline;
> And Friendship wears another garb;
> And Love's delights no more are mind.
> Night comes not, now, with dreams of bliss;
> I chide the slow approach of day;
> Reflection causes painful sighs;
> And I could weep the hours away!

from 'The Author on Himself', 1820 edition, vol. 1

Moving out from the city to the village of Hayton, near Brampton, in 1823 'for want of means', Anderson continued to submit poems submitted to local press – the *Carlisle Journal, Carlisle Patriot* and *The Citizen,* which published his work regularly from its inception in 1821 through to the year of his death. Hopefully the publication was paying for the poems, as the 'Bard' tried to eke out a living in the twilight of his years, although it must be said that the poems published are very far from being the best of his work.

On April 20 1833, just a few months before Anderson's death in September of that year, there appeared in the *Carlisle Journal*'s literature section a review by 'T.A.', allegedly of a of poem by one John Brumwell. However, after opening by praising 'the sons of Cumberland' for their attainments, he goes on mainly to write about Robert Anderson. The 'living bard', he says, showed great promise and 'augured fair to have become a successful rival to the Scottish Poet Burns. Some of his songs display exquisite humour, and an intimate knowledge of the manners, customs, and peculiarities of the people of Cumberland.' If only he had 'cultivated his powers alone in this species of composition, which seems to have been the natural bent of his genius' then he might have acquired the celebrity and status of Burns. It was certainly what the poet had aspired to as a young man, but it was now too late. Robert Anderson passed away on Thursday 26 September 1933 at the house in Annetwell Street, that kind friends provided for him for his final year of life - by means of a monthly subscription, according to Ellwood. His death mask reveals that he died of a stroke.

On Saturday September 28 *The Carlisle Journal*'s reported on the death 'on Thursday evening in Abbey Street, aged 63, Mr Robert Anderson, the Cumberland Bard'. The address published is, however, an error as all later biographies confirm that it was Annetwell Street. The report continues: 'Mr A. was a poet of no mean pretensions; and many of his songs are justly esteemed for their poetic beauty, as well as

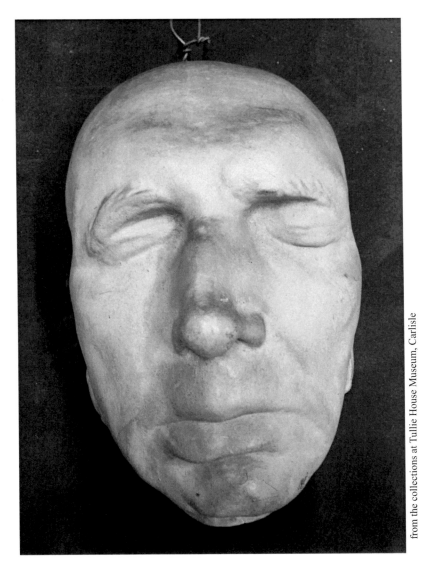

Robert Anderson death mask, clearly showing by the droop on the right side of his face that the poet died of a stroke.

for their truth to nature, and the admirable picture which they afford of the manners and customs of the natives of the County. His ballads will long continue to be favourites amongst our rustics, and he has left behind him a name as a rural poet which will not speedily perish.' A few days later another report appeared, and roundly condemned an obituary that had apparently appeared in some of the London papers stating that Anderson had died in the workhouse 'in a state of great abjectness and poverty'. This was evidently regarded as a slur on the people of Carlisle 'for allowing a man of genius to die thus neglected', the paper being at pains to point out that 'for a considerable period prior to his death, and after he had ceased to labour for his own maintenance, he was comfortably lodged, and every necessary provided for him out of a fund raised amongst a few gentlemen in Carlisle; and though he certainly died in "poverty" (according to the usual acceptation of the word) he had not experienced any real want.' On the morning of Monday September 30, according to Robertson in the biography of his 1843 Anderson edition, 'his remains were respectably interred in St Mary's Church yard, which is in his native parish'.

In February the following year *The Journal* published an article headlined 'The Cumberland Bard' announcing that the anniversary of the birth of the late Robert Anderson had been celebrated at the Three Crowns Inn in English Street 'where a most respectable company, amounting to nearly thirty, sat down to an excellent dinner' at which the late bard was toasted, in the presence of a bust of Anderson, and the evening continued convivially with several of the bard's ballads sung 'with real native *pathos'*. The report concludes by adding that the subject of erecting an appropriate monument to Anderson was 'fully canvassed', resulting in the appointment of a committee to expedite this. Thanks to the popular subscription fund the committee initiated, a marble monument was erected to his memory in Carlisle Cathedral, designed and made by sculptor David Dunbar, who had lived and worked in Carlisle in the early 1820s and known Anderson. The commemorative stone is mounted on the wall just as you enter the cathedral by the south door. Coincidentally, a Carlisle student of David Dunbar, Musgrave Lewthwaite Watson, who studied engraving as well as sculpture, created a set of four illustrations for poems by Anderson. 'The Codbeck Wedding' illustration reproduced in the Robertson edition of 1834 may well be his, but the whereabout of the originals are not known. As Ellwood notes in his 1904 biography, the surplus of the subscription fund was then used to erect a stone above his grave in the churchyard: it can still be seen today just over the low wall of Paternoster Row, in the cathedral grounds.

Robert Anderson memorial in Carlisle Cathedral by sculptor David Dunbar. Erected by subscription in 1834.

6. Anderson in print 1798 – 1904

When Robert Anderson returned home to Carlisle from London in 1796 he continued to write and, no doubt encouraged by his success in getting his Vauxhall songs published, continued writing songs and poetry of a more formal kind. The songs performed at Vauxhall Gardens were turned around very quickly by opportunistic printers, who published what is now known as 'street literature': cheaply produced broadsides and slips - flimsy sheets of ballads, sold by hawkers at markets and fairs as well as by booksellers, along with more substantial chapbooks and songsters. Anderson would not, however, have received any remuneration for these as most 'street literature' publishers were jobbing printers with little regard for copyright, and even less for paying royalties to writers.[13]

Anderson was keen to get into print again, not only for the profile it would give him as a poet but also in order to give him some sort of income from his writing. In 1798 his first volume of poetry appeared, under the catch-all title of *Poems on Various Subjects*, and paid for by enlisting financial support from subscribers and patrons – a common method of financing publishing ventures at the time - possibly with help from his friend and fellow-poet Thomas Sanderson. The poems in the volume were all in Standard English, under the headings 'Miscellanies', 'Epistles', 'Sonnets' and 'Songs', including his 'Lucy Gray' and other songs set by composer

James Hook at Vauxhall Gardens. The first 'epistle' in the book is, tellingly, dedicated to Robert Burns, where we find Anderson attempting to represent Scots rather than Cumbrian, in a form known as 'Standard Habbie', which was popularised by Burnsd:

> Sin' sense and reason baith unite
> In ye to gi'e mankind delight
> Forgi' me gin I bauldly write
>   In lowly strain:
> O man, could I like ye indite,
>   'Twould mak' me fain!
>
> Thought I, I'se try my pen at rhyme,
> If I can hit o' words to chyme;
> Sin poetizin is nae crime,
>   I'll do my best:
> In cam' the Muse -'twas just in time-
>   To do the rest.
>
> But had I sud ha' done lang seyn,
> Excuse this hodge-podge rhyme o' mine;
> And, Rab, gin ye but sen' a line,
>   I vow most fervent,
> I'll thank ye for't, and tak' it kine,
>   Your humble servant.

Carlisle, June, 1796.

Anderson forwarded the epistle to Burns and, judging by the final stanza, expected a reply, but as Burns died just a few weeks later it is quite probable the Scottish bard never saw the letter, let alone be able to 'sen' a line' in reply.

The 1798 volume did receive some local acclaim but sales of the book did not bring Anderson much, if any, income, which sadly was the case for almost all his publications - a source of much frustration. While it is impossible to know whether Anderson selected his own publisher or they chose him, it is interesting to note that the printer was John Mitchell, just recently arrived in Carlisle from Kilmarnock, where he had been apprenticed to the printer of Burns's *Poems, Chiefly in the Scottish Dialect*, commonly known as 'the Kilmarnock edition'. In Mitchell's brief time in Carlisle he also published the 1798 edition of Josiah Relph's poetry, but then moved on to Newcastle in 1799.

In 1801, encouraged by friends, Anderson attempted his first ballad in dialect, 'Betty Brown', which seems to have had a good reception locally, persuading him to write more in the same vein.[14] By 1805 he had sufficient ballads – 58 in all - to publish *Ballads in the Cumberland Dialect*, printed by W. Hodgson in Carlisle, with notes and a glossary provided by Thomas Sanderson. The book sealed his reputation not only in Carlisle and north Cumberland, but also across the wider north. A sure sign of the ballads' popularity was the speed with which they were taken up by the printers of cheap chapbooks and songsters, particularly in Newcastle and in Penrith - both notable centres of chapbook production. As we saw in Anderson's diary entries for this period, the Penrith printer Anthony Soulby was an acquaintance of his, and Soulby included some Anderson songs in *The Harmonist or Musical Olio: A Choice Collection of New and Much Approved Songs. Also Several Cumberland Ballads by Mr Anderson* which was published in 1804. As Soulby did actually take the trouble to register the publication with Stationer's Hall (a copyright law requirement, but one widely flouted by printers of street literature), one assumes that Anderson did get paid for this work.

Expanded editions of *Ballads in the Cumberland Dialect* containing 75 Anderson ballads along with an additional ten pieces in dialect by Cumbrian poets Ewan Clark, Susanna Blamire, Catherine Gilpin, Mark Lonsdale and John Rayson were published by Hetherton of Wigton in 1808, possibly 1809, and 1811– evidence, surely, of increased local interest in dialect literature. Hetherton apparently had purchased the copyright for these, but as almost identical further editions were published in Wigton by John Ismay in 1811 and Rook in 1815, these printers presumably took over the Hetherton business. A later Ismay edition of 1834 features an illustration of 'King Roger'.

All these editions included a glossary, and usually notes as well - both provided by Anderson's friend and supporter Thomas Sanderson. The audience for dialect literature was wide one, but obviously not one that could be expected to be familiar with dialect in a printed form. This was not the way most people came into contact with local dialect, which was of course a form of speech long before it became a form of literature, and individual poets tended to develop own individual spelling system, its 'orthography' in linguistic terms. Anderson's preface to these editions was modest in the extreme, as was the custom of the time: 'The author conceives it unnecessary either to apologize or appeal to the literary world, being aware that provincial expression will not bear critical examination [...] If he has been fortunate enough to give delight, no court-bred bard, basking in the dazzling rays of royalty, will enjoy a greater pleasure; but, as the effusions of the unlettered are too often rashly condemned, the author fears this little volume will only be read, censured, thrown by, and quickly forgotten.' He professes that his 'rural sketches of Cumberland manners' are simply what 'Nature

'King Roger': frontispiece of Ballads in the Cumberland Dialect, *printed by Ismay of Wigton, 1834. Engraving after a painting by G. Sheffield.*

dictated', written in 'the most simple dialect'. Some scenes, he says, are copied from real life while others 'were written with a view of exposing and ridiculing habits that are too often suffered to grow into vices which lead to destruction; and many are unpremeditated attempts at song, composed during the author's solitary rambles on the banks of his favourite stream.' He also notes that 'Living characters respectable as well as odious, he has frequently introduced to the reader, and consequently created many enemies.'

The genesis and reception of the two volumes of *The Poetical Works of Robert Anderson*, published by subscription in 1820 and printed and sold by B. Scott of English Street in Carlisle, were discussed in detail in the previous chapter, so do not need to be repeated here. The volumes contained mostly works in Standard English, including 'An epistle To Robert Anderson' written by Thomas Sanderson, under his pen-name of 'Crito', praising his friend for leaving 'memorials' to rural festivities and claiming that his flute 'will cheer my bow'rs once more'.

In 1823 two editions of *Ballads in the Cumberland Dialect* were published, the first by John Jollie in Carlisle, which includes 33 Anderson pieces along with dialect writings by Ritson, Clark, Lonsdale, and the other by Rooke of Wigton, which contained 37 ballads, all by Anderson – all of which had originally appeared in the earlier Hetherton editions, so either the copyright had lapsed, or was not being enforced. Jollie's edition was re-printed in 1824 with slight amendments to the title page, and then in 1828 H.K. Snowden of Carlisle published an edition incorporating not only the usual notes and glossary, but also reprinting Sanderson's 'Essay' from 1820: the facsimile bound into this book.

In 1839, London publisher John Russell Smith, who produced quite a number of works of antiquarian and philological interest, published *Dialogues, Poems, Songs, and Ballads of Westmorland and Cumberland, &c.*, an anthology of dialect verse and prose from the region, Having a publishers' interest in previous editions, Smith notes that Anderson's 1798 *Selected Poems* had made no money, having brought its author 'little more than dear-bought praise' and despite its popularity, the 1805 edition of *Cumberland Ballads* had 'barely defrayed the expenses attendant upon the publication' owing to much of the subscription money being lost. Nonetheless, he reproduced 36 Anderson ballads - far more than any other writer featured - including some that had never previously been published. One of these, 'The Kurn-

Winnin; or, Shadey an' Jossy' about a traditional harvest time festival, features a repeated refrain in which Anderson compares the 'Famish kurn-winnin at Mowdy-warp farm' to 'murry-neets, clay-daubins, weddin's… Bruff Reaces, the fratch, Cursmess E'en', all references to some of his most popular ballads. This self-referential trick is something Anderson incorporates in other pieces, notably the 'The Ballad Singer' (a late work published by Ellwood in 1904), which largely comprises a litany of Anderson ballads, possibly deliberately done as a marketing ploy, aimed at reminding the public of his other works.

Editions of *Cumberland Ballads* continued to be published throughout the nineteenth century following Anderson's death in 1833, the editions of 1843 and 1904 being the most comprehensive. The first was published by Robertson of Wigton (undated, but as he was only in Wigton 1843-1846, 1843 represents the earliest date he could have published). Robertson apparently knew Anderson and had managed to pull together a huge number of Cumberland ballads wherever he could find them and whatever their quality, including some from a bound manuscript copy owned by Philip Howard of Corby Castle. It seems likely the publication was funded by securing promises from booksellers to purchase quantites of the book, as six different firms are listed on the title page: in London, G. Routledge & Co. (a popular choice for London distribution by Carlisle publishers, as the Routledge family had local roots) and, in Carlisle, C. Thurnam, I. Whitridge, J. Steel, J. Foster and W. Fishburn. Robertson included 193 Cumberland ballads by Anderson – of which 130 had allegedly never before been published - with an additional thirteen ballads from the pens of John Rayson, Ewan Clark, Susanna Blamire and Mark

Lonsdale. It is interesting to read his notes following the familiar Anderson memoir, as someone who actually knew the poet, when he writes that for some years before the poet's death, 'He became sadly changed. His mind became soured and distempered, and his person presented a hapless picture of indigence and misery.'

In 1866 a new edition of *Cumberland Ballads by Robert Anderson,* including 80 Cumberland ballads and four songs from Anderson's *Poems* of 1798, was published by George Coward in Carlisle. By way of a biography of Anderson he printed extracts from the original 'Memoir of the Author' and added further information, where we learn for example that Anderson's later years were 'a sad a mournful chapter in biography', when the poet 'fell into the vice of intemperance' and became 'careless and untidy in his dress. His looks wore a careworn and haggard appearance; and the fear of ending his days in a workhouse haunted his imagination'. In case this seemed too depressive and off-putting, he adds some uplifting lines about Anderson's dialect writing: 'He may fairly be called the bard of our peasantry. There are few ploughmen, shepherds, or buxom country girls throughout the county, who are not in some degree acquainted with his ballads. With many they have been a pocket companion.' Praising his descriptions of fairs and other festive occasions Coward says that 'so truthfully daguerrotyped are some of the characters in his ballads, that we feel as if we had often met them in our daily intercourse, and could hold converse face to face with them.'

That same year Coward published Sidney Gilpin's *Songs and Ballads of Cumberland and the Lake Counties* ('Sidney Gilpin' was the pen-name of Coward), having already released some of it in parts. The book was something of a landmark, certainly with regard to Cumberland song, encompassing as it did a collection of Border Ballads and John Woodcock Graves's song 'D'Ye Ken John Peel', along with ballads from all the Cumberland dialect poets, including 49 by Anderson.

The 1866 *Cumberland Ballads by Robert Anderson* was re-published in 1893, along with a great deal more by way of editorial notes, 'a few fragments', the editor said, 'that had fallen his way at intervals'. One such was a letter to the editor of the *Carlisle Chronicle,* February 15 1808, which had greatly amused Anderson - and reinforces Coward's earlier impression that he had met some of the characters Anderson writes about. The letter reads:

'Sir – I understand you are at present employing your vacant hours in composing a Song, respecting the assembly which was held at Mr. Scarrow, Styled the Butterfly Ball, in hopes to ridicule the characters of those who attended. I have just sent you these few lines to inform you if it be the case you will have reason to repent the hour that ever you began it, for if you do suffer a publication of that description to be made public I can assure you it will be the last you will publish in Carlisle or any place else, for you may depend upon it you must not expect to walk the streets of Carlisle unprotected, therefore I shall leave it to your own judgment to doo what you think proper. – A FRIEND'

Another interesting snippet Coward reports is that while living at Hayton in 1823, in a desperate attempt to make some money, Anderson made an attempt to sell the copyright of his local ballads through the pages of the local press, in an attempt to get some income:

ROBERT ANDERSON, having revised and altered the CUMBERLAND BALLADS, increased their Number from 75 to 177, added Sixty New Stanzas to the old ones, and prepared a copious Glossary to the whole, offers the copyright to any Bookseller inclined to purchase, on reasonable terms. The New Ballads, like the old, are illustrative of Local Feelings, Manners and Customs, and will not, probably, be found inferior to their successful predecessors.

Letters, Post-paid, addressed to R. ANDERSON, at MR. BROWN'S, Hayton, near Brampton, Cumberland, will be duly attended to.

Coward then notes that the appeal was unsuccessful as, 'No local bookseller, or other person, was found to be venturesome enough to risk the publication of the ballads on the terms proposed by the author.' Going on to indulge in what feels like mischievous, if not malicious, gossip about rival publishers, he continues: 'Accordingly, the greater part of the pieces remained in manuscript until an edition–injudiciously edited–was issued by Robertson of Wigton many years after Anderson's death.' This volume he declares to be 'a heterogeneous mass of half digested material' more likely to detract from, rather than enhance, Anderson's reputation.' He then adds in a footnote that an announcement by George Irwin of *The Citizen* of his intention to publish 200 Anderson ballads in twenty fortnightly parts also came to nothing.

In his extended preface he is clear that his admiration for Anderson is tempered with a degree of criticism. Whilst he has 'painted a faithful pictures of manners and customs now almost obsolete' he is 'inferior to Miss Blamire in force of thought – sharp, clear, original reflection – and in fine poetic feeling; to Stagg the blind bard of Wigton, in graphic sketches of character and masculine firmness of language. His models have evidently been the fine old love songs of Scotland.' Furthermore, his works in English prove him to be 'a poor metremonger', saying that whilst even 'his songs in the Cumberland dialect, upon which his reputation is entirely built, possess very unequal merit. Many are of the most commonplace order; while others are faithfully limned and touched in with the nicety of a Dutch painter.' He then goes on to single out 'The Impatient Lassie', 'Will and Kate', 'King Roger', 'The Bashfu' Wooer', 'Gwordie Gill', 'Peggy Penn' and the 'Worton Wedding' as examples of Anderson's best work.

Finally, we come to the so-called 'centenary edition' edited by the Reverend Thomas Ellwood of 1904 which contains the most comprehensive oollection of Cumberland ballads, 200 in all. This he achieved by assiduous work in sourcing manuscripts from friends and relations of Anderson, many of which had never been published before or had only appeared in the local press, not in book form. Ellwood was an enthusiastic promoter of Cumbrian dialect, and in preparing his edition included his own extended biography of Anderson, alongside Sanderson's notes and a 'glossarial concordance' by George Crowther. The designation 'centenary edition' seems to refer not to any aspect of Anderson own life, but to the alleged centenary of Anderson's 'Bleckell Murry Neet', a verse from which is quoted on the title page:

'The last of December, lang may we remember,
At five o' the mworn, eighteen hundred an' twee,' (three)

This reveals, however, a mis-reading of the dialect, for 'twee' is not three but two, and as Anderson dated his rollicking poem 'July 1803', he was evidently referring back to the previous New Year's Eve, the night on which his 'Murry Neet' is supposed to have taken place, ie 1802. Albeit it was 5am on New Year's Day 1803 by the time the revellers stagger back home. As the publication date of Ellwood's book is in any case 1904 not 1903, it does seem to be an odd interpretation of 'centenary'… At the back of the book Ellwood lists 19 editions predating his own, although subsequent research reveals at least 10 further collections, making a total of 30 in all. Other small selections of ballads were reprinted in pamphlets published in 1907 and also in 1933 – the centenary of Anderson's death.[15] Many Cumberland ballads did, however, live on, not necessarily in printed book form but performed and recorded as songs.

7. The poet as songwriter: Vauxhall songs and Cumberland ballads

> 'Tou charms the larn'd fwok in aw quarters;
> I wreyte a bit Cummerlan sang.'
>
> *'To Crito', Cumberland Ballads, 1843*

There is no doubt that Robert Anderson was very musical. His memoir reveals that as a child he was entranced by the old ballads sung to him by his Scottish neighbour and when a little older later would entertain friends and neighbours with his 'German flute', the name used at the time for a transverse flute. Entries in his diary show leisure hours being given over to musical pursuits with the Harmonic Society and the Volunteer Band, for whom he composed at least one march. He also appears to have composed tunes for some of his Cumberland ballads - those which carry the legend 'Tune by the Author' - although sadly none of these survive. For the most part he assigned popular tunes of the day for his songs, and how he went about this is revealed in the note to the ballad 'The Wigton True Singer' in Ellwood's 1904 edition. He prints a letter received from bookseller and printer Thomas McMechan of Wigton which asserts that his ballad refers to Anderson's friend William Johnston, a block cutter at the Wigton calico printing works, who was also a very fine singer:

The Wigton gud singer, lets now justly gie,

For aw that hev hard him, they ay fain will see;
He niver sings onie thing true fwok can bleame,
Pruives just, in sang, music – Owre few dui the seame!

McMechan writes that Johnston and Anderson were 'very intimate', adding that 'the poet almost invariably consulted Mr Johnston for the tune to which to set his songs, his practice being, I understand, to get the air well into his mind and get the rhythm to fit with it, which accounts for the words and tune going so well together.' He adds that Mr Johnson, who was his uncle, 'had an extensive repertoire of Anderson's songs, of which he was an inimitable exponent…

Surprising as it might seem to us today, some degree of musical education was not uncommon in the early nineteenth century for even the most lowly in society. This was usually provided through the church as Thomas Sanderson explains in his essay on 'Manners and Customs' in the 1820 *Poetical Works*: 'Church music generally composes a part of the education of a Cumbrian peasant. They are instructed in it by the parish clerk, or by some itinerant professor, and in the course of a few months, by the means of a good ear and a tuneable voice, acquire as much skill in it as to able to gratify the taste of a country audience, at last as far as an accurate combination of sounds extends.' Then, just like the church musicians and singers Thomas Hardy describes in *Under the Greenwood Tree*, when the school breaks up, 'they who compose the choir, and he who leads it, have generally a ball at the village ale-house, in order to experience joys of a more terrestial nature than those which spring from psalm singing.'

Anderson's first published and performed songs, however, were all written in Standard English, not dialect, following his first visit to Vauxhall Gardens in London in

1794, as he relates in his 'Memoir'. Vauxhall was the first of the London pleasure gardens, dating back to the 1630s and originally known as 'Spring Gardens' or 'New Spring Gardens'. Pleasure gardens provided jaded urban dwellers with a faux-rural retreat in which to amuse themselves, their families and friend. A regular haunt for flâneurs and lovers the Gardens were frequented by celebrities and members of the aristocracy as well as the general public from all classes, Vauxhall also became the perfect setting for novelists like Thackeray and Dickens to send both their heroes and villains. As well as its tree-lined walks, including an infamous 'dark walk', Vauxhall also offered paintings and sculpture, a variety of spectacles from masquerades to fireworks and, of course, music. By the late eighteenth century a raised orchestra building had become a main focal point, from which orchestra works, opera arias and popular songs of the day were performed to the audience below. For both composers and performers, Vauxhall offered the quickest way to attract a public following and some the most celebrated composers of the day were contracted to the gardens, including Thomas Arne and James Hook, who was composer and organist there from 1774 to 1820. Hook wrote over two thousand songs for Vauxhall, as well as performing regular organ concertos there and composing operas and other musical works for performance at Drury Lane and Covent Garden theatres.

Operatic arias and patriotic songs, including sea songs like Charles Dibdin's 'Tom Bowling', were staples of the repertoire, along with 'Scotch songs', a popular genre of the time, the term 'Scotch' tending to cover pastoral songs, as well as songs from Scotland and the north of England. Appalled by the mock pastoral Scottish style he heard, Anderson was convinced that he could produce songs

David Coke

Vauxhall Gardens 'One Half of the World don't know how T'other Lives', sung by Master Charles Dignum (c.1765-1827), who is recorded as having performed some of Anderson's songs. Anonymous hand-coloured engraving, based on Rowlandson's 'Vaux-Hall' aquatint of 1785.

'considered equal, or perhaps superior' and, he says, dashed off four the following day: 'Lucy Gray of Allendale', 'I sigh for the Girl I adore', 'The Lovely Brown Maid' and 'Ellen and I', and offered the songs 'to my friend, Mr Hook, a composer of celebrity', who set them to music. Anderson's very first 'poetic effusion' was sung by Master Phelps at Vauxhall in 1794. He went on to achieve some modest success with his song writing, although his only payment was free entry to Vauxhall Garden. Hook went on to set at least eight other Anderson texts, including the song 'Lucy Gray, which achieved wide popularity and was published many times, including in 1812 by John Bell, in his *Rhymes of Northern Bards*. 'Lucy Gray' is also claimed by some to be the unacknowledged inspiration for Wordsworth's 'Lucy" poems.[16]

LUCY GRAY OF ALLENDALE
SET TO MUSIC BY MR. HOOK,
And sung by Master PHELPS, at VAUXHALL, 1794.

O HAVE you seen the blushing rose,
The blooming pink, or lily pale;
Fairer than any flow'r that blows
Was Lucy Gray of Allendale.

Pensive and sad by rae and burn,
Where oft the nymph they us'd to hail,
The shepherds now are heard to mourn
For Lucy Gray of Allendale.

With her to join the rural dance,
Far have I streay'd o'er hill and vale;
Then pleas'd each rustic stole a glance
At Lucy Gray of Allendale.

'Twas underneath the hawthorn shade
I told her first the tender tale;
But now low lays the lovely maid,
Sweet Lucy Gray of Allendale.

Bleak blows the wind, keen bears the rain,
Upon my cottage in the vale:
Long may I mourn a lonely swain,
For Lucy Gray of Allendale.

Many of the songs performed at Vauxhall Gardens were taken up very quickly after their first performance by opportunistic London printers like Dicey and Marshall, who regularly produced compilations of up to twenty-four songs in cheaply produced eight page octavo booklets. These 'songsters', as they were known, were often named after birds like *The Nightingale* and *The Warbler,* selling wholesale at ten for a penny and probably retailing at a halfpenny each. By 1780 new format song sheets deep-etched on copper were also made available, aimed at a better class of clientele: theatregoers as well as those attending the pleasure gardens.[17] An example of one of these is A *Collection of Favorite Songs Sung at Vauxhall Gardens, with unbounded Applause. Composed by Mr Hook*, published in 1803 by J. Dale of The Royal Exchange. The publication comprises eleven songs, of which two were composed by 'Mr Anderson': 'Content in my Cot', sung by Miss Daniels and 'Ben Bonsor's Maxims', a sea song sung by Mr Denman.

Relatively few of Anderson's total output of Cumberland ballads went on to became popular songs, or what we might today call folk songs – of which more, anon. Almost all of these date from between 1802 and 1805 which, as Anderson singer and scholar Keith Gregson has observed, was undoubtedly the poet's most fruitful period, when Anderson had just begun writing in dialect and was active as a musician as well as a poet.[18] Notable amongst the most popular ballads are 'Betty Brown', 'Barbary Bell', 'Peggy Penn', 'Bleckell Murry Neet', 'Geordie Gill', 'Young Roger', 'Canny Cummerlan'' and 'Sally Gray'. 'Bleckell Murry Neet' went on to acquire something of a legendary status in Carlisle ('Bleckell' is the suburb of Blackwell, originally a village just outside the city), re-enacted at the centenary of its composition in 1902, and for some years after, while 'Canny Aul Cummerlan' became a patriotic county anthem and, along with 'Dye Ken John Peel', was sung at numerous Cumbrian gatherings, including the Carlisle 'Cummerlan' Neets' which began with the celebrations marking Anderson's centenary in 1933 and continuing in similar vein into the 1950s.

My own research into folk songs from Cumbria in the period from the late eighteenth to the mid-twentieth centuries reveals a corpus of some 510 songs, of which around a quarter are songs in dialect, a third of which (37) being Cumberland ballads from the pen of Robert Anderson. The airs the ballads were to be sung to are generally specified by the poet under the title, in the manner of Burns. Many of these tunes are commonly perceived as Scottish, although most were actually in widespread throughout the wider British Isles. Examples include, 'Nancy's Tae the Greenwood Gane', a tune from Allan Ramsay's ballad opera *The Gentle Shepherd*, for 'Jenny's Complaint'; the air 'I am a young fellow' for 'Borrowdale Johnny'; 'Andrew wi' his Cutty Gun' for 'Gwordie Gill'; 'John Anderson my Jo' for 'Betty Brown' and 'The Mucking o' Geordie's Byre', the dance tune 'Humours of Glen' for 'Canny Cummerlan'', 'The Lads o' Dunse' for 'Croglin Watty'. It is perhaps the musicality of these songs, their words and tune complementing each other so well, which made them so popular with singers and audiences, most especially 'Sally Gray', which went on to be arranged and published by three different Carlisle musicians, and continued to be performed by local singers throughout most of the twentieth century.

Anderson's songs in Standard English were already circulating widely in the form of broadsides, chapbooks and songsters by the time he began writing his ballads in Cumberland dialect, which followed the same course. Carlisle's Jackson Library has a few locally printed examples in its chapbook collection, including *A Garland of New Songs: Sally Gray, Barbara Bell, The Unfortunate Wife* (Penrith: Soulby, 1804) and 'Nicholl the Newsmonger' in

Chapbook: Village Present.   A Garland of New Songs – 3
Printed by Ann Bell, Penrith.   Anderson Cumberland ballads.
Printed by A. Soulby, Penrith.

Four New Songs (Penrith: Ann Bell, n.d.). There would have been many more in circulation, particularly from printers in Newcastle, York and Glasgow, with later nineteenth century examples including 'First Luive' and 'It's just three years sin' Carel Fair' printed on a broadside published by Fordyce (Newcastle) and 'The Bashfu' Wooer' in *Selkirk's Songs and Ballads for the People No.1* (Newcastle: 1851).

As noted earlier, Penrith printer Anthony Soulby included a selection of Anderson's songs in his 1804 collection *The Harmonist or Musical Olio, A Choice Selection of new and much approved SONGS, Also several*

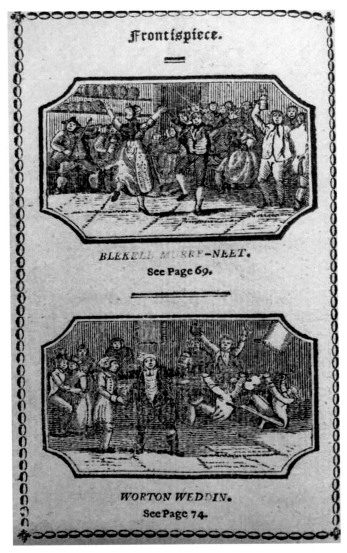

Frontispiece from Soulby's The Harmonist or Musical Olio *published 1804, with illustrations for 'Bleckell Murry Neet' and 'Worton Wedding'.*

Cumberland Ballads by Mr. Anderson. The first section comprised 54 songs, many of a patriotic nature (the market was ripe for them as Britain had declared war on France the year before) from composers including Charles Dibdin and Robert Burns, and five of Anderson's songs in Standard English: 'The Lover's Trial', The Rose of the Valley', 'Britons United the World may Defy' and 'Britannia's Address'. The second section featured fourteen of Anderson's Cumberland ballads, most of which appeared in his *Ballads in the Cumberland Dialect* the following year. We know from his diary that he met up with Soulby on a number of occasions 1801-1803, when one assumes Soulby was already planning *The Harmonist*, while on February 20 1802 Anderson adds: 'Wrote to Penrith with some songs'.

In 1826 volume III of the immensely popular *Universal Songster* was published, and included five Anderson songs: 'The Peck o' Punch', 'Jwohny and Mary', 'Dicky Glendinnin', 'The Thuirsby Witch' and 'Guid Strang Yell'. Although the volume was published within Anderson's lifetime, it is extremely unlikely he saw any royalties from it, as all the songs published were those already circulating in cheap print. Sadly he died before seeing a publication he would have taken great delight and not a little pride in: *Burns' Songs and Anderson's Cumberland Ballads*, a 24-page chapbook published in 1838-40 by W. Stewart of Newcastle which included ballads by the bards of both Scotland and Cumberland.[19] Some twenty-five years later Carlisle composer and singer William Metcalfe (1830-1909) began arranging Cumberland dialect ballads along with for performance on the concert stage, by himself and members of the Carlisle Choral Society, which he conducted. Six of Anderson's ballads were included -'Sally Gray','Reed

William Metcalfe (1830-1909), who published arrangements of 'Reed Robin', 'The Impatient Lassie', 'Sally Gray', 'Gwordie Gill', King Roger' and 'Canny Aul Cumberlan' in the 1870s, as part of a series of sheet music, Songs and Ballads from Cumberland, *printed in Carlisle by Thurnam & Sons and G.T. Coward.*

Robin', 'The Impatient Lassie', 'Gwordie Gill', 'King Roger' and 'Canny Aul Cummerlan' – as well as Alexander Craig Gibson's 'Lal Dinah Grayson' and 'Jwohnny Git Oot' and Susanna Blamire's 'The Waefu' Heart'. Metcalfe bequeathed his music and manuscripts to his young friend James Walter Brown (1851-1930), who was probably better known in Carlisle as a local historian but also sang as a lay-clerk in Carlisle Cathedral. Metcalfe's songs were largely those popular Cumberland ballads of Anderson's best years, 1802-1805, songs which ultimately went on to be sung in the twentieth century, as folk songs.[20]

8. Anderson's legacy:
folk songs, 'Cummerlan' Neets'
and reportage

> The Song beguiles dull Care, at Night's black hour;
> Now calls a starting tear from Sorrow's eye;
> Then grant me, Fate, awhile the nooflllng pow'r,
> To charm the rustic with wild minstrelsy ;
> If, midst coarse weeds, he find a simple flow'r,
> The learned critic's frown l'll proud defy !
>
> *Title page of* Ballads in the Cumberland Dialect,
> *1815 & 1823*

Cumberland ballads as folk songs

According to popular opinion, folk songs are transmitted by word of mouth, never appear in print and are written by 'anon', criteria which would certainly disqualify Robert Anderson's Cumberland ballads. In fact there is no universally agreed definition of what constitutes a folk song. Folk song scholar Steve Roud believes that it is not the origin of a song that makes it 'folk', but the process of learning and performance: its transmission over time. He argues that while it may be possible to agree on some typical folk song characteristics, such as they are usually learnt and performed by non-professionals in non-commercial settings, but there are no hard and fast rules. Before being passed on in that way, however, the songs may have had a commercial life – for example at the pleasure garden or on the stage - or may have been in print as broadsides or chapbooks. Many also have a known composer – a popular poet and songwriter like Anderson perhaps.[21]

The Anderson songs that came to the attention of the Edwardian folk song collectors like Lucy Broadwood, Cecil Sharp and Vaughan Williams were certainly regarded as folk songs. The Folk Song Society was founded in 1898, although even before, in 1893, Broadwood had included 'Sally Gray' in her folk song collection, *English County Songs*. In 1905 a new and very enthusiastic member of the Society, Carlisle Cathedral's Acting Organist Sydney Nicholson sent the tunes of some Cumberland songs sung for him by James Walter Brown, for possible inclusion in the Society's Journal.[22] Of the ten tunes sent (the early collectors were almost all musicians, primarily interested the tunes rather than the words of folk songs) eight were by Anderson: 'Elizabeth's Birthday', 'The Worton Wedding', 'Barbary Bell', 'Geordie Gill', 'Rob Lowry', 'Bleckell Murry Neet', 'Canny Cumberland' and 'Sally Gray', the last three selected for publication in the 1907 Journal'.

In 1906 Nicholson instituted a folk song competition class in the Carlisle and District Musical Festival, offering a prize of £1 (which he donated himself) for 'the best genuine folk-song from the six northern counties.' The competition attracted seven singers, between them performing nine songs, seven of of which were Anderson's, including 'The Worton Wedding', 'Barbary Bell' and 'Gwordie Gill', sung by Messrs. J.W. Brown and J. Carruthers. Also in 1906, probably encouraged by the enthusiastic Nicholson, well-known composer and keen folk song collector Ralph Vaughan Williams paid a flying visit to Carlisle. While on a summer visit to family in Newcastle on August 9 he travelled over to

Ralph Vaughan Williams' transcription of the tune of 'Bleckell Murry Neet', sung for him in Carlisle by John Carruthers on 9 August 1906.

Carlisle for the morning (presumably by train) to meet the singer Mr J. Carruthers, possibly at Nicholson's home, and transcribed the tunes of 'Bleckell Murry Neet', 'Rob Lowry', 'King Roger', 'Barberry Bell', 'A Wife of Willy Miller', 'Rossler Fair' (actually Anderson's 'Betty Brown', which opens 'Come, Gwordie lad, unyoke the yad, Let's gow to Rosley Fair') and 'Geordie Gair'(this should be 'Gwordie Gill'), adding a scribbled note to say that the words 'are in Anderson's book'.[23]

Three years later the London-based but Carlisle-born musician John Graham published his *Dialect Songs of the North*, including in it three Anderson songs, 'Sally Gray', 'The Bashful Wooer' and 'King Roger'. The ex-patriot's customary nostalgia for home comes to the fore in Graham's preface, where he expresses his belief that the dialect, uniquely: 'unlocks the key to the heart of the native. In these days of travel there are exiles from home everywhere. I have sung one or two of these songs in wood and camp in America, and have watched Cumbrian eyes glistening as youthful days were recalled.'[24] This is a theme which recurs throughout the twentieth century.

In 1927 Carlisle-born musician Jeffrey Mark arranged some dialect songs for performance by the Carlisle Male Voice Choir at a concert in 1927, going on to publish these as *Four North Country Songs* in 1928. The voice and piano arrangements of Anderson's 'Sally Gray', along with Blamire's 'Barley Broth' and Craig Gibson's 'L'al Dinah Grayson' and 'Auld Jobby Dixon', proved popular and were performed by Carlisle Musical Society and sung at the Anderson-inspired 'Cummerlan' Neets' in Carlisle in the 1930s and 1940s.[25] Mark went on to become Professor of Composition at the Royal College of Music, but always retained a love for the folk music he had known since childhood – albeit viewed through that prism of nostalgia and Romanticism. Writing in a music journal in 1930 about his recollections of musicians and singers at The Royal Oak in Welton he says: 'We had a few songs, mostly very badly sung, but one man of about sixty presently got up and gave us a version of a once very popular Cumberland song called "Sally Gray", which I have known and sung since boyhood. The actual difference in notes from my own version was quite subtle, but I was chiefly interested in the method and poise of his delivery. His was a voice which came to me directly out of the past'. But it was soon apparent that "Sally Gray" did not suit the company, being 'only tolerated as an old man's quaverings; stale, old-fashioned and unexciting. And this although they were all the genuine article - honest rustics honestly quaffing their honest ale in the manner which a romantically interested society expects of them. According to common report, they should have automatically joined in the chorus and improvised a few verses on the spot. But the next item was a cheap music-hall song of about forty years ago (as I reckoned), with the refrain, "I didn't stop to say good-bye", which pleased tremendously, and soon put everyone in a good humour again after the tedium of "Sally Gray".'

Anderson's songs were still taken up by a few local people with an interest in local songs, notably some of the founding members of The Lakeland Dialect Society, formed in 1939. In the main these were educated, middle-class men who came from working class families: Jonathan Mawson Denwood of Cockermouth, Lance Porter of Eskdale, Frank Warriner of Millom and Harold Forsyth and Robert Forrester of Carlisle. And while in its earlier years the Dialect Society's journals carried a few articles on music including, in 1942, one on Lakeland fiddlers and another on old Westmorland folk singers, and in 1961 an article by Frank Warriner on the late J.M. Denwood's folk song collection – there was nothing on Anderson, despite the fact that Harold Forsyth and others were involved in the Carlisle 'Cummerlan' Neets' inspired by the Anderson centenary celebration of 1933. Forsyth was himself a musician and singer, conducted the Carlisle Male Voice Choir and was a popular wartime entertainer with a number of dialect songs in his repertoire, including Anderson's 'Reed Robin', 'A young wife for me', 'Rob Lowrie', 'The Peck of Punch' and 'Canny Cummerlan'.

In more recent years local folk singers Angie Marchant and Paula and Linda Adams performed and recorded a few dialect songs including 'Sally Gray' and 'Canny Cummerlan" in the 1970s, while Keith Gregson published his *Cumbrian Songs and Ballads* in 1980. This included 38 songs by Cumbrian dialect poets, 21 of them by Robert Anderson, as well as the original tunes specified by the author. However, it should be noted that not all the tunes indicated had stayed with their ballads, with variants evolving and sometimes even completely different tunes being used over the previous 180 years. The changes made, either consciously or unconsciously, by different singers over that time represent 'the folk process' in action, a process that is continuing with a new generation of singers in the twenty-first century.

'Cummerlan' Neets' and commemorations

> The last o' December, lang may we remember,
> At five o' the mworn, eighteen hundred an twee
> Here's health an success to the brave Jwohnny Dawston
> An monie sec meetings may we leeve to see."

Bleckell Murry Neet

Such was the hold of Anderson's rumbustious 'Bleckell Murry Neet', written on July 4 1803 about the previous year's New Year's Eve, that the poem went on to have a life of its own, most memorably when a group of Anderson enthusiasts in Carlisle decided to arrange a celebratory event to mark the hundredth anniversary of the original merry neet in a barn at Blackwell (the 'Bleckell' of the poem), on the edge of the city. It was attended by scores of country people, who walked there as well as some of the 'bettermer swort' ['better sort', as in more middle-class] from Carlisle and elsewhere, who drove out in cabs, some with copies of first editions of Anderson in their pockets.

A pamphlet was produced, by George Crowther, which reproduced a feature from *The Carlisle Patriot* on January 3 1902, where we learn that there were five singing competitions that night: one for best performance of 'Bleckell Murry Neet', one for any Cumberland song, and others for best sentimental song, best comic song and best rendering of 'John Peel', to be judged by James Walter Brown and T.

Lattimer. 'Sally Gray' was the most popular choice of Cumberland song, which a large number of singers selected to perform, followed by 'Canny Cummerlan'', sung by the eventual winner, William Henderson. He also won the 'Bleckell Murry Neet' competition too, with John Carruthers of Wigton coming fourth. The 'Murry Neet' proved so popular it became an annual event, later held in the more salubrious environs of the Racecourse Pavilion, and there was even a suggestion that an Anderson Club should be formed in Carlisle, like the many Burns Clubs that existed around the country and of course in neighbouring Scotland.

In January 1911 *The Cumberland News* reported that almost 100 couples attended that year's 'Murry Neet', including several members of a pantomime troupe appearing at the Palace Theatre. As well as dancing, prizes were offered for the best rendered song, with an additional prize 'given by a few admirers of the local tongue' for the best song in Cumberland dialect. Sadly there were only four entries in the category, which was won once again by Mr Henderson. By 1927, although the committee were anxious to continue the dialect competition, they were finding by then a marked dearth of dialect singers, so opened it up consequently to any kind of songs. As it turned out, in the end the competition was cancelled completely 'owing to the authorities'attitude in regard to entertainment tax.

There were no problems with taxes or singers at the elaborate 1933 Anderson centenary celebration at the Pageant Hall of the Silver Grill restaurant in Carlisle. 'A reet Murry Neet and Centenary Supper: Dialect Stwories and Sangs' ran the headline in *The Cumberland News*, which devoted a whole page to its report on the event. Anderson's own 'Grace before Meat' was said and glasses raised to 'Canny Aul

Canny Aul Cummerlan'

Robert Anderson.

Old Air arranged by F. W. Wadely.

1. 'Twas ae neet last week, wid our wark ef-ter supper, We went owre the geate, cousin Is-bel to see; Ther was Sib-by frae Cur-thet, an lal Bet-ty By-ers, Deef Deb-by, Greace Gill, Bel-la Bun-ton an me; We'd scearce begun spinnin when Sib be-gan sing-in A

*Arrangement of 'Canny Aul Cummerlan" by Dr. Frederick W.
Wadely (1882-1970), organist at Carlisle Cathedral 1910-1960.
The tune is an version of the air popularly used since the early
nineteenth century, not the one specified by Anderson in 1804, 'The
Humours of Glen'*

WHITE OX, BLACKHALL
(SCENE OF ANDERSON'S "BLECKELL MURRY NEET.")

Woodcut of The White Ox at Blackwell (Blackhall is an error), where the original 'Bleckell Murry Neet' was held: front cover of pamphlet Bleckell Rhymes by W.T. Johnston, published by Steel Bros, Carlisle, 1927.

Cummerlan' before guests tucked into a tatie pot supper, the menu written in dialect. The programme included speeches, recitations, songs and a talk about the bard, described as a real musician and singer 'who wrote songs meant to be sung' and these songs 'linked Cumbrians, in whatever part of the world they might be, with their homeland.' A Centenary Celebration Souvenir brochure was produced for the occasion which reprinted a feature by the late James Walter Brown, who claimed that Anderson's best songs were worthy of

Burns, his particular favourites being 'The Worton Wedding', 'The Impatient Lassie' and 'Canny Cummerlan' – a musical setting of which was also printed in the brochure.

Following the success of the 1933 celebrations, 'Cummerlan' Neets' became popular annual events, which the organising committee hoped would foster an interest in local dialect. After the formation of the Lakeland Dialect Society in 1939 the events ceased for a while but were revived in 1954 and ran until at least 1959.[26] The next, and indeed last, Robert Anderson event in Carlisle was in 1983: a celebratory show to mark the 150th anniversary of the poet's death. The show was held at the city's Green Room theatre and produced by Keith Gregson, with a programme interspersing extracts from the poet's biography with performances by local folk musicians of his songs and some of the tunes, dances and clog steps Anderson wove into his 'Bleckell Murry Neet', 'Worton Wedding' and 'The Clay Daubin'.

Reportage: snapshots of local history

George Coward argues in his 1893 edition of the *Anderson's Cumberland Ballads* that the poet painted a faithful picture 'of manners and customs now almost obsolete. In this respect Anderson has had no rival… for does not *Canny auld Cummerland cap them aw still*?' He is here echoing the sentiments of Robertson some fifty years earlier, who claimed that Anderson's descriptions of fairs, merry nights and other merry makings 'stand unrivalled as faithful pictures of these rude and rustic amusement' which were 'fast gliding down the stream of oblivion'. And while Robertson's first statement may be open to question, the second is certainly true.

Dialect poetry can be a valuable but much neglected source for social historians, overlooked because of the perceived problem of its language as well as its veracity. Some of the longer narrative poems of the early-nineteenth century poets like Stagg, Lonsdale and Anderson, represent what scholar Michael Baron calls the tradition of reportage in the Romantic period.[27] Baron specifically notes Anderson's 'Nichol the Newsmonger' and Lonsdale's 'Th'Upshot' as examples of this tradition, although we do need to be wary of treating them as objective history.[28] We need to remember that both writers were keen to create atmosphere, theatre and a good story, and tended to romanticise the past, their youth, their roots in the Cumbrian countryside and the idea of the Cumbrian peasant - all common traits of dialect poets. Anderson in particular always had one eye on his market: he needed to sell books in order to provide an income. That said, neither are the scenes depicted by either poet pure invention, but rather fiction grounded in fact. The names of the tunes, dances and songs interwoven into Anderson's descriptions of merry neets, weddings and other festivities are most certainly genuine, lending an air of authenticity to his 'Bleckell Murry Neet', 'Worton Wedding', 'Codbeck Wedding' and 'Clay Daubin'. His descriptions of Carlisle Fairs in 'Borrowdale Jwohny' and 'Croglin Watty' (also called 'Watty' or 'Daft Watty') are convincing, the place names he mentions are of course real and, as we saw earlier, many of the people were too.

Festive rural gatherings were a popular subject for the early dialect poets, for all human life was there: workers, young folk, old folk, wise men, fools, fighters, lovers, dancers, singers and musicians, with all their foibles and virtues. Sanderson attempts a description of a merry-night, in his 'Essay', not in altogether favourable terms: '…as its name imports, a night appropriated to mirth and festivity. It takes place at some country ale-house, during the holidays of

Christmas, a season in which every Cumbrian peasant refuses to be governed by the cold and niggardly maxims of economy and thrift. That the guests might want nothing to cheer their hearts, the landlord of the house is careful to replenish his cellar with ale and spirits, as well as to provide bread and cheese, pipes and tobacco, cards and music.' He goes on to describe how the company divides into different parties according to their interests, the card players to wherever they can find tables and the sweethearts to some snug corner, while the dancers head either for the kitchen or upstairs to the 'house-loft' where, to the music of a fiddle, they 'exhibit specimens of agility rather than of skill; and, though their heads have often stubborn rencounters with the beams and rafters of the building, they are seldom forsaken by either their spirits or their elasticity.'

Anderson brings this whole scene to life in the opening stanzas of his 1803 poem 'Bleckell Murry Neet':

> Aa, Lad! sec a murry neet we've had at Bleckell,
> The soun' o' the fiddle yet rings in mey ear;
> Aw reet clipt and heel'd were the lads and the lasses,
> An monie a cliver lish hussy was theer;
> The bettermer swort sat snug in the parlour,
> I'th' pantry the sweet hearters cutter'd sae saft;
> The dancers they kickt up a stour i' the kitchen;
> At lanter the card-lakers sat i' the loft.
>
> The clogger o' Dawston's a famish top hero,
> He bangs aw the player fwok twenty to yen;
> He stampt wid his fit, an he shoutet an roystert,
> Till the sweet it ran off at. his varra chin en:
> He held up ae han leyke the spout of a teapot
> An danc'd "cross the buckle" an "ledder te spatch"
> When they cried "Bonny Bell" he lap up to the ceilin,

An aye snapt his thoums fer a bit ov a fratch.

'The Worton Wedding' is also a pretty uproarious affair, where 'Young Sour-milk Sawney' jumped on a stool to dance a hornpipe but was so energetic (as well as drunk) that he fell off and 'brak his left-leg shin'. Not to be outdone, 'cocker Wullie' did a clog dance, although 'Tamer, in her stockin' feet' made a better job of it, even without the clogs. The fiddler for the party is none other than John Stagg, the poet, who was also a regular fiddler at country gatherings:

Blin' Stagg, the fiddler, gat a whack,
The bacon fleek fell on his back,   [bacon flitch, or side]
And neist his fiddle-stick they brack,   [next they broke his bow]
'Twas weel he was nea waur.'   [it was just as well he wasn't worse]

The prefatory note to 'The Codbeck Weddin'' in the 1893 edition of *Anderson's Cumberland Ballads* says the poem depicts a real wedding, that of weaver Joe Bewley who died aged 90 about 1870. We can infer that the wedding was held between 1805 and 1807, as although the ballad is undated it does not appear in Anderson's 1805 collection, but is included in 1808. The dancing after the wedding is lively:

The breyde wad dance 'Coddle me, Cuddy; "
A threesome then caper'd Scotch Reels;
Peter Weir cleek'd up auld Auld Mary Dalton,
Leyke a cock round a hen neist he steeals;
Jwohn Bell yelp'd out 'Sowerby Lasses;'
Young Jwosep, a lang Country Dance,
He'd gat his new pumps Smithson meade him,
And fain wad shew how he cud prance.

'The Clay Daubin' (dated October 21 1804) meanwhile, describes the party which follows a day spent by friends and

'*The Codbeck Wedding*': *frontispiece of* Ballads in the Cumberland Dialect *printed by W. Davison of Alnwick, 1838.*

neighbours of a newly-married couple building for them a
'clay dabbin', a cottage built of compressed earth. After '…
the waws were aw finish'd er dark'nin'; Now grypes, shouls,
and barros thrown by,' [the walls were all finished by dark,
and the forks, shovels and barrows put aside] everyone gets
stuck into the food and drink, intent on having a good time.
When the rum is finished they move on to whisky, and the
fiddler asked to play: 'Come, Adams, asked to 'rasp up a lal
tune!' According to Sanderson's notes, the real Bill Adams
was 'an excellent country musician, particularly noted for
playing jigs and strathspeys; and a man well known at fairs,
merry-nights, kurn-suppers, and clay daubings.' After Adams
has 'kittled up 'Chips and Shavings' (a popular dance tune)
Deavie offers 'a bit of a sang':

> 'He lilted 'The King and the Tinker',
> And Wully struck up 'Robin Hood';
> Dick Mingins tried 'Hooly and Fairly';

And Martha 'The Babs o' the Wood'.

Adams appears again in 'The Kurn-winnin', a late ballad of Anderson's published by John Russell Smith in his 1839 dialect anthology: 'Aul Adams was neist frae the kitchen cawt in, He rosselt the strings, weel he play'd min.' The refrain of the ballad likens the event to previous local events with Anderson in self-referential mode again, advertising some of his most popular poems before boasting that of course the 'Kurn-winnin' was a much better, and wilder, affair – and by implication, his poem about it too?[29]

Ov murry-neets, clay-daubin's, weddin's they tell,
Bruff reaces, the fratch Cursmess eve, min
Leyke the sun till a rushleet the kurn-winnin-pruiv'd.

Of merry neets, clay daubins, weddings they tell,
Burgh races, the quarrel on Christmas Eve, mind,
Like the sun to a rush light the kurn-winnin proved.

(harvest festivities)

The character of 'Nichol the Newsmonger' is an interesting one. He first appears in a poem of July 1802, published in the 1805 edition of *Cumberland Ballads*, where we learn that he is the conduit of all news to and from the outside world – news which comes well-spiced with local gossip:

Our parson he gat drunk as muck,
Then leddert aw t'lads roun about him;   [leathered/beat]
Some said he was nobbet hawf reet [only half-right, ie in the head]
An fwok mud as weel be widout him.
The yell's to be fourpence a whart   [ale is to be 4d. a quart]
Odswinge, lad! Ther will be rare drinkin
Billy Pitt's mad as onie March hare,   [Pitt the Younger]

An niver was reet, fwok er thinkin.'

Nichol pops up elsewhere from time to time, such as in 'The Cram; or, Nichol and Cuddy', where we find him gossiping with Cuddy about a grand ball in the neighbourhood - 'Hut Cuddy! This warl's but a show'- before dissecting the character of various attendees and having a lengthy discussion about music: 'Aye music this weyde warl can please'. As for dancing: 'The warl's but a weyl country dance, Whoar aw caper teane ageane tudder', while he opines how the standard of singing has gone downhill: 'Were sangs but leyke weather, still gud, How happy 'twad pruive to the nation!' He also appears at the end of 'The Kurn-winnin':

> Auld Nichol's the deevil for lees, min.   [lies, mind]
> In towns, aye in villages, stwories grow big,
> Leyke snobaws roll'd up in the street, min!
> But may aw to peace an' to merriment bow,
> Whene'er at kurn-winnins they meet, min.

It is very tempting to read into Nichol the character of Anderson himself - his views on local people and on music, someone who could be a 'deevil for lees' (lies): perhaps defending himself from accusations of depicting acquaintances and neighbours in an unflattering light? And when in 'Nichol the News Monger's Death' we read that he 'keept murry' all the neighbours young and old, gave bread and a penny to every beggar and hated 'feghts, fratches, corruption, war and preyde,' as well as 'slav'ry an priss-gangs', this surely was the real Robert Anderson.

9. Some conclusions:
Anderson, dialect and regional Identity

We help yen anudder, we welcome the stranger,
Ourselves and our country we'll ivver defend;
We pay bits o' taxes as well as we're yebble,
And pray, leyke true Britons, the war hed an end.
Then Cummerlan' lads, an' ye lish rwosy lasses,
If some caw ye clownish, ye needn't think shem.
Be merry and wise, enjoy innocent pleasures,
And still seek for peace and contentment at yem.

('Canny Cummerlan', written August 12, 1804)

As early as 1808 an unknown owner of a copy of Hetherton's edition of *Cumberland Ballads* wrote on the verso of the title page: 'Many of these ballads have a great deal of merit. The author has a talent for painting rustic manners and possesses comic humour in no mean degree. He is of the school of Ramsay in that department – but aspires not to the greater merits of Burns, having little or no turn for the sublime or pathos. The 'Worton Wedding' is a good specimen of the author's happiest manner. His political opinions have a small tincture of the modern popular prejudice in favour of Reform…' Critics throughout the nineteenth century were fairly consistent in their reservations about not considering Robert Anderson a major 'bard', especially when compared with Burns, let alone Wordsworth. In his youth Wordsworth was an admirer of Burns, although we know nothing of his opinion of Anderson. And although there might be some similarities in the stories of fellow-Cumbrians Wordsworth and Anderson, there remain huge divergences - not least in their respective educations.

Dialect writers like Anderson were typically quite self-conscious users of the language, as Stephen Matthews observes in his study of Josiah Relph. Ewan Clark and Susanna Blamire both wrote the majority of their poems in what is described as 'a mildly marked form of standard English', while John Stagg and Mark Lonsdale used dialect 'in a bravura fashion, as a way of foregrounding the social aspects of their verse'.[30] I would argue too that Lonsdale's and Anderson's experience of the London stage also informed and influenced their writing: both knew how to appeal to audiences as performers as well as writers. Burns himself moderated his language in order to appeal to a wider British audience by employing what has been termed 'stage Scots': the use of a limited repertoire of words that characterise Scots speakers - lass, guid, bonny, mickle, ken, frae, laddie and the like. It was a self-conscious and playful performance that brought Burns to a wider audience as well as spawning many imitations in songs and plays of the time.[31]

Native dialect speakers also of course resorted at time to what linguists call 'code-switching': varying the register of speech according to the circumstances and the company.[32] Dialect has always been modified according to need to some extent, and 'putting on a voice' is nothing new. Deliberate code-switching was certainly used by Burns, and also by Anderson, creating a self-conscious 'performance' and stylised use of dialect. This was carried forward by later nineteenth century writers like Lancashire poet Samuel Laycock and Edwin Waugh, and entertainers like Joe Wilson and Tommy Armstrong in the North-East, combining dialect with play or parody whilst also tapping into existing popular traditions of performance and singing.[33] As Annette Wheeler Cafarelli points out, we should also remember that the mainstream Romantics, while they liked the concept of the vernacular, they did not want to compete in the marketplace for book buyers and even scarcer patrons. Peasant poets would surely be regarded by mainstream poets as 'unjust usurpers' and 'cultural rivals' – especially when Anderson's poetry proved more popular locally than that of Wordsworth.[34]

Cafarelli also oberves that it was their authenticity in rendering scenes of rural life that was viewed as the special virtue of writers like Anderson, with working-class writers generally being deemed custodians of nature: the simple voice of rural Britain. The working-class poets themselves understood this very well, realising that by styling themselves as simple, peasant poets they could 'capitalize on sentimentalized rurality', in the (usually forlorn) hope of acquiring wealth, a distinguished literary reputation and higher social status. Burns was the master of this: far from being a 'heaven-taught ploughman', he was a sophisticated writer for whom writing in Scots was 'a poetic option… not an educational necessity'.[35]

Dialect poetry is complex: its significance less to do with accurate re-creation of the dialect speech of the past, and more to do with the language's ability to invoke for its audience nostalgia for a time when living, loving, working and playing were altogether simpler: a mythical golden age. Most of all dialect poetry and song promote a sense of place, of identity and belonging and just as Burns's Scots songs came to be seen as standing for Scotland itself, we have seen

Anderson's 'Canny Cummerlan'' acting in just the same way. It is the authentic voice of the region, and rather than being emblematic of a dead or dying language and culture, as I hope Anderson's verse shows, the most enduring dialect works bring colour and add texture to the stories being told through the language they use.

Attachment to dialect in Cumberland and Westmorland runs deep. Particularly when framed as song it encapsulates an idea of 'Cumbrian-ness', as was identified in 1961 by Richard Kelly, producer of the BBC Northern Region's 'Voice of Cumberland' programme - on which Joe Wallace's songs were often heard [36] Whilst the county might be more sparsely populated and more parochial than the North East, he said, it had 'a strong cultural and linguistic tradition' along with 'a good deal of local music, and one or two singers and musicians worth encouraging.' Or, as George Coward put it in 1893: 'Most of the songs which Anderson has left us are intensely and thoroughly Cumberland songs, and belong to no other county; they are Cumberland in expression, feeling, and sentiment; they are Cumberland even in their prejudices and braggings, for does not Canny auld Cummerlan' cap them aw still?'

from the collections at Tullie House Museum, Carlisle

Portrait in oils of Robert Anderson,
attributed to John Hazlitt (1767-1837).

FAREWELL TO CAREL
Tune: 'The lovely brown maid'.

Fareweel canny Carel! hoo oft by thy streams
I've studied mankeynd to amuse;
An gain'd praise frae monie, but monie it seems
Will sneer at whate'er they peruse:
To paint rustic manners ov Cumbrians aw roun,
To rid them ov sorrow an care;
The wretch to expwose that wad boo puir fwok doon,
May please when puir Robbin's nae mair.

Fareweel canny Carel! on Hayton's hee hills,
Tho' winter is noo stealin on,
I view what wi' plishure the meynd ever fills,
Variety niver is gone!
By Celt's murm'rin river I offen perceive,
Weyl scenery aw praise that mun claim;
Hills, rocks, woods an watters deleyte can aye give
Mair than the girt city can neame.

Fareweel canny Carel! the pleace o' my birth,
Whoar years o' true plishure I spent;
Whate'er I may suffer wheyle gaz'n on earth,
May I pillow my heed wi' content!
Hoo chang'd are thy manners sin I was in youth,
For Modesty's gien way to Preyde;
Then innocent pasteymes fwok sowt for an truth;
Noo, Virtue owre monie dereyde.

Fareweel my dear Friens! may ye bliss langenjoy ;
Yer keyndness I'll niver forget;
Ther are whee my happiness fain wad destroy,
Tho' oft wi' my frienship they've met:
At neet owre the ingle or strayin by day,
I iver reflect on the past;
Whate'er may beteyde me for you I'll ay pray,
The others I'll scworn to the last.

Fareweel my dear Friens! when deame Nature we view,
Dress'd ever in beauteous attire;
Ow'rjoy'd let aw gaze on her scenes iver new,
An gazing still mair they'll admire:
Let panders ov veyce court the joys ov the toon,
Owre offen fause plishures that lure,
Then eager leyfe's cares in oblivion to droon,
They show what owre monie endure.

Fareweel my dear Friens! wheyles I'll wander alang,
Deleyted a few but to see;
For oft I hae pass'd thro' the midst o' the thrang,
Just view'd as a leafless aul tree.
Leyke weyld burds aroun us retirement I luive ;
A neybor I ne'er will begueyle;
Sud Captain Deeth caw he'd a tyrant nit pruive,
My welcome I'd gie wid a smeyle !

Notes

1. Taryn Hakala, A Great Man in Clogs: Performing Authenticity in Victorian Lancashire', *Victorian Studies,* 52 (2010), pp. 400 & 407.

2. Michael Baron, *Language and Relationship in Wordsworth's Writing* (London: 1995), pp. 17-18; William Wordsworth, *Lyrical Ballads with other poems. In two volumes,* (London: 1800).

3. Robert Crawford, *The Bard: Robert Burns, A Biography* (London, 2009), p. 195. Dave Russell, *Looking North: Northern England and the national imagination,* p. 111.

4. Katie Wales, *Northern English: A Cultural and Social History,* pp. 105, 151.

5. Mark Lonsdale's 'Th'Upshot' was published, with explanatory notes, in Francis Jollie's *Sketch of Cumberland Manners and Customs* (Carlisle: 1811), pp.5-23. Stagg's 'Rosley Fair' and 5. 5. 'The Bridewain' are published in John Stagg, *Miscellaneous Poems some of which are in the Cumberland Dialect* (Wigton: 1807), pp. 125-138. Robert Anderson editions are listed separately, see p.103.

6. John Russell Smith, *A biographical list of the works that have been published, towards illustrating the provincial dialects of England* (London: 1839); Josiah Relph, *A Miscellany of Poems* (Wigton: 1747).

7. Alexander Craig Gibson, *The Folk Speech of Cumberland and some districts adjacent: Being short stories and rhymes in the dialects of the West Border Counties* (London, 1869). Robert Anderson (Carlisle: 1893). Addenda, p. 19.

8. Archibald Sparke, *A Bibliography of the Dialect Literature of Cumberland, Westmorland and Lancashire North-of-the-Sands* (Kendal: 1907).

9. J. D. Marshall and John Walton, *The Lake Counties from 1830 to the Mid-Twentieth Century: a Study in Regional Change* (Manchester: 1981), pp. 15, 138.

10. Marshall and Walton, *The Lake Counties,* p. 49.

11. John Goodridge, 'Some Rhetorical Strategies in Later Nineteenth Century Laboring-Class Poetry', *Criticism,* 47 (2005), p. 534. Nikolas Coupland, 'Dialect Stylization in Radio Talk', *Language in Society,* 30 (2001), p. 348.

12. Charlotte Deans, *Memoirs of the life of Mrs Charlotte Deans,* (Wigton: 1837).

13. Broadsides generally featured two songs on one sheet, often decorated with woodcut illustrations, while a slip was a single song cut from a broadside. Chapbooks were small, cheaply produced eight to 24-page publications, also illustrated by woodcuts. Their content ranged from primers to fairy tales and religious tracts to history, but 'garlands' or collections of songs were especially popular. 'Songsters' were larger collections of songs.

14. Although the date of composition of 'Betty Brown' is given in Anderson's memoir, it is not clear when the poem was first published. It could perhaps have come from the press of his friend, the Carlisle printer Francis Jollie as there are three references in his diary to visiting Jollie in October and November 1800.

15. *Robert Anderson, the Cumberland bard: centenary celebration souvenir* (Carlisle: 1933).

16. Other Anderson texts set by James Hook include: 'A poor helpless wand'rer, the wide world before me', 'Orphan Bess the beggar girl', 'Canst thou love me, Mary?','Kate of Dover', 'Muirland Willy', 'The press gang forc'd my love to go', 'The cottage boy', 'The death of Crazy Jane', as well as 'Lucy Gray, of Allendale'.

17. Jonathan Conlin, *The Pleasure Garden, from Vauxhall to Coney Island* (Pennsylvania, 2013). David Stoker, 'Street Literature of the Long Nineteenth Century: Producers, Sellers, Consumers', in *Street Literature of the Long Nineteenth Century: Producers, Sellers, Consumers*, ed. David Atkinson and Steve Roud (Newcastle: 2017), pp. 60-97,

18. Keith Gregson, 'The Cumberland Bard: An Anniversary Reflection', *Folk Music Journal*, 4 (1983).

19. George Cruikshank, *The Universal Songster or Museum of Mirth* (London: 1825 -1826), pp. 239-240, 271-272, 347, 380 404. Robert Burns and Robert Anderson, *Burns' songs and Anderson's Cumberland ballads* (Newcastle-upon-Tyne: 1838).

20. Gregson, 'The Cumberland Bard: An Anniversary Reflection.'

21. Steve Roud, *Folk Song in England* (London: 2017). Steve Roud and Julia Bishop, *The New Penguin Book of English Folk Songs* (London: 2012).

22. Nicholson was also conductor of Carlisle Choral Society, and went on to become Organist of Manchester Cathedral in 1908 and Westminster Abbey in 1919. In 1929 he founded the Royal School of

Church Music and was knighted in 1938 for services to church music; 'Sydney Nicholson', *Oxford Dictionary of National Biography online*.

23. Songs collected at Carlisle, Vaughan Williams Memorial Library, Ralph Vaughan Williams Collection, Vol. 3, Book 11.

24. *Graham, Dialect Songs of the North: Lancashire, Cheshire, Westmorland & Cumberland* (London: 1910). Preface.

25. Jeffrey Mark, *Four North Country Songs* (Oxford: 1928).

26. Ted Relph, *Hoo's ta gaan on? Harold Forsyth's Cumberland Tales* (Carlisle: 2002), pp. 96-97 and 103.

27. Michael Baron, 'Dialect, Gender and the Politics of the Local: The Writing of Ann Wheeler', in *Romantic Masculinities* (Keele: 1997), p. 51.

28. Terminology varied from place to place, but 'merry neet' is a term still understood, and sometimes used, in Cumbria today. As Sanderson says, it originally referred to a Christmas gathering organised by the landlord of a local inn, where ale, food, music, dancing and card playing were enjoyed until the early hours of the morning. Similar gatherings at other times of the year were privately organised 'upshots' usually held in a barn in summer, while 'kurn suppers' or 'kurn-winnins' were harvest suppers.

29. He does something similar in another late poem, 'The Ballad Singer', which largely consists of a list of his own ballads (see Ellwood, 1904).

30. Steve Matthews, *Josiah Relph of Sebergham, England's First Dialect Poet* (Carlisle: 2015) pp. 250-251.

31. Alex Broadhead, 'A Sprinkling of Stage Scots: Burns, Linguistic Stereotypes and Place', *Scottish Literary Review*, 3 (2011), p. 21, 24.

32. Simon Elmes, *The Routes of English*, Vol. 1 (London: 2000) p. 29.

33. John Goodridge, 'Some Rhetorical Strategies,' pp. 534, 538.

34. Annette Wheeler Cafarelli, 'The Romantic "Peasant" Poets and their Patrons', *The Wordsworth Circle*, 26 (1995).

35. Murray Pittock, 'Scottish and Irish Romanticism', *Oxford Scholarship Online* (2008).

36. *Voice of Cumberland,* BBC Written Record Archive, 959-002-024, N25/40/1: memo dated 18 July 1961 from Richard Kelly, about a report suggesting axing 'Voice of Cumberland' programme on BBC Northern Service.

Robert Anderson in print: collections, anthologies and street literature 1798 - 1907

Anderson collections:

Poems on Various Subjects by R. Anderson, of Carlisle (Carlisle: J. Mitchell, 1798)

Ballads, in the Cumberland Dialect, by Robert Anderson; with Notes and a Glossary
(Carlisle: W. Hodgson, 1805)

Select ballads, in the Cumberland dialect, chiefly humorous, from the works of R. Anderson & others (Wigton: R. Hetherton, 1807)

Ballads, in the Cumberland Dialect, chiefly by R. Anderson, with Notes and a Glossary; the Remainder by various Authors, several of which have been never before published (Wigton: R. Hetherton, 1808)

Another edition, as above, 1809 (mentioned by Ellwood)

Anderson's Popular Songs, selected from his Works, calculated to enliven the Mind and exhilarate the Spirits in difficult Times (Wigton: R. Hetherton, 1811)

Another edition: as above but different printer (Wigton: J. Ismay, 1811)

Ballads, in the Cumberland Dialect, chiefly by R. Anderson, with Notes and a Glossary; the Remainder by various Authors, several of which have been never before published (Wigton: E. Rook, 1815)

The Poetical Works of Robert Anderson, Author of "Cumberland Ballads," &c., to which is prefixed the Life of the Author, written by himself; an Essay on the Character, Manners, and Customs of the Peasantry of Cumberland ; and Observations on the Style and Genius of the Author, by Thomas Sanderson. Two vols. (Carlisle: B. Scott, English Street, 1820).

Ballads in the Cumberland dialect by R. Anderson, with Notes & a Glossary (Wigton: E. Rooke, 1823).

Ballads in the Cumberland Dialect, by Robert Anderson and others ... [A selection.] To which is added, the Borrowdale Letter." (Carlisle: John Jollie, 1823) .

Another edition, also by Jollie, 1824.

Ballads, in the Cumberland Dialect, by R. Anderson, with Notes and a Glossary; and an Essay on the Manners & Customs of the Cumberland Peasantry, by Thomas Sanderson (Carlisle: H. K. Snowden, 1828).

Ballads, in the Cumberland Dialect, by R. Anderson, with Notes, a

Glossary, and a Biographical Sketch of the Author (Wigton: John Ismay, 1834).

Ballads in the Cumberland Dialect, by Robert Anderson, with Notes descriptive of the Manners and Customs of the Cumberland Peasantry; a Glossary of Local Words; and a Life of the Author (Alnwick: W. Davison, no date but probably c.1838-1840).

Note: Ellwood says this edition was stereotyped, the types then sold to T.W. Arthur of Carlisle, who re-issued it under his own name. 'A large portion of the stock in sheets' was then purchased by Crosthwaite and Co., Whitehaven, who used it under their own name as did their successors, Pagen and Gill.

Anderson's Cumberland Ballads, carefully compiled from the Author's MS., containing above one hundred pieces never before published, with a Memoir of his Life, written by himself, Notes, Glossary, &c., to which is added several other songs in the Cumberland Dialect, by various authors (Wigton: William Robertson, n.d., possibly 1843). Note: Publication must post-date 1843, when Robertson set up in business in Wigton.

Anderson's Cumberland ballads with notes, descriptive of the manners and Customs of the Cumberland Peasantry: a glossary of local words; and a life of the author (Cockermouth: D. Fidler, 1859).

Ballads in the Cumberland Dialect, by Robert Anderson, with Notes descriptive of the Manners and Customs of the Cumberland Peasantry ; a Glossary of Local Words, and a Life of the Author (Carlisle: B. Stewart. Printed in Glasgw, 1864).

Ballads in the Cumberland Dialect, by Robert Anderson (Whitehaven: Pagan & Gill, n.d.)

Note: only known from Ellwood's bibliography.

Cumberland Ballads by Robert Anderson, with Autobiography, Notes, and Glossary, edited by Sidney Gilpin (Carlisle: Geo. Coward, 1866).

Ballads in the Cumberland Dialect, by Robert Anderson, with Notes, descriptive of the Manners and Cusdtoms of the Cumberlad Peasantry; A Glossary of Local Words, and a Life of the Author. (Whitehaven: Crosthwaite & Co, n.d. probably c. 1870).

Ballads in the Cumberland Dialect, chiefly by R. Anderson, with Notes and a Glossary. The remainder by various authors (Cockermouth: I. Evening, 1870). Note: Essentially the same as editions of 1808 and 1815.

Anderson's Cumberland Ballads, with Notes, descriptive of the Manners and Customs of the Cumberland Peasantry; a Glossary of Local Words; and a Life of the Author (Carlisle: T. W. Arthur, c.1870). Note: Cheaply printed paperback edition.

Cumberland Ballads with Notes and a Glossary, edited by Sidney Gilpin (Carlisle: G, & T. Coward, 1881).

Anderson's Cumberland Ballads, Autobiography, Notes and Glossary, ed. Sidney Gilpin (Carlisle: G & T. Coward, 1893).

Anderson's Cumberland Ballads and Songs: Centenary Edition, edited, with Life of Anderson & Notes, by Rev. T. Ellwood, Also with Glossarial Concordance by Geo. Crowther (Ulverston: W. Holmes Ltd, 1904).

Cumberland Dialect. Selections from the Cumberland Ballads of Robert Anderson, edited by Geo. Crowther (Ulverston: W. Holmes, 1907).

Anthologies including Anderson ballads

Miscellaneous poems, songs, and ballads, in the Cumberland Dialect, with an essay on the manners and customs of Cumberland, a memoir oif the late Robert Anderson, the Cumberland Bard, and notices of other distinguished Cumberland writers, by John Rayson (Carlisle: Jollie and Steel, 1835)

Dialogues, Poems, Songs, and Ballads of Westmorland and Cumberland (London: John Russell Smith, 1839) Note: includes newly published Anderson ballads provided by his nephew.

The Songs and Ballads of Cumberland, edited by Sidney Gilpin (Carlisle: Geo. Coward, 1866) Note: includes 49 Anderson ballads.

The Songs and Ballads of Cumberland and the Lake Country, edited by Sidney Gilpin (Carlisle: G. & T. Coward, 1874)

Selected bibliography of street literature: Anderson ballads in broadsides, chapbooks and songsters

'Lucy Gray' in chapbook (Penrith: Ann Bell, c. 1798)

'The Sweetest Flower of Yarrow' in *The Whim of the Day* songster (London: J. Roach, 1795)

Sung by Mrs Rosamond Mountain (1768-1841) at Vauxhall Gardens

'Bonny Jem that's o'er the Sea' in songster *The Favourite Songs Sung at Vauxhall Gardens by Mrs Mountain, Mrs Franklin, Master Welsh, Mr Denman & Mr Dignum, Composed by Mr Hook*, Book 2 (London: Preston & Son, 1796) Includes music for all songs.

'Bonny Jem that's o'er the Sea' in songster *The New Whim of the Night* (London: C. Sheppard, S. Symonds, T. Bellamy, 1797)

'I rang'd the Banks of Tweed' in songster *The Whim of the Day* (London: J. Roach, 1799)

'Betty Brown' printed on broadside (London: J. Evans, c.1802)

'Sally Gray', 'Barbara Bell' and 'The Unfortunate Wife' in chapbook *A Garland of New Songs* (Penrith: A. Soulby, c.1803).

'Crazy Jane' in chapbook *New Songs* (Penrith: Ann Bell, 1804)

'The Cottage Boy' in chapbook *New Songs* (Penrith: Ann Bell, 1804)

The Harmonist, or Musical Olio: a choice selection of new and much-approved songs. Also, several Cumberland ballads, by Mr. Anderson. Songster (Penrith: Anthony Soulby, 1804)

'The Beggar Girl' in *A Garland containing Four Excellent Songs* (Alston: J.Harrop, n.d. c.1800)

'Polly' and 'The Beggar Girl' in chapbook *A Garland Containing Three Excellent New Songs* (no printer or date given)

'Crazy Jane' and 'Lovely Polly' in chapbook *Favourite Songs* (Alston: J. Harrop, n.d. c.1800?)

'Nichol the Newsmonger' and 'Biddy' in chapbook *The Two Cumberland Ballads called Nichol the Newsmonger: And Biddy: To which is added the Scottish song called The Wee Thing.* (Cumberland: Printed for the Booksellers, 1809)

'Canst Thou Love me, Mary' in *The Fashionable Songster, No.30* (Plymouth: W. Gray, c.1805) Note: 'Written by Mr Anderson, composed by Mr Hook, sung by Mr Dignum at Vauxhall Gardens'.

'Barbary Bell' broadside (London: J. Pitts, 1802-1819)

'Sweet Sally Gray' broadside (London: J. Pitts, c.1802-1855)

'Daft Watty's Ramble to Carlisle' in chapbook *A Garland of New Songs* (Newcastle/Hull: Fordyce, 1810-1828)

'Daft Watty's Ramble to Carlisle' in chapbook *A Garland of New Songs* (Newcastle: J.Marshall, c.1810-1831)

Burns Songs and Anderson's Cumberland Ballads: songster (Newcastle-upon-Tyne: W. Stewart, c.1838-1840)

'Dick Watters' broadside (Carlisle: B.Stewart, n.d.)

'It's just three weeks sin' Carel Fair '('First Liuve'), broadside (Newcastle & Hull: Fordyce; Carlisle: Whinham, n.d.)

'The Redbreast' broadside (Whitehaven: Wilson, n.d.)

'The Worton Wedding' in chapbook (Penrith: Allison, n.d. c. 1809)

'Nichol the Newsmonger' and 'The Worton Wedding' in chapbook *Select Cumberland Ballads* (Carlisle: C. Thurnam, n.d.)

'The Worton Wedding' in songster *Songs, Glees, duets, chorusses &c, sung at the Grand Concerts, at the Theatre-Royal,* Oct 5th, 6th & 8th 1824, by Madame Calala… &c … also the admired song, 'O say not Woman's heart is brought' and 'Worton Wedding' in the Cumberland Dialect. (Newcastle: J. Marshall, 1824)

The Universal Songster, or, Museum of Mirth […], Vol. III. Volume includes in the 'Yorks & Provincial' section, the followin - each designated 'A Cumberland Ballad': 'The Peck o'Punch', 'Jwohnny and Mary', 'The Thuirsby Witch 'Guid Strang Yell' and 'Dick Glendinin'(London: John Fairburn, 1826)

'The Bashfu' Wooer' and 'The Impatient Lass' in songster *Selkirk's Songs & Ballads for the People, No.2* (Newcastle: Selkirk, 1851)

'Peggy Penn - A Cumberland Ballad', air: The Barley Mow in songster *The Whistle-Binkie*, 1890 edition, no 2, part 4, (Glasgow: David Robertson, 1878)

Selected Bibliography

Manuscripts and fragments of diary of Robert Anderson, Carlisle, Jackson Library 2F. AND, 1A J417.

Chapbooks, some of which include Anderson's Ballads, Carlisle, Jackson Library M.175 Vol.1

Robert Anderson, The Cumberland Bard: Centenary Celebration Souvenir (Carlisle: 1933).

Burns' songs and Anderson's Cumberland ballads (Newcastle-upon-Tyne: Printed and published by W. Stewart, No. 5, Grainger Street, 1838).

Baron, Michael, *Language and Relationship in Wordsworth's Writing* (London: Longman, 1995).

Brown, James Walter, 'Omnium Gatherum', *Jackson Collection* Various.

Cafarelli, Annette Wheeler, 'The Romantic "Peasant" Poets and their Patrons', *The Wordsworth Circle,* 26 (1995).

Conlin, Jonathan, ed., *The Pleasure Garden, from Vauxhall to Coney Island* (Pennsylvania: University of Pennsylvania Press, 2013).

Coupland, Nikolas, 'Dialect Stylization in Radio Talk', *Language in Society,* 30 (2001)

Crowther, George, ed., *Bleckell Murry Neet: Ballad by Robert Anderson, the Cumberland Bard* (Carlisle: James Beaty & Sons, 1906).

Cruikshank, George, *The Universal Songster or Museum of Mirth*, Vol. 3 (London: John Fairburn, 1825 -1826).

Deans, Charlotte, *Memoirs of the life of Mrs Charlotte Deans from her earliest infancy* (Wigton: H Hoodless, Market-Place, 1837),.

Goodridge   John, 'Some Rhetorical Strategies in Later Nineteenth Century Laboring-Class Poetry', *Criticism,* 47 (2005).

Gregson, Keith, 'The Cumberland Bard: An Anniversary Reflection', *Folk Music Journal,* 4 (1983).

Hakala, Taryn, 'A Great Man in Clogs: Performing Authenticity in Victorian Lancashire', *Victorian Studies,* 52 (2010).

Huggins, Mike, 'Popular Culture and Sporting Life in the Rural Margins of Late Eighteenth Century England: The World of Robert Anderson, "The Cumberland Bard"', *Eighteenth-Century Studies,* 45 (2012).

Joyce, Patrick, *Visions of the People: Industrial England and the Question of Class* (Cambridge: Cambridge University Press, 1991).

K.I., 'Cumberland Free and Easy in London', *The Citizen*, May 1829 1829, pp. 289-292.

Mark, Jeffrey, *Four North Country Songs* (Oxford: Oxford University Press, 1928).

Marshall J.D, and Walton J., *The Lake Counties from 1830 to the Mid-Twentieth Century: a Study in Regional Change* (Manchester: Manchester University Press, 1981).

Pegg, Joseph W., *Newcastle's Musical Heritage: An* Introduction (Newcastle: Newcastle City Council, 2003).

Pittock, Murray, 'Scottish and Irish Romanticism', in *Oxford Scholarship Online* (Oxford, 2008).

Rayson, John, *Miscellaneous Poems and Ballads, Chiefly in the Dialects of Cumberland and the English and Scotch Borders* (Carlisle and London: Charles Thurnam and Sons; Piper, Stephenson, and Spence, 1858).

Relph, Ted, ed., *Hoo's ta gaan on? Harold Forsyth's Cumberland Tales* (Carlisle: Lakeland Dialect Society, 2002).

Roud, Steve, *Folk Song in England* (London: Faber & Faber Ltd, 2017).

Roud, Steve and Bishop, Julia, *The New Penguin Book of English Folk Songs* (London: Penguin Books Ltd, 2012).

Sparke, Archibald, *A Bibliography of the Dialect Literature of Cumberland, Westmorland and Lancashire North-of-the-Sands*

(Kendal: CWAAS, 1907).

Stoker, David, Street Literature of the Long Nineteenth Century: Producers, Sellers, Consumers', in *Street Literature of the Long Nineteenth Century: Producers, Sellers, Consumers*, ed. by David Atkinson and Steve Roud (Newcastle: Cambridge Scholars Publishing, 2017).

Wales, Katie, *Northern English: A Cultural and Social History* (Cambridge: Cambridge University Press, 2006).

Wordsworth, William, *Lyrical Ballads with other poems. In two volumes* (London: Printed for T.N. Longman and O. Rees, by Biggs and Co., Bristol, 1800).

Acknowledgements

I owe a debt of gratitude to a whole range of people and institutions for assistance with getting this anniversary celebration of Robert Anderson into print. As my research into the man and his ballads now spans more than thirty years however, there are inevitably those who I will forget to name simply because of the passage of time, so please forgive any omissions here.

Thanks are due first of all to Steve Matthews of Bookcase for commissioning the book in the first place - and putting up with delays in getting my manuscript to him. Thanks too to my PhD supervisor at Lancaster University, Professor Angus Winchester, whose comments and advice when I was writing about Anderson for my thesis on folk song in Cumbria were always apposite and helpful.

Keith Gregson's 1980s Anderson researches and publications were also hugely helpful, both for inspiring me to learn more about the poet and also for guiding my early explorations of the poet and his work. Steve Roud's folk song and broadside indexes at the Vaughan Williams Memorial Library proved to be sources of information on ballads published in more ephemeral print publications–broadsides, chapbooks and songsters–and Steve invariably generous with advice and support.

I am grateful too to the staff of Tullie House Museum and Art Gallery in Carlisle, where I have been able to inspect and photograph a number of Anderson artefacts at close quarters, and to Anderson family member Joan Williams, who provided information on Anderson's Northern Ireland letters.

The finest collection of Anderson books and manuscripts, is at Carlisle Library, and I would like to thank in particular retired Carlisle librarian Kath Barling, who transcribed Anderson's diary and indexed the manuscripts in the collection. Above all though, heartfelt thanks to Local Studies Librarian Stephen White for his unfailingly invaluable assistance over the years. I have relied heavily on the breadth and depth of his knowledge of the Jackson Library (local studies collection) which holds the Anderson material, but must also thank him for his patience when dealing with my many awkward queries - and his enthusiasm for this study of 'The Cumberland Bard'.

Index

Facsimile of 1828 Snowden edition:

Ballads in the Cumberland Dialect
by R. Anderson

with Notes and a Glossary:
and an Essay on the Manners and
Customs of the Cumberland Peasantry
by Thomas Sanderson.

BALLADS,
IN THE
CUMBERLAND DIALECT,
BY
ROBERT ANDERSON.

Drawn & Engraved   by W.H.Lizars

BALLAD 50. TIB AND HER MAISTER.

what think ye o' me?
Tib! gi'es thy hand: a bargain be't –
We'll off to kurk to-mworn: –
A young weyfe for me. Tib.

CARLISLE.
Printed for H. K. Snowden; and sold by Oliver and Boyd, Edinburgh; Mozley,
Derby; and most other Booksellers 1828.

BALLADS,

IN THE CUMBERLAND DIALECT,

BY

R. ANDERSON,

WITH NOTES AND A GLOSSARY;

AND

AN ESSAY

ON THE

MANNERS AND CUSTOMS OF THE CUMBERLAND
PEASANTRY,

BY THOMAS SANDERSON.

———

CARLISLE:

PRINTED FOR H. K. SNOWDEN;

AND SOLD BY OLIVER AND BOYD, EDINBURGH;
H. MOZLEY, DERBY.

—

1828.

CONTENTS.

lv.

CONTENTS.

AN ESSAY

ON THE

CHARACTER, MANNERS, AND CUSTOMS,

OF THE

PEASANTRY OF CUMBERLAND.

THE manners of the Cumbrian peasantry have undergone a great change within the last half century, especially in the neighbourhood of manufacturing towns. He who wishes to view them in their original simplicity, must make a tour into those sequestered parts where herds and flocks constitute the chief wealth of the inhabitants, and where the country, unintersected by turnpike roads, presents to the eye a widely extended waste of uncultivated land. He will there find men who speak their sentiments with honest bluntness, and (strangers to the courtly phrases which the fashionable world has introduced as the standard of politeness) express themselves in the unstudied simplicity of nature, and, in every look and feature, discover the natural feelings of the heart.

Hospitality is their distinguishing virtue. Should a stranger seek shelter in one of their cottages during a shower of rain, or be induced to visit it from motives of curiosity, he is immediately accommodated

B

with the best seat that their humble habitation affords; and after the hearth has been swept clean, and the fire supplied with an additional load of fuel, is invited to partake of their oaten cake, butter, and cheese. If his taste has not been vitiated by more luxurious viands, this simple fare will not be unpalatable to him ; and the more freely he uses his knife, the more will it gratify his hospitable entertainers. On his departure, a glass of whisky (the favourite liquor of a Cumbrian borderer) will be probably offered to him ; while a cordial FAREWELL is pronounced by every tongue in the family. This is certainly *politeness* in the genuine import of the word. Courtesy, says a great poet,

" Is sooner found in lonely sheds
With smoky rafters, than in tap'stry halls
And courts of princes, where it first was nam'd,
And yet is most pretended."—*Milton's Masque.*

The houses of the inhabitants in these remote districts, though seldom more than a story high, and covered generally with straw, are neat and commodious structures, sufficiently capacious to hold the family and a visiting friend or two. Nor does the interior of the building disappoint the expectations raised by the exterior. The furniture is neat, though not costly, —is nicely arranged,—and, at least once a week, receives a varnish from bees' wax. Opposite to the window usually stands what they call a *dresser*, which not only contains such earthen plates and basins as are in daily use, but also an assortment of pewter dishes, trenchers, piggins, and other utensils, on which TIME has impressed his stamp, and which the refinement of the age has made unfashionable. The walls are neatly white-washed, and, in some parts, ornamented with maps and prints executed in a sufficient style of elegance to please the tastes of rustic connoisseurs. Two or three shelves, affixed to the wall, contain the family library. One of the chimney corners is generally occupied by a massive arm chair; that has held a contest

with time for a century or more. It is the seat of the
venerable grandsire of the family, and, during the winter evenings, is commonly surrounded by a groupe of
boys and girls, listening to his " *tales of the times of old
—to the deeds of other days.*"*

It is pleasing to remark, that the moral and religious improvement of the inhabitants of these districts
have kept pace with the amelioration of their external
circumstances, and the increase of their domestic comforts. When we compare their condition to that of
their forefathers before the union of the two kingdoms,
in what a striking light appear the advantages flowing
from a free constitution, and the impartial adminis-
tration of equable laws ! It is difficult to find adequate
words to describe their situation during the inroads of
the Moss-troopers. The day was passed under per-
petual alarm, and even their repose at night was frequently broken by the shouts of a marauding party,
and the HUE and CRY of the plundered peasant. Among
those freebooters no infamy attached to their predatory
incursions, which laid waste the border districts. They
considered pillage and robbery, beyond their own fron-
tiers, not as crimes, but as valorous achievements de-
serving applause. Our German ancestors, according
to Cæsar, entertained the same opinions. " Latrocinia
(says that elegant historian) nullum habent infamiam
quo extra fines cujusque civitatis fiunt." The condition
of the peasantry in those days may be imagined, but
cannot be described. Every thing around them indicated their abject poverty and wretchedness. They
and their cattle reposed at night under the same roof ;
and, as husbandry then was at a low ebb, the dung
which their quadruped neighbours produced, being of
no value, was suffered to accumulate till it formed
a mass that required Herculean labour to remove.—
Their habitations were but mere hovels, built of mud,
covered with fern or rushes, and pervious to every

* Ossian.

shower that fell, and to every blast that blew. In
these huts, surrounded by their shivering offspring,
involved in smoke, and almost destitute of clothing,
they past the cold and dreary months of winter. But
let us turn from a picture at which the heart sickens,
to scenes that are gratifying to every patriotic heart.

The union of the two kingdoms, at length, removed
the evil which had long afflicted Cumberland; but the
poverty of her peasantry continued long after the original cause of it had ceased. Broken down by a series
of calamities, their minds could not rise to that vigour
of thought, necessary to project, and that energy of
action, requisite to execute, any great and important
enterprise. It is only within the last half century,
that they began to rouse themselves from a state of in-
efficacy and inertness, to exertions that have raised
Cumberland to her proper station among her sister
counties. The superior intelligence of her people had
been long acknowledged: they only wanted industry
and exertion to rival, if not surpass, their southern
countrymen, in all the arts that improve or embellish
life. In literature, science, trade, manufactures, and
in agriculture, they have made considerable advances.
Their agricultural improvements have been particularly rapid, extensive, and important. They have almost every where changed the aspect of the country,
and augmented its opulence and population. Extensive commons, which only afforded a scanty pasturage
to a few half-starved sheep and cattle, have been in-
closed and cultivated, and rendered capable of producing
luxuriant crops of grain and grass. Morases have
been drained and converted into meadows, commodious farm-buildings been erected, and travelling facili-
tated by good roads and good bridges. Even the most
sterile lands have been planted with larches, and other
hardy trees; and, by their thriving plantations, are
made to contribute to the general opulence, as well
as to the ornament, of the county. Such have been
the achievements of Cumbrian industry.

In the northern and eastern parts of Cumberland, little attention was paid, till of late years, to the culture of the mind. Even the most opulent *laird** did not possess the advantages of a learned education. To read the psalter, to write their own name legibly, and cast up a mechanic's bill, generally satisfied their literary ambition. Nor had they any desire that the education of their sons should extend beyond these limits, lest such an enlarged erudition should have tempted them to become *forgers*.

With respect to the peasantry of those districts, few at that time could read, and still fewer were acquainted with writing and arithmetic. When their signature became necessary to any legal instrument, they made a *cross*, as a testimony, I suppose, that they were Christians, though they were unable to write. If any one of their class could write and indite, so as to be capable of carrying on an epistolary correspondence with a distant friend, he was considered as a prodigy in literature, and was generally employed as an amanuensis to those who had not made the same literary acquisitions. This general want of learning does not, however, characterize the peasants of the present day. Most of them can read, write, and cast up accounts. They are (to use one of their own phrases) good *Bible scholars*, which implies an ability to read, with tolerable ease and correctness, a chapter in the Old or New Testament ; and let none of us despise that humble mediocrity of learning that reaches not beyond the BIBLE—a book that brings consolation to the heart, under all the distresses to which the unsearchable providence of GOD has subjected our species. " Young man," said the learned Dr. JOHNSON, in his last illness, to a gentleman who sate by his bed-side, " attend to the advice of one who has possessed some degree of

* In some parts of Cumberland, the proprietor of a landed estate is styled a *laird*.

fame in the world, and who will shortly appear before his Maker : " *Read the Bible every day of your life !*"

Of late years, the education of the peasantry has become more general by the erection of new schools ; some of which are endowed, and the rest supported by pecuniary subscriptions among the inhabitants, or by the quarter-pence of the scholars. Where the quarter-pay is inadequate to the support of the master, he is allowed what is called a *whittle-gait*, or the privi- lege of using his knife, in rotation, at the tables of those who send children to his school ; and, if he be not a bashful *trencherman*, he never finds any reason to regret this mode of dining by rotation, as every good housewife always provides, against his WHITTLE-DAY, a *cowed lword*,† and a piece of beef or mutton.

Church music generally composes a part of the edu- cation of a Cumbrian peasant. They are instructed in it by the parish clerk, or by some itinerant profes- sor ; and in the course of a few months, by the means of a good ear, and a tuneable voice, acquire as much skill in it, as to be able to gratify the taste of a coun- try audience, at least as far as an accurate combination of sound extends. As to the principles of the science, they and their instructors are equally ignorant. When the school breaks up, they who compose the choir, and he who leads it, have generally a *ball* at the village ale-house, in order to experience joys of a more *terres- trial* nature than those which spring from PSALM- SINGING. Fiddling, dancing, and drinking continue to a late hour : the divine strains, which they lately sung, are forgotten ; and the heart shut against all the devout feelings which they are calculated to inspire. A practice so offensive to every pious and religious mind, cannot certainly be too soon abolished:

Most of the Cumbrian peasantry are instructed in their early years in DANCING, by some teacher who wanders from village to village, generally carrying more merit in his heels than in his head. His pupils

† A favourite dish among the Cumbrian peasantry, made of oat- meal and hog's lard.

are taught country dances, hornpipes, jigs, and reels ; and, if they have any *springyness* in them, generally attain, after a few months' instruction, sufficient skill and agility in the art, as to be able to amuse the spectators in a rustic assembly-room.

Dancing has so many advocates among the lower, as well as among the higher, classes of the community, that to censure it would probably be to incur the charge of puritanical austerity ; but I should think that the time and money expended in acquiring this art, might be more usefully applied. Life is too short to waste any portion of it in frivolous amusements—in such as have no tendency to advance us in the scale of thinking beings. But the frivolity of dancing might be passed over, if it were not reprehensible in a moral light. In attaining the regulated movement and the measured step, a girl too often loses those retiring and sweetly blushing graces which are the chief ornaments of her sex. Few readers of poetry are strangers to the beautiful episode of PALEMON and LAVINIA, in Thomson's Autumn. It was not the accomplishments acquired in a dancing-school which struck the heart of the generous PALEMON, when he observed LAVINIA gleaning in his field : it was " her *native* graces—her *modest* virtues—her *unaffected* blushes—her *down-cast* eyes, darting all their beams into the blooming flowers" that made " love and chaste desire spring in his bosom." If a painter wishes to draw a rural BEAUTY, with all the magic charms of nature about her, he must not go into a dancing-room for an archetype.

Amidst all the fatiguing labours which his condition of life subjects him to, the Cumbrian peasant has his festive scenes, which throw a temporary sunshine around him ; and by the gratifications which they afford *to-day*, suspend the thoughts of the hardships and toils of *to-morrow*. In these he mingles with such ardour and vivacity, as if he belonged rather to the train of COMUS, than to those terrestrial beings who journey in a vale of sorrow. FAIRS, MERRY-NIGHTS, UPSHOTS, and other festive meetings present themselves, in rapid succession, to his joyous heart, and offer a sufficient channel for the most redundant flow of animal spirits. Every market-town in Cumberland has its annual fair, which draws together a great concourse of people. Carlisle fair, or, as it is called by the country people, *Carel fair*, is so noted for the number and variety of its amusements and choice of commodities, that there is hardly a villager within the circuit of ten miles who does not attend it, except perhaps two or three unhappy swains and nymphs, whom the authority of a morose parent, or a churlish master or mistress, confines at home. A Cumberland lad, when he meets his sweetheart at a fair, whether by appointment or accident, throws his arms round her waist in all the raptures of love, conducts her to a dancing room, places her beside him on a bench, and treats her liberally with cake and punch. When a vacancy happens on the floor, he leads her out to dance a jig or a reel. If her choice be a reel, another partner being necessary, he makes a bow to some other girl in the company, and at the end of the dance he salutes each of his fair partners with a cordial kiss, if its cordiality can be ascertained by the loudness of its sound ; for a plain, honest rustic, impresses his kisses with so much vehemence on the roseate lips of his fair one, that they have been compared by BURNS to the crack of a waggoner's whip; and, with equal happiness, by the author of the following Ballads, to the sound of a gate's latch. At the close of the day, a Cumbrian rustic would think himself deficient in common gallantry, if he omitted to escort his sweetheart to her own house,—a favour that she always repays by a more than usual portion of smiles on his next visit. Rosley-hill is also celebrated for its fairs, some of which are as numerously attended as that which takes place in the metropolis of the county, of which I have given a description. They

are held on an extensive common, where sufficient
room is given to the crowd to expand themselves.
They commence on Whit-Monday, and continue once
a fortnight till Michaelmas. It is impossible to con-
vey an adequate idea of them by description. One
part of the hill is covered with horses and black cattle
—with dealers, drovers, and jockies ; who, if the day
be windy and sultry, are involved in a hurricane of
dust, almost as violent in its duration as that which
sweeps the arid deserts of Africa : another part is
overspread with the booths of mercers, milliners, hard-
waremen, and bread-bakers. Here you see the moun-
tebank, hawker, and auctioneer, addressing the gaping
crowd from a wooden platform ; and there you hear
the discordant strains of the ballad-singer, the music
of the bagpipe and the violin, of the fife, and " the
spirit-stirring drum." Tents of innkeepers, crowded
with bottles and barrels, are interspersed in every part
of the festal ground, but particularly in the vicinity of
the horse-fair, where the heat and dust of the day occasion a more than usual thirst ; and, much to the prudence
of these *knights of the cork* and *spigot*, the malt and spi-
rituous liquors which they retail to their thirsty cus-
tomers, are so judiciously diluted with water, that
they operate with all the innocence of simple dieure-
tics ; so that it is not uncommon to see a company of
hale farmers, after having exhausted all the casks and
bottles in these *moving cellars*, returning to their own
houses with all the sobriety and gravity in which they
left them in the morning.—Of these fairs, which are
prolonged till they dwindle into insignificance, the second is particularly noted for a fine assemblage of
Cumbrian lasses, who, in different parties, parade
the hill, in all the artless simplicity of rural beauty,
till some rustic admirer displays his gallantry and his
love, by escorting a select number of them to some
neighbouring tent, and treating them with cake and
punch, and the music of the bagpipe and fiddle.—

When these acknowledgements have been paid to their beauty, they return to the field to attack and to conquer ; for to a girl, who has received from nature her share of beauty, the whole day is distinguished by a succession of triumphs. The cakes, ribbons, and handkerchiefs, (the tributes of rural gallantry,) are, on their return home, carefully deposited, as so many illustrious trophies of their victories. At these fairs are sold a species of cheese called *Whyllymer*, or, as some whimsically style it, *Rosley Cheshire*. It is as remarkable for its poverty as that of Stilton is for its richness ; and its surface is so hard, that it frequently bids defiance to the keenest edge of a Cumbrian *gully*, and its interior substance so very tough, that it affords rather occupation to the teeth of a rustic than nourishment to his body, making his hour of repast the severest part of his day's labours.—About noon the boundaries of the fair are perambulated, or, as it is provincially called, "*ridden*,"—whioh exhibits a spectacle "sufficient," (to use the words of Dr. Johnson) "to awaken the most torpid risibility." A number of lairds, farmers, tradesmen and mechanics, mount their horses, and, in a slow and solemn pace, wind round the circuit of the hill, accompanied by a train of venerable fiddlers, many of whom have been the tormentors of cat-gut for almost half a century. These minstrels, who, during the rest of the year, travel on foot from village to village, giving music in return for oats or barley, are on these occasions, by the favour of their friends, mounted on horseback, and provided with better clothes.

A " MERRY-NIGHT" is, as its name imports, a night dedicated to mirth and festivity, and always takes place at some country ale-house, during the Christmas holidays. It is generally attended by a numerous company of lads and lasses, the pride and flower of the neighbouring villages, for whose entertainment the landlord takes care to provide pies of different kinds, cards, music, and a competent quantity of ale, whisky, gin, and rum. The dancing commences early in the evening, and continues, with unabating spirit, till after midnight. The music, if it be not able to produce the wonderful effects attributed to the strains of Orpheus,* has always sufficient powers to move the muscular limbs of an athletic ploughman, and urge him to acts of agility, that often bring his head in contact with the ceiling, or beams of the dancing-room—a *feat* that never fails to give celebrity to a country performer.

> " He jumps, and his heels *knack* and *rattle*,
> At turns of the music so sweet;
> He makes such a thund'ring brattle,
> That the floor seems afraid of his feet."
> *The Collier's Pay Week.*

At the conclusion of a jig, the fiddler makes his instrument squeak out two notes that say, or are understood to say, " *Kiss her !*"—a command which the rustic youth immediately obeys, by giving his fair partner a salute equal, as far as relates to *sound*, to that which PETRUCIO bestowed upon his bride :

> " He took the bride about the neck,
> And kiss'd her lips with such a *clam'rous smack*,
> That, at the parting, all the church did echo !"
> *Shakspeare's* " *Taming of the Shrew.*"

This familiarity between a dancing couple is of an ancient standing. The anonymous author of an old poem, entitled " The use and abuse of dancing and minstrelsie," appears to think, in the following stanza, that a dance would give no pleasure, if not terminated by a parting salute :

> " But some reply what fool would daunce,
> If that when daunce were doone,
> He may not have a ladyes lips,
> That which in daunce he woon."

* ——————————————The Poets
Did feign that Orpheus drew trees, stones, and floods.
Shakspeare's " *Merchant of Venice.*"

In Shakspeare's Henry VIII. the prince says to his partner :

> " I were unmannerly to take you out,
> And not to kiss you."

But all these authorities in favour of the custom, will not be able to keep it up, I fear, against the refinements of the age, which, in some parts of Cumberland, have, in a great measure, already done it away, and induced the country girls to be less lavish of the balmy fragrance of their lips—at least in public.

MERRY-NIGHTS are certainly well calculated to facilitate an intercourse between the two sexes. A courtship commonly commences at them, which is carried on by an ardour of spirit that would have done honour to a cavalier in the days of chivalry. The enamoured youth, in order to escape the observation of his inquisitive neighbours, sets out for the habitation of his DULCINEA at a late hour of the night, and often in the depth of winter, regardless of the inclemency of the weather, of the badness of the roads, and of the moors, mosses, and hills that intervene between him and his fair charmer. He surmounts every difficulty, and announces his arrival to his fair one, by a tap on the window of her chamber, on which, if he be one of her favourite swains, she immediately rises, and opens to him the kitchen door. The wooing scene commences in one of the chimney corners, where a few embers diffuse a sort of glimmering light ; and the lovers seldom separate till the " cock's shrill clarion" announces the approach of day. As a well wisher to my fair countrywomen, I cannot help representing to them the danger and impropriety of admitting the addresses of lovers during those hours of the night which are usually appropriated to repose. Nothing more encourages unbecoming familiarities, nothing more endangers female chastity, and nothing more promotes the designs of the seducer, than these *night-courtships*. A custom, from which so many evils result, however general it may be, and whatever antiquity it may claim, cannot be too soon abolished; and I am so much convinced of the general good sense and purity of the heart of the CUMBRIAN FAIR, that I am encouraged to hope that, as soon as they reflect on the guilt and misery which it is likely to lead to, their virtue will take the alarm, and they will see the danger of admitting the visits of their lovers in improper situations and at improper times.

An UPSHOT is a meeting among a number of merry-hearted swains and nymphs, most of them fond of music and dancing, and all of them prepared to say to melancholy:

> " Hence, loathed Melanchely
> ' Of Cerberus and blackest midnight born,
> In Stygian cave forlorn
> 'Mongst horrid shapes, and shrieks, and sights unholy,
> Find out some uncouth cell,
> Where brooding darkness spreads his jealous wings,
> And the night-raven sings;
> There under cbon shades, and low-brow'd rocks,
> As ragged as thy locke,
> In dark Cimmerian desart ever dwell."
> *Milton's L' Allegro.*

It generally takes place in a BARN, during the summer season, when there are no " merry-nights" to animate the lagging moments of a leisure hour; and

> " Though no *golden sconces* hang upon the walls,
> To light the costly suppers and the balls,"—*Dryden.*

the humble assembly-room is commonly well illuminated by a number of tallow-lights, stuck in tin and iron sockets, and sometimes in cloven sticks, and excavated turnips or potatoes; and the company are sufficiently regaled by liberal slices of bread and cheese, and flowing bumpers of home-brewed ale. The dance is always kept up with unabating spirit, till what Shakspeare calls " the witching time of night," and, when it terminates, each rustic lover accompanies his fair one to her own habitation.

c

Among the peasantry of Cumberland, a WEDDING-DAY is one continued scene of mirth and feasting, from morning till midnight. Early in the day, the bridegroom, attended by a select party of his friends, well-mounted, and all in their holiday dresses, proceed, at a quick trot, to the bride's house, where the nuptial festival is always held. On alighting, he takes a seat near his intended spouse, gives her a salute, and then joins the breakfasting company, in order to taste something more substantial, if not as fragrant, than a lady's vermil lips. After banqueting amidst all the luxuries of a tea-table, he and his friends re-mount their horses, and, accompanied by the bride and her retinue, proceed, at a steady pace, to the church, sometimes animated on the road by the strains of the violin or bagpipe.

> " The pipers wind and take their post,
> And go before to clear the coast '
> > *The Collier's Wedding.*

The bridegroom, after he is indissolubly united to the maid of his choice, invites the company to the village ale-house, which is often but a few paces from the church : for, as an old satirist observes,

> " Where'er the Lord erects a house of prayer,
> The devil always builds a chapel near."

With their courage elevated by drams and punch, they re-mount their steeds, and, with the ardour of Newmarket sportsmen, contend who shall first reach the bride's habitation. The victor at this Hymenial race is rewarded by a kiss from the bridemaid, or what is more valuable to a man who has more sweethearts than pence—with a silken handkerchief.

After dinner, the dancing commences, the glass circulates briskly round, to the health of the new-married couple ; and slices of bride-cake are thrice, and sometimes oftener, put through the wedding-ring, and given to the unmarried youngsters, who place them under their pillows, in consequence of which, they have nothing but sweet dreams of love and marriage. When the bride has been put to bed by her female attendants, one of her stockings is thrown among the lads and lasses; and the person whom it hits will, it is supposed, be sooner married than any other of the company.

Some of the Cumbrians, particularly those who are in poor circumstances, have, on their entrance into the married state, what is called A BIDDING or BIDDEN WEDDING, at which a pecuniary collection is made among the company for the purpose of setting the wedded pair forward in the world. It is always attended with music and dancing; and the fiddler, when the contributions begin, takes care to remind the assembly of their duties, by notes imitative of the following couplet:

"Come, my friends, and freely offer,
Here's the Bride who has no Tocher."[*]

A BRIDEWAIN[†] or INFAIR is also a festive meeting called together for the same purpose, and held at the house of the bridegroom, when he brings home his bride and her furniture. The whole country, for several miles round, is invited to it, and various diversions are exhibited for their entertainment. A plate or dish is placed upon a table, where every one of the company contributes according to his inclination and circumstances. The contributions, amounting to fifty, and sometimes to a hundred pounds, enable a couple to begin the world with advantage; and are also a convincing testimony of the high estimation in which they are held by their neighbours.

[*] Dower.
[†] The bride and her furniture were formerly brought to the bridegroom's house in a *wain* or waggon.

The Cumbrian peasantry were formerly so fond of athletic exercises, such as wrestling, leaping, throwing the stone, and playing at foot-ball and quoits, that they were frequently practised on the Sabbath. The growing piety of the age at length did away these rustic diversions, or at least, operated as a bar to their taking place on the day set apart for public worship, and I wish I could add that the Sunday afternoons, which were spent by our forefathers in idle amusements, are appropriated by my young countrymen to religious reading and meditation.

In some parts of Cumberland, a number of boys and girls, on the eve of New Year Day, go about from house to house singing a sort of a carol, of which the following lines are the first couplet :—

Hagnuna, Trolola,
Give us some pie, and let us go away.

When they receive their present of pie, they depart peaceably, wishing the donor a happy new year. In Northumberland, the first word in the couplet is *Hagmena,* which some derive from the two Greek words, *agia mene,* signifying the holy month. The custom is not unknown in Scotland. Some years ago, one of her ministers endeavoured to abolish it by censuring it from the pulpit. " Sirs, (said he to his audience,) do you know what *Hogmane* signifies? It is, The Devil be in the house!—that is the meaning of its *Hebrew original.*" Our little strolling Cumbrian boys and girls will not, I think, be easily persuaded that any part of their begging-song conveys an imprecation on the houses which they visit.

A few years ago, many superstitious notions, with respect to the existence of supernatural beings, prevailed in Cumberland, which, as learning and science advanced, gave way to more rational opinions. Some of them, however, still linger in the sequestered districts of the county, where the mind has not been improved by education, and the manners polished by an extended intercourse with the world. Stories of boggles, ghosts, wraiths, and fairies, have there a general currency, and afford ample materials for a long winter night's conversation. The boggle, as described by those who have seen it, is a being of a terrified aspect, of a gigantic size, and generally in the human shape, with an enormous head and two saucer eyes, flaming like a beacon. Its favourite haunts are dark and secluded lonnings, the ruins of old castles, and dilapidated mansion-houses. It loves darkness, and never appears till those hours, which Shakespeare calls the "witching time of night." Like other spectres, it is generally silent; but when it does break silence, its unearthly cries "make night hideous," and operate so much on the fears of the poor benighted rustic, that he hastens home with precipitated steps, sometimes leaving his clogs in the flight—a loss that he does not regret when he reaches in safety his fire-side; for who would not part with articles of the greatest value for the sake of being able to breathe awhile longer in this sublunary scene?

Of the ghost, the village chroniclers relate the following particulars:—It is, according to them, the spirit of a person deceased, who is permitted to revisit the world for various purposes; sometimes to discover murder,—sometimes to procure restitution of some real or personal estate, unjustly withheld from an orphan or a widow,—sometimes to inform the heir in what private place the title deeds of the estate are deposited,—or in what spot of ground plate or money has been buried. Some ghosts of persons who have been murdered make their appearance, that they may shew the grave where their bones lie, in order to have them taken up, and interred in consecrated ground, with the rites of Christian burial; and some ghosts are said to be the spirits of those who, having committed some theft or injustice in their life-time, cannot rest till the stolen articles be restored, or the injury redressed.

The *wraith, swarth,* or *swath,* is an apparition in the form and garb of some living person that is seen by some of his acquaintances. If it appears in the morning, it betokens health and long life to the person whose semblance it bears ; but if it is seen in the evening, it is considered as a prognostic of his approaching dissolution.

The fairies are a sort of intermediate beings between men and spirits, very diminutive in stature, but active and fond of gambols. They have their habitations under-ground,—from which, in a summer evening, they frequently issue, to enjoy in our meadows their favourite diversion of dancing. They are said to be of a fair complexion, with dishevelled hair, floating over their shoulders, and are always clothed in green attire.

Such of the Cumbrian peasantry, whose ideas have not been enlarged by education, have a firm belief in witchcraft and necromancy ; and discover, in the person of every deformed old woman, a witch and a magician, whose favour they are anxious to conciliate, and whose vengeance they are solicitous to avert.   If poor Hodge fall from his cart, and dislocate his neck— if he be wildered on some dreary moor—if some contagious distemper destroy his cattle, or some pestilential sickness afflict his family—in short, all the calamities and misfortunes that visit him or his neighbours, are imputed to her infernal incantations.

The manners and customs peculiar to the peasantry of Cumberland, have furnished subjects to the pastoral Muse of several of her provincial Bards.   The late Josiah Relph, a native of Sebergham, a man of learning and genius, was, if I mistake not, the first Cumbrian poet that attempted to write pastorals in the county dialect ; and the great talents which he has displayed in this species of writing, leave us to regret that he did not write more. In his "Cursty and Peggy," he has pourtrayed the effects and operation of love in humble life, with all that picturesque accuracy, which characterizes the masterly delineations of Burns. He was followed in the same walks of poetry by the late Ewan Clark; but the attempts of this gentleman reached no further than mere imitations of his distinguished predecessor, and fell far short of his prototype in all the characteristical qualities of pastoral poetry. The late ingenious Mark Lonsdale, in his "Upshot," has ably and humourously described a festive scene among his countrymen, and given faithful portraits of characters when the heart of a peasant throws off all restraint, and indulges itself in rustic jollity.

The Cumberland Ballads by Mr. Robert Anderson, display uncommon merit; and may be considered as the most perfect specimens of pastoral writing that have yet appeared. The Author has taken a wider view of rural life than any of his predecessors, and has been more happy in describing the peculiar cast of thought and expression, by which individual manners are distinguished. In delineating the characters of his peasants, he has closely adhered to nature and truth, never raising them above their condition in life by too much refinement, and never depressing them below it by too much vulgarity. He holds them up often to laughter, but never to contempt. He has the happy talent of catching the ludicrous in every thing that comes before him, and of expressing it in that felicity which gives it in its full force to the reader.

The locality and peculiar phraseology of his Cumberland Ballads must necessarily circumscribe their popularity; but their general merit is such as will always find them admirers among those who are acquainted with the provincial idiom in which they are written, and with the manners and scenes which they delineate.

CUMBERLAND BALLADS.

BETTY BROWN.

Tune—"*John Anderson my jo.*"

WULLY.

Come, Gwordie lad, unyoke the yad,
    Let's gow to Rosley fair;
Lang Ned's afore, wi' Symie' lad,
    Peed Dick, and monie mair:
My titty Greace and Jenny Bell
    Are gangen bye and bye,
Sae doff thy clogs, and don thysel—
    Let fadder luik to t' kye.

GWORDIE.

O, Wully! leetsome may ye be!
    For me, I downa gang;
I've often shek'd a leg w' tee,
    But now I's aw wheyte wrang;
My stomich's gaene, nae sleep I get;
    At neet I lig me down,
But nobbet pech, and gowl, and fret,
    And aw for Betty Brown.

Sin' Cuddy Wulson' murry-neet,
    When Deavie brees'd his shin,
I've niver, niver yence been reet,
    And aw for her, I fin:
Tou kens we danc'd a threesome reel,
    And Betty set to me—
She luik'd sae neyce, and danc'd sae weel,
    What cud a body de?

My fadder fratches sair enough,
　　If I but steal frae heame ;
My mudder caws me ɟeer deyl'd guff,
　　If Betty I but neame :
Atween the twee there's sec a frase,
　　O but it's bad to beyde !
Yet, what's far war, aye Betty says
　　She wunnet be my Lreyde.

WULLY.

Wey, Gworge ! tou's owther fuil or font,
　　To think o' sec a frow ;
In au her flegmagɪries donn'd,
　　What is she—nought 'at dow.
There's skeape-greace Ben, the neybors ken,
　　Can git her onie day—
Ere I'd be fash'd wi' sec a yen,
　　I'd list, or rin away !

Wi' aw her trinkums on her back,
　　She's feyne enough for t' squire ;
A sairy weyfe, I trow, she'd mak,
　　At cudn't muck a byre.
But whisht ! here comes my titty Greace,
　　She'll guess what we're about—
To mworn-o'mworn, i' this seame pleace,
　　We'll hae the stwory out.

———

BARBARY BELL.

TUNE—" *Cuddle and cuddle us aw thegether,*"

O but this luive is a serious thing !
　　It's the beginner o' monie waes ;
And yen had as guid in a helter swing,
　　As luik at a bonny feace now-a-days :
Was there ever peer deevil sae fash'd as me ?
　　Nobbet sit your ways still, the truth I's tell,
For I wish I'd been hung on our codlin tree,
　　The varra furst time I seed Barbary Bell !

Quite lish, and nit owr thrang wi' wark,
   · I went my ways down to Carel fair,†
Wi' bran new cwoat, and brave ruffl'd sark,
   And Dicky the shaver pat flour i' my hair ;
Our seyde lads are aw for fun,
   Some tuik ceyder, and some drank yell ;
Diddlen Deavie he strack up a tune,
   And I caper'd away wi' Barbary Bell.

Says I " Bab," says I, " we'll de weel eneugh,
   For tou can kurn, and darn, and spin ;
I can deyke, men car-gear, and hod the pleugh ;
   Sae at Whussenday neist we'll t' warld begin :
I's turn'd a gayshen awt' neybors say,
   I sit like a sumph, nae mair mysel,'
And up or a bed, at heame or away,
   I think o' nought but Barbary Bell."

Then whee sud steal in but Robbin Parknuik,
   And Jowhn of the Stubb,‡ and twee or three mair ;
Suin Barb'ry frae off my knee they tuik,
   " Wey, dang it !" says I, " but this is nit fair !"
Robbie he kick'd up a dust in a crack,
   And sticks and neeves they went pel-mel,
The bottles forby the clock feace they brack,
   ' But, fares-te-weel, wheyte-fit, Barbary Bell !

'Twas nobbet last week, nae langer seyne,
   I wheyn'd i' the nuik, I can't tell how ;
" Get up," says my fadder, " and sarra the sweyne !"
   " I's bravely, Bab !" says I, " how's tou ?"
Neist mworn to t' cwoals I was fworc'd to gang,
   But cowp'd the cars at Tindle Fell,
For I cruin'd aw the way, as I trotted alang,
   O that I'd never kent Barbary Bell !

That varra seame neet up to Barbary' house,
   When aw t' auld fwok were liggin asleep,

---

† Carlisle fair: ‡ Noted pugilists.

I off wi' my clogs, and as whisht as a mouse,
　　Claver'd up to the window, and tuik a peep;

There whee sud I see, but Watty the laird—
　　Od, wheyte leet on him! I munnet tell!
But on Setterday neist, if I live and be spar'd,
　　I'll wear a reed cwot for Barbary Bell.

NICHOL THE NEWSMONGER.

Tune—"*The Night before Larry was stretch'd.*"

Come, Nichol, and gi'e us thy cracks,
　　I seed te gang down to the smiddy;
I've fodder'd the naigs and the nowt,
　　And wanted to see thee 'at did e.
Ay, Andrew lad! draw in a stuil,
　　And gi'e us a shek o' thy daddle;
I got aw the news, far and nar, [1]
　　Sae set off as fast's e could waddle.

In France they've but sworrofu' times,
　　For Bonnyprat's* nit as he sud be;
America's nobbet sae sae;
　　And England nit quite as she mud be:
Sad wark there's amang blacks and wheytes,†
　　Sec tellin plain teales to their feaces,
Wi' murders, and wars, and aw that—
　　But, hod—I forget where the pleace is.

Our parson he gat drunk as muck,
　　Then ledder'd aw t' lads round about him;
They said he was nobbet hawf reet,
　　And fwok mud as weel be widout him:
The yell's to be fourpence a whart—
　　Odswinge, lad, there will be rare drinking!
Billy Pitt's mad as onie March hare,
　　And niver was reet, fwok are thinking.

---

† Bonaparte.   ‡ Alluding to the insurrection of the Blacks.

A weddin we'll hev or it's lang,
  Wi' Bet Brag and lal Tommy Tagwally;
Jack Bunton's far off to the sea—
  It'll e'en be the deeth of our Sally.
The clogger has bowt a new wig;
  Dalston singers come here agean Sunday;
Lord Nelson's ta'en three Spanish fleets,
  And the dancin schuil opens on Monday.

Carel badgers are monstrous sad fwok,
  The silly peer de'ils how they wring up!
Lal bairns ha'e got pox frae the kye,†
  And fact'ries, like mushrooms, they spring up;
If they sud keep their feet for awhile,
  And government nobbet pruive civil,
They'll build up as hee as the muin,
  For Carel's a match for the deevil.

The king's meade a bit of a speech,
  And gentlefwok say it's a topper;
An alderman deet tudder neet,
  Efter eatin' a turkey to supper;
Our squire's to be parliament man,
  Mess, lad, but he'll keep them aw busy!
Whee thinks te's come heame i' the cwoach,
  Frae Lunnon, but grater-feac'd Lizzy.

The cock-feights are ninth o' neist month,
  I've twee, nit aw England can bang them;
In Ireland they're aw up in arms,
  It's whop'd there's nee Frenchmen amang them;
A boggle's been seen wi' twee heeds,
  Lord help us! ayont Wully Carras,
Wi' girt saucer een, and a tail—
  They dui say 'twas auld Jobby Barras.

The muin was at full this neet week;
  The weather is turn'd monstrous daggy;

† Cow Pox.

D

I' th' loft, just at seeben last neet,
   Lal Stephen sweethearted lang Aggy.
There'll be bonny wark bye and bye,
   The truth 'll be out there's nee fear on't,
But I niver say nought, nay, nit I,
   For fear hawf the parish sud hear on't.

Our Tib at the cwose-house has been,
   She tells us they're aw monstrous murry;
At Carel the brig's tummel'd down,
   And they tek the fwok owr in a whurry;
I carried our whye to the bull;
   They've ta'en seeben spies up at Dover;
My fadder compleens of his hip;
   And the Grand Turk has enter'd Hanover.

Daft Peg's got hersel, man, wi' bairn,
   And silly pilgarlic's the fadder;
Lal Sim's geane and swapp'd the black cowt,
   And cwoley hes wurried the wedder;
My mudder hes got frostet heels,   ·
   And peace is the talk of the nation,
For papers say varra neist week,
   There's to be a grand humiliation.†

Aunt Meable has lost her best sark,
   And Cleutie is bleam'd varra mickle;
Nought's seafe out o' duirs now-a-days,
   Frae a millstone e'en down to a sickle;
The clock it streykes eight, I mun heame,
   Or I's git a deuce of a fratchin;
When neist we've a few hours to spare,
   We'll fin out what mischief's a hatchin.

THE WORTON WEDDING.

TUNE—"*Dainty Davie.*"

O, sec a weddin I've been at!
   De'il bin, what cap'rin, feghtin, vap'rin! 2

† Illumination.

Priest and clark, and aw gat drunk—
　　Rare deins there were there :
The Thuirsby lads they fit the best ;
The Worton weavers drank the meast ;
But Brough seyde lairds bang'd aw the rest
　　For braggin o' their gear,
And singin,—Whurry whum, whuddle whum,
　　　　　Whulty whalty, wha-wha-wha,
　　　　And derry dum, diddle dum,
　　　　　Derry eyden dee.

Furst helter skelter frae the kurk ;
　　Some off like fire, through dub and mire ;
" De'il tek the hindmost !" Meer lad cries—
Suin head owre heels he flew :
" God speed ye weel !" the priest rwoar'd out,
" Or neet we's hae a hearty bout"—
Peer Meer' lad gat a bleaken'd snout—
　　He'd mickle cause to rue—
　　　It spoil'd his—Whurry whum, &c.

When on the teable furst they set
　　The butter'd sops, sec greasy chops,
'Tween lug and laggen ! oh what fun,
　　To see them girn and eat !
Then lisping Isbel talk'd sae feyne,
'Twas ' vathly thockin* thuth to dine ;
' Theck griveth† wark ! ta eat like thweyne !'‡
　　It meade her sick to se'et ;
　　　Then we sung—Whurry whum, &c.

Neist stut'rin Cursty, up he ruse,
　　Wi' a-a-a, and ba-ba-ba ;
He'd kiss Jen Jakes, for aw lang seyne,
　　And fearfu' wark meade he ;
But Cursty, souple gammerstang !
Ned Wulson brong his lug a whang :
Then owre he flew, the peets amang,
　　And grean'd as he wad dee ;
　　　But some sang—Whurry whum, &c.

† Vastly shocking.　　‡ Such grievous.　　§ Swine.

Aunt Ester spoil'd the gurdle keakes,
 The speyce left out, was wrang, nae doubt;
Tim Trummel tuik nine cups o' tea,
 And fairly capp'd tem aw:
The kiss went roun ; but Sally Slee,
When Trummel cleek'd her on his knee,
She dunch'd and punch'd, cried, ' fuil, let be !'
 Then strack him owre the jaw,
  And we sang—Whurry whum, &c.

Far maist I leugh at Grizzy Brown,
 Frae Lunnon town she'd just come down,
In furbelows, and feyne silk gown,
 Oh, man, but she was crouse !
Wi' Dick the footman she wad dance,
And ' wonder'd people could so prance;'
Then curtchey'd as they dui in France,
 And pautet like a geuse.
  While aw sang—Whurry whum, &c.

Young sour-milk Sawney, on the stuil,
 A whornpeype danc'd, and keav'd and pranc'd,
He slipp'd, and brak his left-leg-shin,
 And hirpl'd sair about :
Then cocker Wully lap bawk heet,
And in his clogs top teyme did beat ;
But Tamer, in her stockin feet,
 She bang'd him out and out,
  And lilted—Whurry whum, &c.

Now aw began to talk at yence,
 O' naigs and kye, and wots and rye,
And laugh'd and jwok'd, and cough'd & smuik'd,
 And meade a fearfu' reek ;
The furm it brak, and down they fell,
Lang Isaac leam'd auld granny Bell ;
They up, and drank het suggar'd yell,
 Till monie cud'nt speak,
  But some sang—Whurry whum, &c.

The breyde she kest up her accounts
  In Rachael's lap, then poud her cap ;
The parson' wig stuid aw ajy ;
  The clark sang Andrew Car ;
Blin Staig, the fiddler, gat a whack,
The bacon fleek fell on his back,
And neist his fiddle stick they brak,
  'Twas weel it was nee war,
    For he sang—Whurry whum, &c.

Now on the midden some were laid,
  Aw havey scavey, and kelavey ;
The clogger and the teayler fit,
  Peer Snip gat twee black een :
·Dick Wawby he began the fray,
But Jemmy Moffat ran away,
And crap owre head amang the hay,
  Fwok say nit varra clean ;
    Then they sang—Whurry whum, &c.

Neist Windy ·Wull, o' Wample seyde,
  He bang'd them aw, beath girt and smaw ;
He flang them east, he flang them west,
  And bluidy pates they gat ;
To him they were but caff and san ;
He split the teable wi' his han,
But in the dust wi' dancin Dan,
  They brunt his Sunday hat .
    Then aw sang—Whurry whum, &c.

The breyde now thowt it time for bed ;
  Her stockin doff'd, and flang't quite soft—
It hat Bess Bleane—Wull Webster blush'd,
  And luik'd anudder way :
The lads down frae the loft did steal ;
The parish howdey, Greacey Peel,
She happ'd her up, aw wish'd her weel,
  Then whop'd to meet neist day,
    And sing her—Whurry whum, &c.

The best on't was, the parson swore
　　His wig was lost, a crown it cost,
He belsh'd and heccupp'd, in and out,
　　And said it wasn't fair :
Now day-leet it began to peep,
The breydegruim off to bed did creep,
I trow he waddn't mickle sleep,
　　But—whisht! I'll say nee mair,
　Nobbet sing—Whurry whum, whuddle whum,
　　　　　　Whulty, whalty, wha-wha-wha,
　　　　　　And derry dum, diddle dum,
　　　　　　Derry eyden dee.

SALLY GRAY.

Tune—" *The mucking o' Geordie's byre.*"

Come, Deavie, I'll tell thee a secret,
　　But tou mun lock't up i' thee breast,
I wadden't for aw Dalston parish
　　It com to the ears o' the rest ;
Now I'll hod te a bit of a weager,
　　A groat to thy tuppens I'll lay,
Tou cannot guess whee I's in luive wi,
　　And nobbet keep off Sally Gray.

There's Cumwhitton, Cumwhinton, Cumranton,
　　Cumrangen, Cumrew, and Cumcatch,
And mony mair cums i' the county,
　　But nin wi' Cumdivock can match ;
It's sae neyce to luik owre the black pasture,
　　Wi' the fells abuin aw, far away—
There is nee sec pleace, nit in England,
　　For there lives the sweet Sally Gray !

I was sebenteen last Collop-Monday,[3]
　　And she's just the varra seame yage ;
For ae kiss o' the sweet lips o' Sally,
　　I'd freely give up a year's wage ;
For in lang winter neets when she's spinnin,
　　And singin about Jemmy Gay,

I keek by the hay stack, and listen,
　For fain wad I see Sally Gray.

Had tou seen her at kurk, man, last Sunday,
　Tou cou'dn't ha'e thought o' the text ;
But she sat neist to Tom o' the Lonnin,
　Tou may think that meade me quite vext ;
Then I pass'd her gawn owre the lang meedow,
　Says I, ' Here's a canny wet day !'
I wad ha'e said mair, but how cou'd e,
　When luikin at sweet Sally Gray !

I caw'd to sup cruds wi' Dick Miller,
　And hear aw his cracks and his jwokes ;
The dumb wife was tellin their fortunes,
　What ! I mud be like other fwokes !
Wi' chawk, on a pair of auld bellows,
　Twee letters she meade in her way—
S means Sally, the wide warl owre,
　And G stands for nought else but Gray.

O was I but lword o' the manor,
　A nabob, or parliament man,
What thousands on thousands I'd gi' her,
　Wad she nobbet gi' me her han !
A cwoach and six horses I'd buy her,
　And gar fwok stan out o' the way,
Then I'd lowp up behint like a footman—
　Oh ! the warl for my sweet Sally Gray !

They may brag o' their feyne Carel lasses,
　Their feathers, their durtment, and leace ;
God help them ! peer deeth-luikin bodies,
　Widout a bit reed i' their feace !
But Sally's just like allyblaster,
　Her cheeks are twee rwose-buds in May—
O lad ! I cou'd sit here for ever,
　And talk about sweet Sally Gray !

WILL AND KATE.

Tune—"*John Anderson my jo.*"

Now, Kate, full forty years ha'e flown,
  Sin we met on the green ;
Frae that to this the saut, saut tear
  Has oft stuid i' my een :
For when the bairns were some peet-heet,
  Tou kens I leam'd my knee—
Lal todlen things, in want o' bread—
  O that went hard wi' me !

Then tou wad cry, ' Come, Wully, lad,
  ' Keep up thy heart—ne'er fear !
' Our bits o' bairns 'll scraffle up,
  ' Sae dry that sworry tear ;
' There's Matthew's be an alderman ;
  ' A bishop we'll mak Guy ;
' Lal Ned sal be a clogger ;
  ' Dik sal work for tee and I.'

Then when our crops were spoil'd wi' rain,
  Sir Jwohn mud hev his rent ;
What cud we de ? nee geer had we—
  Sae I to jail was sent.
'Twas hard to starve i' sec a place,
  Widout a frien to trust ;
But when I thought o' thee and bairns,
  My heart was like to brust.

Neist, Etty, God was pleas'd to tek,
  What than, we'd seeven still ;
But whee kens what may happen—suin
  The smaw-pox did for Bill :
I think I see his slee-black een,
  Then he wad chirm and talk,
And say, Ded, ded ; Mam, mam, and aw,
  Lang, lang ere he cud walk.

At Carel, when, for six pound ten,
  I selt twee Scotty kye,
They pick'd my pocket i' the thrang,
  And de'il a plack had I ;
'Ne'er ack !' says tou, ' we'll work for mair,'
  ' It's time enough to fret ;
' A pun o' sorrow wunnet pay
  ' Ae single ounce o' debt.'

Now, todlen down the hill o' leyfe,
  Auld yage has brought content ;
And, God be thank'd our bairns are up,
  And pay Sir Jwohn his rent :
When, seyde by seyde aw day we sit,
  I often think and grieve,
It's hard that deeth sud part auld fwok,
  When happy they can leve.

THE IMPATIENT LASSIE.[4]

Tune—" *Low down in the broom.*"

Deuce tek the clock ! click-clackin sae,
  Still in a body's ear ;
It tells and tells the time is past,
  When Jwohnie sud been here :
Deuce tek the wheel ! 'twill nit rin roun—
  Nae mair to-neet I'll spin,
But count each minute wi' a seegh,
  Till Jwohnie he steels in.

How neyce the spunky fire it burns,
  For twee to sit beside !
And there's the seat where Jwohnie sits,
  And I forget to cheyde !
My fadder, tui, how sweet he snwores !
  My mudder's fast asleep :
He promis'd oft, but, oh ! I fear
  His word be wunnet keep !

What can it be keeps him frae me?
 The ways are nit sae lang,
And sleet and snaw are nought at aw,
 If yen were fain to gang!
Some ither lass, wi' bonnier feace,
 Has catch'd his wicked ee,
And I'll be pointed at at kurk—
 Nay! suiner let me dee!

O durst we lasses nobbet gang,
 And sweetheart them we like,
I'd rin to thee, my Jwohnie lad,
 Nor stop at bog or dyke;
But custom's sec a silly thing,
 For men mun hae their way,
And mony a bonny lassy sit,
 And wish frae day to day.

But, whisht! I hear my Jwohnie's fit—
 Aye! that's his varra clog!
He steeks the faul yeat softly tui—
 O hang that cwoley dog!
Now, hey for seeghs and suggar words,
 Wi' kisses nit a few—
O but this warl's a paradise,
 When lovers they pruive true!

THE BUNDLE OF ODDITIES.

Tune—"*Fie let us a' to the bridal!*"

Sit down, and I'll count owre my sweethearts,[5]
 For faith a brave number I've had,
Sin I furst went to schuil wi' Dik Railton,
 But Dick's in his greave, honest lad!
I mind, when he cross'd the deep watter,
 To get me the shilapple's est,
How he fell owrehead, and I skirl'd sae,
 Then off we ran heame, sair distrest.

Then there was a bit of teaylear,
　　That work'd at our house a heale week,
He was sheap'd aw the warl like a trippet,
　·　But niver a word durst he speak ;
I just think I see how he squinted
　　At me, when we sat down to meat ;
Owre went his het keale on his blue breeks,
　　And de'il a bit Snippy cud eat.

At partin he poud up his spirits,
　　Says he, " Tou hes bodder'd my head,
' And it sheks yen to rags and to tatters,
　' To sew wi' a lang double thread :'
Then, in meakin a cwoat for my fadder,
　　(How luive dis the senses deceive !)
Forby usin marrowless buttons,
　　To th' pocket-whol he stitch'd a sleeve.[6]

The neist was a Whaker, caw'd Jacob,
　　He turn'd up the wheyte o' his een,
And talk'd about flesh and the spirit—
　　Thowt I, what can Gravity mean ?
In dark winter neets, i' the lonnins,
　　He'd weade thro' the durt 'buin his knee,
It cuil'd his het heart, silly gander !
　　And there let him stowter for me.

A lang blue-lipt chap, like a guidepwost,
　　(Lord help us and keep us frae harm !)
Neist talk'd about car-gear and middens,
　　And the reet way to manage a farm ;
'Twas last Leady Fair[7] I leet on him,
　　He grummell'd and spent hawf-a-crown—
God bless him ! hed he gowd i' gowpens,
　　I wadn't ha'e hed sec a clown.

But, stop ! there was lal wee deef Dicky,
　　Wad dance for a heale winter neet,
And at me aw the time wad keep glowrin—
　·　Peer man, he was nobbet hawf reet !—

He grew jealous o' reed-headed Ellek,
  Wi, a feace like a full harvest muin ;
Sea they fit till they just gat eneugh on't,
  And I laugh'd at beath when 'twas duin.

There' anudder worth aw put together,
  I cud, if I wad, tell his neame ;
He gangs past our house to the market,
  And monie a time he's set me heame :
O wad he but ax me this question,
  ' Will tou be my partner for life ?'
I'd answer without ony blushes,
  And aye try to mek a guid wife.

LUCKLESS JONATHAN.

Tune,—" *Erin go bragh*"

O heale be thy heart ! my peer merry auld cronie,
  And never may trouble draw tears frae thy e'e ;
It's reet, when he can, man sud rise abuin sorrow,
  For pity's nit common to peer fwok like me.
When I think how we lap about mountain an' meedow,
  Like larks in a mwornin, a young happy pair,
Then I luik at mysel, and I see but a shadow,
  That's suffered sae mickle, it cannot beyde mair.

Tou minds, when I buried my honest auld fadder,
  O how could I ever get owre that sad day !—
His last words were, ' Jonathan, luik to thy mudder,
  ' And God 'll reward thee :' nae mair could he say.
My mudder she stuid, and she fain wad ha'e spoken,
  But tears wadn't let her— O man, it was hard !—
She tuik till her bed, and just thurteen weeks efter,
  Was laid down ayont him in Aikton kurk-yard.

My friend, Jemmy Gunston, went owre seas to Inde,
  For me, his auld comrade, a venture he'd tak ;
I'd scrap'd up a lock money—he gat it—but leately
  Peer Jemmy was puzzen'd, they say, by a black :

'Twas nit for my money I fretted, but Jemmy,
  I'll ne'er forget him, as lang as I've breath ;
He said, ' Don't cry, mudder ! I'll mek you a leady!'
  But sairy auld Tamer ! 'twill e'en be her death.

To mek bad far war, then I courted lal Matty,
  Her bonnie blue een, how they shot to my heart !
The neet niver com but I went owre to see her,
  And when the clock struck we were sworry to part:
An aunt ayont Banton a canny house left her,
  (What but health & contentment can money nit buy?)
Wi' laird Hodgson o' Burgh [8] off she canter'd to Gretna,
  The varra seame mworn we our fortune sud try.

'Twas nobbet last Cursmas I fain wad be murry,
  Sae caw'd in Dick Toppin, Tom Clarke, and Jwohn
    Howe;
We sung, and we crack'd, but lal thowt ere neist
    mwornin,
  That aw our heale onset wad be in a lowe ;
They gat me poud out, and reet weel I renember,
  I stamp'd, ay, like mad, when the sad seet I saw,
For that was the pleace my grandfadder was bworn in,[9]
  Forbye my twee uncles, my fadder and aw.

Now, widout owther fadder, or mudder, or sweatheart,
  A friend, or a shelter to cover my head,
I mazle and wander, nor ken what I's dein,
  And wad, (if I nobbet durst,) wish I were dead.
O heale be thy heart ! my peer merry auld cronie,
  And niver may trouble draw tears frae thy e'e ;
It's reet, when he can, man sud rise abuin sorrow,
  For pity's nit common to peer fwok like me.

DICK WATTERS.

TUNE—" *Crowdy.*"

O, Jenny ! Jenny ! where's tou been?
  Thy fadder is just mad at tee ;

E

He seed somebody i' the croft,
  And gulders as he'd worry me.

O monie are a mudder's whopes,
  And monie are a mudder's fears,
And monie a bitter, bitter pang,
  Beath suin and late her bosom tears!

We brong thee up, pat thee to schuil,
  And clead the weel as peer fwok can;
We larn'd thee beath to dance and read,
  But now tou's crazy for a man.
                    O monie, &c.

When tou was young, and at my knee,
  I dwoated on thee, day and neet;
But now tou's rakin, rakin still,
  And niver, niver i' thy seet.
                    O, monie, &c.

Tou's proud, and past aw guid adveyce—
  Yen mud as weel speak till a stean;
Still, still thy awn way, reet or wrang—
  Mess, but tou'll rue't when I am geane!
                    O, monie, &c.

Dick Watters, I ha'e telt thee oft,
  Ne'er means to be a son o' mine;
He seeks thy ruin sure as deeth,
  Then like Bet Baxter tou may whine.
                    O, monie, &c.

Thy fadder's comin frae the croft,
  A bonny hunsup faith he'll mek;
Put on the clogs and auld blue brat—
  Heaste, Jenny, heaste! he lifts the sneck!

O monie are a mudder's whopes,
  And monie are a mudder's fears,
And monie a bitter, bitter pang,
  Beath suin and late her bosom tears!

THE LASS ABUIN THIRTY.

Tune—Jocky's grey breeks."

I've wonder'd sin I kent mysel,
  What keeps the men fwok aw frae me;
I's as guid-like as cousin Tib,
  And she can ha'e her choice o' three;
For me, still moilin by mysel,
  Life's just a bitter widout sweets;
The simmer brings nae pleasant days,
  And winter tires wi' lang, lang neets.

I had some whopes o' Wully yence,
  And Wully was the only yen;
I dreamt and dreamt about him lang,
  But whopes and Wully aw are geane:
A kiss he'd hev, I gev him twee,
  Reeght weel I mind amang the hay;
Neist time we met, he glump'd and gloom'd,
  And turn'd his head anither way.

A feyne pink sash my uncle sent
  Frae Lunnon yence; about my waist
I wore't and wore't, but de'il a lad
  At me or sash a luik e'er cast:
My yellow gown I thought was sure
  To catch sonte yen at Carel Fair,
But, oh fareweel to gown and sash,
  I'll niver, never wear them mair!

The throssle, when cauld winter's geane,
  Aye in our worchet welcomes spring;—
It mun be luive, did we but ken,
  Gars him aroun his partner sing.
The cock and hen, the duck and drake,
  Nay e'en the smawest birds that flee,
Ilk thing that lives can get a mate,
  Except sec sworry things as me.

I often think how married fwok
　　Mun lead a sweet and happy life;
The prattlin bairns rin toddlin roun,
　　And tie the husband to the wife:
Then, oh! what joy when neet draws on!
　　She meets him gangen frae his wark:
But nin can tell what cheerfu' cracks
　　The tweesome ha'e lang efter dark.

The wise man lives nit far frae this,
　　I'll hunt him out suin as I can;
He telt Nan Dobson whee she'd wed,
　　And I'm as likely, sure, as Nan.
But still, still moilin by mysel,
　　Life's just a bitter widout sweets:
The summer brings nae pleasant days,
　　And winter tires wi' lang, lang neets!

TOM LINTON.[10]

TUNE—"*Come under my plaidie.*"

Tom Linton was bworn till a brave canny fortune,
　　His auld fadder screap'd aw the gear up he cud;
But Tom, country booby, luik'd owre hee abuin him,
　　And mix'd wi' the bad, nor e'er heeded the good;
At the town he'd whore, gammle, play hell & the deevil,
　　He wad hev his caper, nor ca'ed how it com;
Then he mud hev his greyhounds, guns, setter & hunter,
　　And king o' the cockers they aw cursened Tom.

I think I just see how the lads wad flock roun him,
　　And, oh! they were fain to shek Tom by the hand!
Then he'd tell how he fit wi' the barbers and bullies,
　　And drank wi' the waiter till nowther cud stan:
His watch he wad show, and his list o' the horses,
　　And pou out a guinea, and offer to lay,
Till our peer country lads grew uneasy and lazy,
　　And Tom cud ha'e coax'd hawf the parish away.

Then he drank wi' the 'squire, and laugh'd wid his
 worship,
And talk'd of the duke, and the deevil kens whee:
He gat aw the new-fangled oaths i' the nation,
 And mock'd a peer beggar-man wanting an e'e :
His fields they were mortgag'd; about it was whisper'd,
 A farmer was robb'd nit owre far frae his house :
At last aw was selt his auld fadder had toil'd for,
 And silly Tom Linton left nit worth a sous.

His fortune aw spent, what! he'd ha'e the laird's dowter,
 But she pack'd him off wid a flee in his ear ;
Neist thing, an auld comrade (for money Tom borrow'd)
 E'en pat him in prison, and bad him lig there :
At last he gat out, efter lang he had suffered,
 And sair had repented the sad life he'd led :
Widout shoon till his feet, in a soldier's auld jacket,
 He works on the turnpike reet hard for his bread.

Now folly seen into, ragg'd, peer, and down-hearted,
 He toils and he frets, and keen wants daily press :
If cronies ride by, wey, alas! they've forgot him,
 For whee can remember auld friends in distress?
O pity, what pity, that, in every county,
 Sae monie Tom Lintons may always be found !
Deuce tek aw girt nwotions, and whurligig fashions,
 Contentment's a kingdom, aye, aw the warl round!

THE HAPPY FAMILY.[11]

Tune—" *O'er bogie.*"

The hollow blast blows owre the hill,
 And comin down's the sleet ;
God help them, widout house or hauld,
 This dark and stormy neet !
Come, Jobby, gi'e the fire a prod,
 Then steek the entry duir ;
It's wise to keep cauld winter out,
 When we ha'e't in our pow'r.

Heaste, Jenny! put the bairns to bed,
   And mind they say their pray'rs;
Sweet innocents! their heads yence down,
   They sleep away their cares!
But gi' them furst a butter-shag,
   When young, they munnet want,
Nor ever sal a bairn o' mine,
   While I've a bite to grant.

O wife! that weary rheumatism,
   E'en gars thee luik but thin;
I mind when tou was fresh and fair,
   And fattest o' thy kin;
But yage comes on, dui what we can;
   We munnet think it hard:
A week at Gilsland tou salt try,
   Neist summer, if I be spared.

Now, seated at my awn fire-nuik,
   Content as onie king,
For hawf an hour afore we sleep,
   Bess, quit thy wark and sing:
Try that about the beggar lass,
   'Twill please thy mudder best,
For she, tou kens, can always feel
   For peer fwok when distrest.

Nay, what its owre! tou cannot sing,
   But weel I guess the cause;
Young Wulliam sud ha'e come to neet—
   Consider, lass, it snaws!
Another neet 'll suin be here,
   Sae divvent freet and whine:
Come when he will, he's welcome still
   To onie bairn o' mine.

I'll ne'er forget, when we were young,
   (Thy mudder kens as weel,)
We met but yence a month, and then
   Out she was fworc'd to steel:

The happiest day we e'er had known,
Was when I caw'd her mine,
But monie a thousand happier days
We beath ha'e kent sin-syne.

— — —

THE AUTHOR ON HIMSELF.

TUNE—" *The Campbells are coming.*"

O, Eden, whenever I range thy green banks,
And view aw the scenes o' my infantine pranks,
Where wi' pleasure I spworted, ere sorrow began,
I sigh to trace onward frae boy to the man :
To memory dear are the days o' yen's youth,
When, enraptur'd, we luik'd at each object wi' truth,
And, like fairies, a thousand wild frolics we play'd—
But manhood has chang'd what youth fondly pourtray'd.

I think o' my playmates,[12] dear imps, I lov'd best !
Now divided, like larks efter leaving the nest !
How we trembl'd to schuil, and wi' copy and buik,
Oft read our hard fate in the maister's stern luik ;
In summer, let lowse, how we brush'd thro' the wood,
And meade seevy caps on the brink o' the flood ;
Or watch'd the seap-bubbles, or ran wi' the kite,
Or launch'd paper navies, how dear the delight !

There was Jock Smith the boggle,—I mind him reet
    weel,
We twee to Blain's hay-loft together wad steal ;
And of giants, ghosts, witches, and fairies oft read,
Till sae freeten'd, we hardly durst creep off to bed :
Then, in winter, we'd caw out the lasses to play,
And tell them the muin shone as breet as the day ;
Or scamper, like wild things, at hunting the hare,
Tig-touch-wood, four corners, or twenty gams mair.

Then my fadder, God bless him ! at thurteen oft said,
' My lad, I mun get the bit of a trade ;

' O, cud I afford it, mair larnin thou'd get !'
But peer was my fadder, and I's unlarned yet.
And then my furst sweetheart, an angel was she !
But I only meade luive thro' the tail o' my e'e :
I mind when I met her I panted to speak,
But stood silent, and blushes spread aw owre my cheek.

At last, aw the play-things o' youth laid aside,
Now luive, whope, and fear did my moments divide,
And wi' restless ambition deep sorrow began,
But I sigh to trace onward frae boy to the man :
To memory dear are the days o' yen's youth,
When, enraptur'd, we luik'd at ilk object wi' truth.
And, like fairies, a thousand wild frolics we play'd—
But manhood has chang'd what youth fondly pour-
    tray'd.

PEACE.

Tune—" *There's nae luck about the house.*"

Now, God be praised ! we've peace at last,
    For Nichol he's been down,
And sec a durdem, Nichol says,
    They've hed in Lunnon toun ;
The king thowt war wad ruin aw,
    And Bonnyprat the seame,
And some say teane, and some say beath,
    Ha'e lang been much to bleame.

Now monie a wefe will weep for joy,[13]
    And monie a bairn be fain,
To see the fadders they'd forgot,
    Come seafe and sound agean ;
And monie a yen will watch in vain,
    Wi' painfu' whopes and fears,
And oft the guilty wretches bleame,
    That set fwok by the ears.

My cousin Tommy went to sea,
   And lost his left-hand thum ;
He tells sec teales about the feight,
   They mek us aw sit dum ;
He says it is reet fearfu' wark,
   For them that's fworc'd to see't—
The bullets whuzzing past yen's lugs,
   And droppen down like sleet.

But Peter, our peer sarvant man,
   Was far owre proud to work,—
They said a captain he sud be,
   Alang wi't Duke o' York :
Wi' powdered heed away he marched,
   And gat a wooden leg ;
But monie a time he's rued sin syne,
   For now he's fworced to beg.

Ay, but our Sally wull be fain,
   Sud Lanty but cum back !
Then owre the fire, i' winter neets,
   We wull ha'e monie a crack ;—
He'll tell us aw the ins and outs,
   For he can write and read ;
But Sally's heart for sure 'll brek,
   If he's amang the dead.

O ! but I us'd to wonder much,
   And think what thousands fell ;
Now what they've aw been feightin for,
   The de'il a yen can tell ;—
But, God be praised ! we've peace at last,
   The news hes spread afar ;
O may our bairns and bairns' bairns hear
   Nae mair o' murderous war.

THE CUMBERLAND FARMER.

I've thought and I've thought, agean and agean,
Sin I was peat-heat, now I see it quite plain,
That farmers [14] are happier far, tho' we're peer,
Than thur they caw gentlefwok, wi' aw their gear;
Then why about riches aye mek sec a fuss,
Gi'e us meat, drink, and cleading, it's plenty for us:
Frae the prince to the ploughman, ilk hes but his day,
And when Deeth gi'es a beckon we aw mun obey.

There's our 'squire, wi' his thousand's, jant jantin about,
What! he'd gi'e aw his gear to get shot o' the gout:
Nowther heart-ach nor gout e'er wi' rakin had I,
For labour brings that aw his gold cannot buy:
Then he'll say to me, ' Jacob, thou whussels and sings,
' Mess, lad, but you've ten times mair pleasure than
      kings;
' I mean honest simplicity, freedom, and health;
' These are dearer to man than the trappings o' wealth.'

Can ought be mair sweet than, like larks in a mworn,
To rise wi' the sunshine, and luik at the cworn?
Tho' in winter, its true, dull and lang are the neets,
But thro' life fwok mun aye tek the bitters wi' sweets.
When God grants us plenty, and hous'd are the crops,
How we feast on cruds, collops, and guid butter-sops.
Let your feyne fwok in town brag o' dainties whee will,
Content and the country for my money still.

They may tell o' their gardens as lang as they like,
Don't the flow'rs bluim as fair under ony thworn dike?
The de'il a guid bite they wad e'er get I trow,
Wer't not for the peer man that follows the plough.
If we nobbet get plenty to pay the laird's rent,
And keep the bairns teydey, we aye sleep content;
Then, ye girt little fwok, niver happy in town,
Blush, blush, when ye laugh at a peer country clown.

THE DISAPPOINTMENT.

TUNE—" *Etrick banks.* "

The muin shone breet at nine last neet,
  When Jemmy Sharp com owre the muir;
Weel did I ken a lover's fit,
  And heard him softly tap the duir :
My fadder started i' the nuik,
  ' Rin, Jenny ! see what's that,' he said :
I whisper'd, ' Jemmy, come to-mworn,'
  And then a leame excuse suin meade.

I went to bed, but cudn't sleep,
  This luive sae breks a body's rest ;
The mwornin dawn'd, then up I gat,
  And seegh'd, and aye luik'd tow'rds the west ;
But when far off I saw the wood,
  Where he unlock'd his heart to me,
I thought o' monie a happy hour,
  And then a tear gush'd frae my e'e.

To-neet my fadder's far frae heame,
  And wunnet come this three hours yet ;
But, O ! it pours, and I'd be leath
  That Jemmy sud for me get wet !
Yet, if he dis, guid heame-brew'd yell
  Will warm his chearfu' honest heart ;
Wi' him, my varra life o' life !
  I's fain to meet, but leath to part.

AULD MARGARET.

Auld Margaret in the fauld she sits,
And spins, and sings, and smuiks by fits,
And cries as she had lost her wits—
    ' O this weary, weary warl !'15

Yence Margaret was as lish a lass
As e'er in summer trod the grass ;
But fearfu' changes come to pass
    In this weary, weary warl !

Then, at a murry-neet or fair,
Her beauty meade the young fwok stare;
Now wrinkled is that feace wi' care—
    O this weary, weary warl!

Yence Marget she hed dowters twee,
And bonnier lasses cudna be;
Now nowther kith nor kin has she—
    O this weary, weary warl!

The eldest, wi' a soldier gay,
Ran frae her heame ae luckless day,
And e'en lies buried far away—
    O this weary, weary warl!

The youngest she did nought but whine,
And for the lads wad fret and pine,
Till hurried off by a decline—
    O this weary, weary warl!

Auld Andrew toil'd reet sair for bread—
Ae neet they fan him cauld, cauld dead,
Nae wonder that turned Marget's head—
    O this weary, weary warl!

Peer Marget! oft I pity thee,
Wi' care-worn cheek and hollow e'e,
Bowed down by yage and poverty—
    O this weary, weary warl!

FIRST LUIVE.

Tune—"*Cold and raw.*"

It's just three weeks sin' Carel fair,
    This sixteenth o' September;
There the furst loff of a sweetheart I gat,
    Sae that day I'll remember.

This luive meks yen stupid—ever sin seyne
    I's thinkin and thinkin o' Wully;
I dung owre the knop, and scawder'd my fit,
    And cut aw my thoum wi' the gully.

O, how he danc'd ! and, O how he talk'd !
    For my life I cannot forget him ;
He wad hev a kiss—I gev him a slap—
    But if he were here I'd let him.

Says he, ' Mally Maudlin, my heart is thine !
    And he brong sec a seegh, I believ'd him :
Thought I, Wully Wintrep, thou's welcome to mine,
    But my head I hung down to deceive him.

Twee yards o' reed ribbon to wear for his seake,
    Forby ledder mittens, he bought me ;
But when we were thinkin o' nought but luive,
    My titty, de'il bin ! com and sought me :

The deuce tek aw clashes ! off she ran heame,
    And e'en telt my tarn'd auld mudder ;
There's sec a te-dui—but let them fratch on—
    Miss him, I'll ne'er get sec anudder !

Neist Sunday, God wullin ! we promis'd to meet,
    I'll get frae our tweesome a baitin ;
But a lee mun patch up, be't rang or be't reet,
    For Wully he sha'not stan waitin :

The days they seem lang, and lang are the neets,
    And, waes me ! this is but Monday !
I seegh, and I think, and I say to mysel,
    O that to-morrow were Sunday !

LAL STEPHEN.

TUNE—" Hallow Fair."

Lal Stephen[16] was bworn at Kurkbanton,
    Just five feet three inches was he ;
But at ploughing, or mowing, or shearin,
    His match you but seldom cud see ;
Then at dancin, O he was a capper !
    He'd shuffle and lowp till he sweat ;
And for singin he ne'er hed a marrow,
    I just think I hear his voice yet.

F

And then wid a sleate and a pencil,
  He capp'd aw our larned young lairds;
And played on twee jew-trumps together,
  And aye come off winner at cards :
At huntin a brock or an otter,
  At trackin a foumert or hare,
At pittin a cock or at shootin,
  Nae lad cud wi' Stephen compare.

And then he wad feight like a fury,
  And count fast as hops aw the stars,
And read aw the news i' the paper,
  And talk about weddins and wars ;
And then he wad drink like a Briton,
  And spend the last penny he had,
And aw the peer lasses about him,
  For Stephen were runnin stark mad.

Our Jenny she writ him a letter,
  And monie a feyne thing she said—
But my fadder he just gat a gliff on't,
  And faith a rare durdum he meade ;
Then Debby, that leev'd at Drumleenin,
  She wad hev him aw till hersel,
For ae neet when he stuil owre to see her,
  Wi' sugger she sweetened his keale.

Then Judy she darned aw his stockins,
  And Sally she meade him a sark,
And Lizzy, the laird's youngest dowter,
  Kens weel whe she met efter dark ;
Aunt Ann, o' the wrang seyde o' fifty,
  E'en thowt him the flower o' the flock—
Nay, to count yen by yen aw his sweethearts,
  Wad tek a full hour by the clock.

O ! but I was vext to hear tell on't,
  When Nichol the teydins he brought,
That Stephen was geane for a soldier—
  Our Jenny she gowled, ay, like ought :—

Sin' that we've nae spwort efter supper,
  We nowther get sang or a crack ;
Our lasses sit beytin their fingers,
  Aw wishin for Stephen seafe back.

THE BASHFUL WOOER.

Tune—"*Dainty Davie.*"

Whene'er ye come to woo me, Tom,
  Dunnet at the window tap,
  Or cough, or hem, or gi'e a clap,
    To let my fadder hear, man ;
He's auld and fealed, and wants his sleep,
Sae by the hallan softly creep,
Ye need nae watch, and glower, and peep,
    I'll meet ye, niver fear, man :
      If a lassie ye wad win,
        Be chearfu' iver, bashfu' niver ;
      Ilka Jock may get a Jen,
        If he has sense to try, man.

Whene'er we at the market meet,
  Dunnet luik like yen hawf daft,
  Or talk about the cauld and heat,
    As ye were weather-wise, man ;
Haud up yer head, and bauldly speak,
And keep the blushes frae yer cheek,
For he whee hes his teale to seek,
  We lasses aw despise, man.
        If a lassie, &c.

I met ye leately, aw yer leane,
  Ye seemed like yen stown frae the dead,
  Yer teeth e'en chattered i' yer head,
    But ne'er a word o' luive, man ;
I spak, ye luik'd anudder way,
Then trimmeled as ye'd got a flay,
And owre yer shou'der cried " guid day,"
  Nor yence to win me struive, man.
        If a lassie, &c.

My aunty left me threescwore pun,
  But de'il a yen of aw the men,
  Till then, did bare-legged Elcy ken,
    Or care a stree for me, man ;
Now, tiggin at me suin and late,
They're cleekin but the yellow bait;
Yet, mind me, Tom, I needn't wait,
    When I ha'e choice o' three, man.
        If a lassie, &c.

There lives a lad owre yonder muir,
He hes nae fau't but yen—he's puir ;
  Whene'er we meet, wi' kisses sweet,
   He's like to be my deeth, man ;
And there's a lad ahint yon trees,
Wad weade for me abuin the knees ;
Sae tell yer mind, or, if ye please,
    Nae langer fash us beath, man.

      If a lassie ye wad win,
        Be cheerfu' iver, bashfu' niver ;
      Ilka Jock may get a Jen,
        If he hes sense to try, man.

THE AUNTY.

We've roughness amang hands, we've kye i' the byre,
Come live wi' us, lassie, it's aw I desire;
I'll lig i' the loft, and gi'e my bed to thee,
Nor sal out else be wantin that guidness can gi'e :
Sin the last o' thy kin, thy peer aunty, we've lost,
Thou freets aw the day, and e'en luiks like a ghost.

I mind, when she sat i' the nuik at her wheel,
How she'd tweyne the slow thread, and aye counsel
    us weel,
Then oft whisper me, ' Thou wad mek a top wife,
' And pray God to see the weel sattl'd for life ;'
Then what brave funny teales she cud tell the neet
    through,
And wad bless the peer fwok, if the stormy win blew.

That time when we saunter'd owre leate at the town,
'Twas the day, I weel mind, when tou gat thy chintz
      gown,
For the watters were up, and pick dark was the neet,
And she lissen'd and cry'd, and thought aw was'nt reet;
But, oh! when you met, what a luik did she give!—
I can niver forget her as lang as I live.

How I like thee, dear lassie! thou's oft heard me tell;
Nay, I like thee far better than I like mysel;
And when sorrow forseakes thee, to kurk we'll e'en
      gang,
But tou munnet sit pinin thy leane aw day lang;
Come owre the geate, lassie, my titty sal be
A companion to her that's aye dearest to me.

THE RURAL VISIT.

TUNE—"*The sutor's dowter.*"

I went to see young Susy,
  Bonny, teydey, blithe was she;
I slyly kiss'd her cherry lips,
    And mark'd the magic o' her e'e,
      That in my fancy rais'd desire;
But purer passion never burn'd
  In onie lover's bosom;
And aye may sorrow wet his cheek,
  Who'd crush sae rare a blossom!

And now the rwosie lassie
  The cleath she laid, and teable spread
Wi' monie a dainty quickly,
    And monie a welcome thing she said;
      But nit sae sweet the honeycwom,
As Susy's temptin cherry lips,
  That fir'd at once my bosom:
O may no rude destroyer dare
  To crop sae fair a blossom!

And now, to greet the stranger,
 The wearied auld fwok dander'd heame,
And village news recounted :
 The guid man bade his sonsy deame
  Trim up the fire and mek the tea ;
The gurdle-cakes, as Susy turn'd,
 I watch'd her heaving bosom,
And pleasure beam'd in ilka feace,
 To see sae sweet a blossom.

And now, to please the auld fwok,
 The sang and teale went gaily round,
Till neet had drawn her curtain
 Some five full hours ; I ruse, and fan
  Young Susy half consenting
To set me out a mile o'geate ;[17]
 I held her to my bosom,
And, parting, kiss'd, and pray'd kind Heav'n
 To guard this beauteous blossom.

WATTY.

Tune—" *The Lads o' Dunce.*"

If ye ax where I come frae, I say the Fell-seyde,
Where fadder and mudder, and honest fwok beyde ;
And my sweetheart, O bless her! she thowt nin like me,
For when we shuik hans the tears gushed frae her e'e:
Says I, ' I mun e'en git a spot if I can,
' But, whatever beteyde me, I'll think o' thee, Nan !'

 Nan was a parfet beauty, wi' twee cheeks like
codlin blossoms ; the varra seet on her meade my
mouth aw watter. ' Fares-te-weel, Watty !' says
she ; ' tou's a wag amang t' lasses, and I'll see thee
nae mair !'—' Nay, dunnet gowl, Nan !' says I,

' For, mappen, ere lang, I's be maister mysel;'
Sae we buss'd, and I tuik a last luik at the fell.

On I whussel'd and wonder'd ; my bundle I flung
Owre my shouder, when Cwoley he efter me sprung,
And howled, silly fellow ! and fawned at my fit,
As if to say—Watty, we munnet part yet !
At Carel I stuid wi' a strea i' my mouth,[18]
And they tuik me, nae doubt, for a promisen youth.

    The weyves com roun me in clusters : ' What
weage dus te ax, canny lad ?' says yen.—' Wey,
three pun and a crown ; wunnet beate a hair o'
my beard.' ' What can te dui ?' says anudder.—
' Dui ! wey I can plough, sow, mow, sheer, thresh,
deyke, milk, kurn, muck a byer, sing a psalm,
mend car-gear, dance a whornpeype, nick a naig's
tail, hunt a brock, or feight iver a yen o' my
weight in aw Croglin parish.'

An auld bearded hussey suin caw'd me her man—
But that day, I may say't, aw my sorrows began.

Furst Cwoley, peer fellow ! they hanged i' the street,
And skinned, God forgie them ! for shoon to their feet !
I cry'd, and they cawd me peer hawf-witted clown,
And bantered and followed me aw up and down :
Neist me deame she e'en starv'd me, that niver leev'd
    weel,—
Her hard words and luiks wad hae freeten'd the dei'l :

    She hed a lang beard, for aw t' warl leyke a
billy gwoat, wi' a kil-dried frosty feace ; and then
the smawest leg o' mutton in aw Carel market
sarrat the cat, me, and her, for a week. The
bairns meade sec gam on us, and thundered at
the rapper, as if to waken a corp ; when I opened
the duir, they threw stour i' my e'en, and caw'd
me daft Watty ;

Sae I packed up my duds when my quarter was out,
And, wi' weage i' my pocket, I sauntered about.

Suin my reet-hand breek pocket they picked in a fray,
And wi' fifteen wheyte shillings they slipped clean away,
Forby my twee letters frae mudder and Nan,
Where they said Carel lasses wad Watty trepan ;—
But 'twad tek a lang day just to tell what I saw—
How I skeap'd frae the gallows, the sowdgers and aw.

Ay! there were some fworgery chaps bad me
just sign my neame. 'Nay,' says I, 'you've gotten a wrang pig by the lug, for I canno write.'
Then a fellow like a lobster, aw leaced and fea-
thered, ax'd me, 'Watty, wull te list? thou's
owther be a general or a gomoral.'—'Nay, I wunnet—that's plain : I's content wi' a cwoat o' mudder's spinnin.'

Now, wi' twee groats and tuppence, I'll e'en toddle
      heame,
But ne'er be a sowdger wheyle Watty's my neame.

How my mudder 'll gowl, and my fadder 'll stare,
When I tell them peer Cwoley they'll never see mair.
Then they'll bring me a stuil ;—as for Nan, she'll be fain,
When I kiss her, God bless her, agean and agean !
The barn and the byre, and the auld hollow tree,
Will just seem like cronies yen's fidgin to see.

The sheep 'll nit ken Watty's voice now! The
peat-stack we us'd to lake roun 'll be brunt ere
this! As for Nan, she'll be owther married or
broken-hearted ; but sud aw be weel at Croglin,
we'll ha'e feastin, fiddlin, dancin, drinkin, singin,
and smuikin, aye, till aw's blue about us :

Amang aw our neybors sec wonders I'll tell,
But niver mair leave my auld friens or the fell.

JENNY'S COMPLAINT.

TÜNE—"*Nancy's to the greenwood gane.*"

O, lass! I've fearfu' news to tell!
　What thinks te's come owre Jemmy?
The sowdgers hev e'en pick'd him up,
　And sent him far, far frae me:
To Carel he set off wi' wheat;
　Them ill reed-cwoted fellows
Suin wil'd him in [19]—then meade him drnnk:
　He'd better geane to th' gallows.

The varra seet o' his cockade
　It set us aw a-crying;
For me, I fairly fainted tweyce,
　Tou may think that was tryin:
My fadder wad ha'e paid the smart,
　And show'd a gowden guinea,
But, lack-a-day! he'd kiss'd the buik,
　And that 'll e'en kill Jenny.

When Nichol tells about the wars,
　It's war than deeth to hear him;
I oft steal out, to hide my tears,
　And cannot, cannot bear him:
For aye he jeybes, and cracks his jwokes,
　And bids me nit forseake him;
A brigadier, or grandidier,
　He says, they're sure to meake him.

If owre the stibble fields I gang,
　I think I see him ploughin,
And ev'ry bit o' bread I eat,
　It seems o' Jemmy's sowin:
He led the varra cwoals we burn,
　And when the fire I's leetin,
To think the peats were in his hands,
　It sets my heart a beatin.

What can I de ? I nought can de,
 But whinge, and think about him :
For three lang years he follow'd me,
 Now I mun live widout him !
Brek heart, at yence, and then it's owre !
 Life's nought widout yen's dearie.
I'll suin lig in my cauld, cauld grave,
 For, oh ! of life I'm weary !

MATTHEW MACREE.[20]

TUNE—" *The wee pickle tow.* "

Sin I furst work'd a sampleth at Biddy Forsyth's,
 I ne'er saw the marrow o' Matthew Macree ;
For down his braid back hing his lang yellow locks,
 And he hes sec a cast wi' his bonny grey e'e ;
Then he meks us aw laugh, on the stuil when he stands,
And acts like the players, and gangs wi' his hands,
And talks sec hard words as nit yen understands—
 O, what a top scholar is Matthew Macree !

'Twas nobbet last Easter his cock wan the main,
 I stuid i' the ring rejoicin to see ;
The bairns they aw shouted, the lasses were fain,
 And the lads o' their shou'ders bore Matthew Macree :
Then at lowpin he'll gang a full yard owre them aw,
And at rustlin, whilk o' them dare try him a faw ?
And whee is't that aye carries off the fit-baw,
 But the king of aw Cumberland, Matthew Macree.

That time when he fit full twee hours at the fair,
 And lang Jemmy Smith gat a famish black e'e ;
Peer Jemmy I yence thought wad niver paw mair,
 And I was reet sworry for Matthew Macree :
Then he wad shek the bull-ring, & brag the heale town,
And to feght, rin, or russle, he put down a crown ;
Saint Gworge, the girt champion, o' fame and renown,
 Was nobbet a waffler to Matthew Macree.

On Sundays, in bonny wheyte weastcwoat when dress'd,
  He sings i' the kurk, what a topper is he!
I hear his strang voice far abuin aw the rest,
  And my heart still beats time to Matthew Macree:
Then his feyne eight-page ditties, & garlands sae sweet,
They mek us aw merry the lang winter neet;
But, when he's nit amang us, we niver seem reet,
  Sae fond are the lasses o' Matthew Macree.

My fadder he left me a house on the hill,
  And I's get a bit lan sud my aunty dee,
Then I'll wed bonny Matthew whenever he will,
  For gear is but trash widout Matthew Macree:
We'll try to shew girt fwok content in a cot,
And when in our last heame together we've got,
May our bairns and their neybors oft point to the spot,
  Where lig honest Matthew and Jenny Macree.

CALEP CROSBY.

Tune—"*Auld Rob Morris.*"

O wife! I wad fain see our Sukey dui reet,
But she's out wi' the fellows, aye neet efter neet:
Them that's fash'd wi' nae bairns iver happy mun be,
For we've yen, and she's maister o' baith thee and me!

I can't for the life o' me get her to work,[21]
Nor aw the lang Sunday to ga near a kurk,
Nor frae week en to week en a chapter to read,
For the Bible ligs stoury abuin the duir head.

She yence cud ha'e scrammel'd, and writ her awn neame,
And, Sunday and warday, was teydey at heame;
Now, to see her whol'd stockins, her brat, and her gown,
She's a shem and a byzen to aw the heale town.

O wad she be guided, and stick till her wheel,
There's nin kens how fain I wad see her dui weel;
For she's thy varra picture, and aw that we have,
But thur neets'warks'll bring my grey hairs to the grave.

'Twas nobbet last week, in a passion I flew,
And gev her a trouncin—but sair did I rue;
Then I bad her e'en pack up her duds, and we'd part,
For to streyke my awn bairn it just breks my auld heart.

There's that ill Calep Crosby, he's niver away,
He's gleymin and watchin her beath neet and day;
Sud he come i' my clutches a ken-guid he's get,
For, tho' auld, leame, and feeble, I'll maister him yet.

I'll away owre to Whitten* a press-gang to seek,
And they's lig him in irons, ay this varra week;
On his back he may tie her, a donnet is she,
And sha'not be maister o' beath thee and me!

FECKLESS WULLY.

Wee Wully wuns on yonder brow,
  And Wully he hes dowters twee;
But nought cud feckless Wully dui,
  To get them sweethearts weel to see.

For Meg she luik'd baith reet and left,
  Her een they bwor'd a body thro';
And Jen was deef, and dun, and daft,
  And de'il a yen com there to woo.

The neybor's wink'd, the neybors jeer'd,
  The neybors flyr'd at them in scworn,
And monie a wicked trick they play'd
  Peer Meg and Jen, beath neet and mworn.

As Wully went ae day to wark,
  He kick'd a *summet* wid his shoe;
And Wully glowr'd, and Wully girn'd,
  ' Guide us!' quoth he, ' what ha'e we now?'

And Wully cunn'd owre six scwore pun,
  And back he ran wi' nimmle heel,
And aye he owre his shou'der glym'd,
  And thought he'd dealins wi' the de'il.

* Whitehaven.

And Wully's bought a reet snug house,
    And Wully's bought a bit o' lan ;
And Meg and Jen are trig and crouse,
    Sin he the yellow pwokie fan.

Nae mair the neybors wink and jeer,
    But aw shek hans wi' them, I trow ;
And ilk yen talks o' William's gear,
    For Wully's chang'd to William now.

And some come east, and some come west,
    And some come monie a mile to woo ;
And Meg luiks straight, and Jen has sense,
    And we aw see what gear 'll dui.

Ye rich fwok aw, ye'll aye dui reet ;
    Ye peer fwok aw, ye'll aye dui wrang ;
Let wise men aw say what they will,
    It's money meks the meer to gang.

THE BLECKELL MURRY-NEET.

Ay, lad ! sec a murry-neet we've hed at Bleckell,
    The sound o' the fiddle yet rings in my ear ;
Aw reet clipt and heeled were the lads and the lasses,
    And monie a cliver lish hizzy was there :
The bettermer swort sat snug i' the parlour,
    ·I' the pantry the sweethearters cutter'd sae soft ;
The dancers they kick'd up a stour in the kitchen ;
    At lanter the caird-lakers sat in the loft.

The clogger o' Dawston's a famish top hero,
    And bangs aw the player-fwok twenty to yen ;
He stampt wid his fit, and he shouted and roystered,
    Till the sweat it ran off at his varra chin en ;
Then he held up ae han like the spout of a tea-pot,
    And danc'd cross the buckle and leather-te-patch ;
When they cry'd ' bonny Bell !' he lap up to the ceilin,
    And aye cracked his thoums for a bit of a fratch.

G

The Hiverby lads at fair drinkin are seypers ;
　At cockin the Dawstoners niver were bet ;
The Buckabank chaps are reet famish sweethearters,
　Their kisses just sound like the sneck of a yeat ;
The lasses o' Bleckell are sae monie angels ;
　The Cummersdale beauties aye glory in fun—
God help the peer fellow that gleymes at them dancin,
　He'll steal away heartless as sure as a gun.

The 'bacco was strang, and the yell it was lythey,
　And monie a yen bottomed a whart leyke a kurn ;
Daft Fred. i' the nuik, leyke a hawf-rwoasted deevil,
　Telt sly smutty stwories, and meade them aw gurn ;
• Then yen sung *Tom Linton*, anudder *Dick Watters*,
　The auld farmers bragg'd o' their fillies and fwoals,
Wi' jeybin and jwokin, and hotchin and laughin,
　Till some thowt it teyme to set off to the cwoals.

But, hod ! I forgat—when the clock strack eleeben,
　The dubbler was brong in, wi' wheyte breed & brown ;
The gully was sharp, the girt cheese was a topper,
　And lumps big as lapsteans our lads gobbled down :
Aye the douse dapper lanleddy cried, ' Eat and welcome,
　' I' God's neame step forret ; nay, dunnet be bleate !'
Our guts aw weel pang'd, we buck'd up for blin Jenny,
　And neist paid the shot on a girt pewder plate.

Now full to the thropple, wi' head-warks & heart-aches,
　Some crap to the clock-kease instead o' the duir ;
Then sleepin and snworin tuik pleace o' their rwoarin,
　And teane abuin tudder they laid on the fluir.
The last o' December, lang lang we'll remember,
　At five i' the mworn, eighteen hundred and twee :
Here's health & success to the brave Jwohney Dawston,
　And monie sec meetings may we leeve to see !

THE DELIGHTS OF LOVE.

Tune—" Farewell to Bamf."

The summer sun was out o' seet,
  His partin beams danc'd on the fluid :
The fisher watch'd the silver fry,
  As i' the stream he bending stuid ;
The blackburd mourn'd the clowsin day,
  And caw'd his partner to his nest ;
When I up Caldew tuik my way,
  And met the lass I aye like best.

I gaz'd upon her matchless feace,
  That fairer than a lily seem'd ;
I mark'd the magic o' her e'e,
  That wi' luive's powerfu' leetnin beam'd ;
I saw her cheek of breetest red,
  That, blushing, telt a lover's pain,
And seiz'd a kiss, if 'twas a crime,
  Ye God's ! oft may I sin again !

Fast flew the hours—now ruse the muin,
  And telt us it was time to part ;
I set her to her mudder's duir,
  She wisper'd low, ' Thou's stown my heart !'
I thro' the lattice stule a glance,
  And heard her angry mudder chide :
Then thought of aw a parent's cares,
  As frae her cottage heame I hied.

I've teasted plasures dearly bought,
  And read mankind in monie a page :
But woman, woman, sweetens life,
  Frae giddy youth to feeble age.
Ye fuils, aye court coy Fortune's smile ;
  Ye rakes, in quest of pleasure rove :
Ye drunkards, drown each sense in wine ;
  Be mine the dear delights of love !

RUTH.

TUNE—" *My auld guidman.*

The crackets were chirpin on the hearth ;
   Our wife reel'd gairn, and sat i'th' nuik ;
I tuik a whiff o' my cutty black peype ;
   Lal Dick by fire-leet plied his buik ;
The youngermer bairns, at heeds and cross,
   Sat lakin merrily in a row ;
The wind clash'd tui the entry duir,
   And down the chimney fell the snow.

' O ! says our weyfe, then fetch'd a seegh,
   ' Guidman, we sud reet thankfu' be !
' How monie a scwore this angry neet,
   ' Wad like to sit wi' tee and me ;
' Sae wad our dowter Ruth, I trow,
   ' A silly peer luckless bairn she's been ;
' For her, nae day gangs owre my head,
   ' But painfu' tears gush frae my een.

' She aye was honest and weel to see,
   ' I say't—she hed nae faut but yen—
' She off wid a taistrel sowdger lad,
   ' And niver yence sent the scribe of a pen :
' O man ! we sud forget and forgive ;
   ' The brute beast for its awn 'll feel ;
' Were mine awt' warl, ay ten times mair,
   ' I'd gi'e't to see her alive and weel.

' Whea kens, peer thing ! what she's endur'd,
   ' Sin that sad hour she left her heame ;
' Thou turn'd her out ; it hurt me sair,
   ' And aw our neibors cried out shem.'
Here stopped our weyfe, and shuik her head,
   While tears ran tricklin down her cheek ;
I fan the truth o' what she said,
   But de'il a word cud owther speak.

Just then the latch was lifted up ;
 ' Ay, that's a boggle !' cried out lal Ann ;
In bounc'd my bairn, and, at my feet,
 Cried. ' O, forgi'e me !—here's my guidman !'
Our dame she shriek'd, and dropp'd her wark ;
 I bless'd them beath—the bairns were fain ;
We talk'd the stormy neet away,
 And, God be prais'd, we've met again !

THE PECK O' PUNCH.

'Twas Rob and Jock, and Hal and Jack,
 And Tom and Ned forby,
Wi' Archy drank a Peck o' Punch,
 Ae neet when they were dry ;
And aye they jwok'd, and laugh'd, and smuik'd,
 And sang wi' heartfelt glee,
" To-night we're yen, to-morrow geane,
 " Syne let us merry be !"

Saint Mary's muckle clock bumm'd eight,
 When each popp'd in his head ;
But ere they rose, they'd fairly drank
 The sheame-feac'd muin to bed ;
    And aye they jwok'd, &c.

To monie a bonny Carel lass,
 The fairest o' the town,
And monie a manly British chiel,
 The noggin glass went roun ;
    And aye they jwok'd, &c.

A neybor's faut's they ne'er turn'd owre,
 Nor yence conceal'd their ain—
Had Care keek'd in, wi' wae-worn feace,
 They'd kick'd him out again ;
    For aye they jwok'd, &c.

The daily toil, the hunter's spoil,
  The faithless foreign pow'rs,
The Consul's fate, his o'ergrown state,
  By turns beguil'd the hours ;
          And aye they laugh'd, &c.

Let others cringe, and bow the head,
  A purse-proud sumph to please ;
Fate, grant to me aye liberty
  To mix with souls like these ;
Then oft we'll jwoke, and laugh, and smuik,
  And sing wi' heartfelt glee,
" To-night we're yen, to-morrow geane,
  " Syne let us merry be !"

THE THUIRSBY WITCH.

TUNE—" *O'er Bogie.*"

There's Harraby and Tarraby,
  And Wigganby beseyde ;
There's Oughterby and Souterby,*
  And bys beath far and weyde ;—
Of strappin, sonsy, rwosy queens,
  They aw may brag a few ;
But Thuirsby for a bonny lass
  Can cap them aw I trow.

Her mudder sells a swope o' drink,
  It is beath stout and brown,
And Etty is the hinny fowt
  Of aw the country roun ;
Frae east and west, beath rich and peer,
  A-horse, a-fit, caw in—
For whee can pass sae rare a lass,
  He's owther daft or blin.

Her een are leyke twee Cursmass sleas,
  But twice as breet and clear ;

* Names of Cumberland villages.

Nae rwose cud iver match her feace,
    That yet grew on a breer ;
At toun, kurk, market, dance or fair,[23]
    She meks their hearts aw stoun,
And conquers mair than Bonyprat,
    Whene'er she keeks aroun.

Oft graith'd in aw their kurk-gawn gear,
    Leyke nwoble lwords at cwort,
Our lads slink in, and gaze and grin,
    Nor heed their Sunday spwort ;
If stranger leets, her een he meets,
    And fins he can't tell how ;
To touch the glass her hand has touch'd,
    It sets him in a lowe.

Yence Thuirsby lads were—whea but we,
    And cud ha'e bang'd the lave,
But now they hing their lugs, and luik
    Leyke fwok stown frae the grave ;
And what they ail in head or heart
    Nae potticary knows—
The little glancin Thuirsby Witch,
    She is the varra cause.

Of Black-eyed Susan, Mary Scott,
    · The Lass o' Patie's Mill,
Of Barbara Allan, Sally Gray,
    The Lass o' Richmond-hill,
Of Nancy Dawson, Molly Mog,
    Though thousands sing wl' glee,
This village beauty, out and out,
    She bangs them aw to see.

THE VILLAGE GANG.

Tune—" *Jenny dang the weaver.* "

There's sec a gang in our town,
    The deevil cannot wrang them,

And cud yen get tem put i' prent,
   Aw England cuddent bang them ;
Our dogs e'en bite aw decent fwok,
   Our varra naigs they kick them,
And if they nobbet ax their way,
   Our lads set on and lick them.

Furst wi' Dick Wiggem we'll begin,
   The teyney, greasy wobster ;
He's got a gob frae lug to lug,
   And neb like onie lobster :
Dick' Weyfe, they say, was Branton bred,
   Her mudder was a howdy,
And when peer Dick's thrang on the luim,
   She's off to Jwohnie Gowdy.

But as for Jwohnie, silly man,[24]
   He threeps about the nation,
And talks o' stocks and Charley Fox,
   And meakes a blusteration ;
He reads the paper yence a week,
   The auld fwok geape and wonder—
Were Jwohnie king, we'd aw be rich,
   And France mud e'en knock under.

Lang Peel the laird's a dispert chap,
   His weyfe's a famous fratcher—
She brays the lasses, starves the lads,
   Nae bandylan can match her :
We aw ken how they gat their gear,
   But that's a fearfu' stwory,
And sud he hing on Carel Sands,
   Nit yen wad e'er be sworry.

Beane-breaker Jwohn we weel may neam ,
   He's tir'd o' wark, confound him !
By manglin limbs and streenin joints,
   He's meade aw cripples round him :
Mair hurt he's duin than onie yen
   That iver sceap'd a helter ;

When sec like guffs leame decent fwok,
  It's time some laws sud alter.

The schuilmaister's a conjurer,
  For when our lads are drinkin,
Aw maks o' tricks he'll dui wi' cairds,
  And tell fwok what they're thinkin ;
He'll glower at maps and spell hard words,
  For hours and hours together,
And in the muin he kens what's duin—
  Nay he can coin the weather !

Then there's the blacksmith wi' ae e'e,
  And his hawf-witted mudder,
'Twad mek a deed man laugh to see
  Them glyme at yen anudder ;
A three-quart piggen, full o' keale,
  He'll sup, the greedy sinner,
Then eat a cow'd-lword like his head,
  Ay, onie day at dinner.

Jack Mar, the hirplin piper's son,
  Can bang them aw at leein ;
He'll brek a lock, or steal a cock,
  W' onie yen in bein :
He eats guid meat, and drinks strang drink,
  And gangs weel graith'd o' Sunday,
And weel he may, a bonny fray
  Com out last Whissen-Monday.

The doctor he's a parfet pleague,
  And hawf the parish puzzens ;
The lawyer sets fwok by the lugs,
  And cheats them neist by duzzens ;
The parson swears a bonny stick
  Amang our sackless asses ;
The 'Squire's ruin'd scwores and scwores
  O' canny country lasses.

There's twenty mair, course as neck beef,
   If yen hed time to neame them;
Left-handed Sim, slape-finger'd Sam,
   Nae law cou'd iver teame them;
There's blue-nebb'd Watt and ewe-chin'd Dick,
   Weel wordy o' the gallows—
O happy is the country seyde
   That's free frae sec like fellows!

DICKY GLENDININ.

Tune—"*As Patie cam up frae the glen.*"

My fadder was down at the mill,
   My mudder was out wid her spinnin,
When, whea sud slip whietly in,
   But canny lal Dicky Glendinin;
He poud off his muckle top cwoat,
   And drew in a stuil by the hallen,
Then fworc'd me to sit on his knee,
   And suin a sad teale began tellin.

" O, Jenny! O Jenny!" says he,
   " My leykin for tee I can't smudder;
It meade me as sick as a peat,
   To think tou'd teane up wid anudder:
What! there's been a bonny te-dui
   About a lang hulk of a miller!
He's weyde-gobb'd and ill-nature'd tui,
   But ae word says aw—he hes siller.

" The lasses aye flyre and mak gam,
   And ax me, what's got Jenny Forster?
The lads, when we meet i' the lwones,
   Cry out, ' Sairy Dick! what, tou's lost her!'
When Rowley, the miller, last neet
   I met, as we com in frae sheerin,
Had the sickle but been our lang gun,
   I'd shot him, ay, dead as a herrin.

" O ! hes te forgotten the time,
    Tou said tou leyk'd me best of onie ?
And hes te forgotten the teyme,
    Tou said luive was better than monie?
And hes te forgotten the teyme,
    I mark'd our twea neames on a shillin ?
Tou promised to wear't neist thy heart,
    And then to wed me tou was willin.

" The furst teyme you're cried i' the kurk,
    I'll step my ways up and forbid it ;
When cauld i' my coffin, they'll say,
    'Twas e'en Jenny Forster that did it !
My ghost, the lang neet, aw in wheyte,
    Will shek thee, and gar thee aw shiver—
O the tears how they hop owre my cheeks,
    To think I sud lwose thee for ever !"

" O, Dicky ! O, Dicky !" says I,
    " I nowther heed house, lan, or siller ;
Tou's twenty teymes dearer to me,
    Than onie lang hulk of a miller !"
A match we struck up in a crack,
    And Dicky's got sticks and got beddin ;
My fadder and mudder are fain—
    Then hey for a guid merry weddin !

THE INVASION.

Tune—" Lingo's Wedding."

How fens te, Dick ?   There's fearfu' news—
    Udsbreed ! the French are comin !
There's nought at Carel but parades,
    And sec a drum, drum, drummin :
The volunteers and brigadiers
    Are aw just mad to meet them ;
And England e'en mun hing her head,
    If Britons dunnet beat them.

Then there's the Rangers aw in green,
    Commanded by brave HOWARD—
Of aw his nowble kin, nit yen
    Was iver caw'd a coward ;—
They'll pop the French off leyke steyfe,
    If e'er they meet, I'll bail them :
Wi' sec true Britons at their heads,
    True courage cannot fail them.

Thur French are dispert wicked chiels,
    If it be true they tell us,
For where they've been, fwok curse the day
    They e'er saw sec sad fellows ;—
They plant the tree o' liberty,
    And hirelings dance around it;
But millions water't wi' their tears,
    And bid the de'il confound it.

Our parson says,[25] " We bang'd them still,
    And bang them still we mun, man ;
For he desarves a coward's deeth,
    That frae them e'er wad run, man :
What feckless courts and worn-out states,
    They've conquered just by knavery ;
But every volunteer will pruive,
    A Briton kens nae slavery."

'"ve thowt and thowt, sin I kent ought,
    Content's the greatest blissin,—
ind he that seizes my bit lan
    Desarves a guid soun drissin.
:uld England, though we count thy fau'ts,
    For iver we'll defend thee !
'o foreign tyrants sud we bow,—
    They'll mar, but niver mend thee !

GRIZZY.

TUNE—"*My auld guidman.*"

The witch weyfe begg'd in our backseyde,[26]
    But went unsarra'd away i' th' pet ;
Our Ester kurn'd at e'er she kurn'd,
    But butter the deuce a crum cou'd get.
The pez-stack fell, and crush'd my fadder ;
    My mudder cowp'd owre, and leam'd hersel ;
Neist, war and war, what dud we see,
    But Jenny' pet lam drown'd i' the well.

Auld Grizzy the witch, as some fwok say,
    Meks paddock-rud ointment for sair een,
And cures the tuith-wark wi' a charm,
    Of hard words neane ken what they mean.
She milks the kye, the urchin's bleam'd ;
    She bleets the cworn wi' her bad e'e ;
When cross'd by lasses, they pruive wi' bairn;
    And if she grummel, they're seafe o' twee.

I yence sweethearted Madge o' th' Mill,
    And whea sae thick as she and I ;
Auld Whang he promised tweescore pun,
    A weel-theek'd house, and bit of a stye ;
Ae neet we met at our croft head,
    But Grizzy was daund'ring aw her leane,
And scarce a week o' days were owre,
    Till Madge to kurk Wull Weer had teane.

When deef Dick Maudlin lost his weyfe,
    And said 'twas weel it was nae war ;
When Jerry' black filly pick'd the fwoal,
    And hawf-blin Calep fell owre the scar ;
When manten Marget brunt her rock ;
    When smuggler Mat was lost i' the snaw ;
When wheezlin Wully was set i' the stocks ;
    Auld Grizzy aye gat the wheyte of aw.

Her feace is like the stump of a yek ;
　She stoops and stowters, sheks and walks ;
Bleer-e'e'd and tuithless, wi' a beard :
　She cough's aud granes, and mumps and talks ;
She lives in a shill-house, burns dried sticks,
　And there hes dealins wi' the de'il.
O war she whietly in her grave,
　For where she bides few can dui weel.

GWORDIE GILL.

Tune—" *Andrew wi' his cutty gun.*"

Of aw the lads I see or ken,
　There's yen I like abuin the rest ;
He's neycer in his war day duds,
　Than others donn'd in aw their best.
A body's heart's a body's awn,
　And they may gi'e't to whea they will ;
Had I got ten where I ha'e neane,
　I'd gi'e them aw to Gwordie Gill.

Whea was't that brak our lanlword' garth,[27]
　For me, when bairns we went to schuil ?
Whea was't durst venture mid-thie deep,
　To get my clog out o' the puil ?
And when the filly flang me off,
　And lang and lang I laid sae ill,
Whea was't gowl'd owre me day and neet,
　And wish'd me weel ? 'Twas Gwordie Gill.

Oft mounted on his lang-tail'd naig,
　Wi' feyne new buits up till his knee,
The laird's daft son leets i' the faul,
　And keaves as he wad wurry me ;
Tho' fadder, mudder, uncle tui,
　To wed this maz'lin teaze me still,
I hear of aw his lan and brass,
　But oft steal out to Gwordie Gill.

Frae Carel cousin Fanny com,
  And brong her whey-feac'd sweetheart down,
Wi' sark-neck stuck abuin his lugs,
  A peer clipt dinment frae the town :
He minc'd and talk'd, and skipp'd and walk'd,
  But tir'd a gangin up the hill,
And luik'd as pale as onie corp,
  Compar'd to rwosie Gwordie Gill.

My Gwordie's whussle weel I ken,[28]
  Lang ere we meet, the darkest neet ;
And when he lilts and sings Skewball,
  Nit playhouse music's hawf sae sweet.
A body's heart's a body's awn,
  And they may gi'e't to whea they will ;
I yence had yen, now I ha'e neane,
  For it belangs to Gwordie Gill.

A WEYFE FOR WULLY MILLER.

Tune—"*Maggy Lawder.*"

Hout, Wully, lad ! cock up thy head,
  Nor fash thysel about her ;
Nought comes o' nought, sae tek nae thought,
  · Tou's better far widout her.
Peer man ! her fadder weel we ken,
  He's but an ass-buird meaker ;
But she's town-bred, and, silly gowk !
  Thou'd gi'e thy teeth to teake her.

I've seen thee flyre and jwoke like mad,
  At aw our country fellows ;
But now thou seeghs and luiks like death,
  Or yen gawn to the gallows ;
Thou's sous'd owre head and ears i' luive —
  Nay, nobbet luik at Cwoley !
He wags his tail, as if to say,
  ' Wey, what's the matter, Wully ?'

There's lads but few in our town,
  And lasses wanters plenty,
And he that fain wad wed a weyfe
  May weale yen out o' twenty :—
There's Tamer Toppin, Aggy Sharp,
  And clogger Wilkin' Tibby ;
There's Greacy Gurvin, Matty Meer,
  And thingumbob' lal Debby :

Then there's Wully Guffy' dowter Nan
  At thee aye keeks and glances,
For tou's the apple o' their e'en
  At cairdin neets and dances ;
My titty, tui, ae neet asleep,
  Cried, ' Canny Wully Miller !'
I poud her hair, she blush'd rwose reed,
  Sae gang thy ways een till her.

Tell mudder aw the news tou kens ;
  To fadder talk o' th' weather ;
Then lilt tem up a sang or twea,
  To please tem aw together ;
She'll set thee out, then speak thy mind—
  She'll suit thee till a shevin ;
But town-bred deames, to sec as we,
  Are seldom worth the hevin.

THE TWEE AULD MEN.
MATTHEW.

What, Gabriel! come swat thy ways down on the sattle,
  I lang for a bit of a crack ;
Thy granson I sent owre the geate for some 'bacco—
  The varment 'll never come back !—
Nay, keep on thy hat : we heed nought about manners :
  What news about your en o' the town ?
They say the king's badly ; thur times gang but oddly ;
  The warl just seems turn'd upseyde down ;
Ay, what alterations, and out-o'-way fashions,
  Sin lal todlin callans were we !

GABRIEL.

O, Matthew! they've cutten the yeks and the eshes,
    That grew owre anent the kurk waw!
How oft dud we lake just like wild things amang them;
    But suin we, like them, mun lig low!
The schuil-house is fawn, where we beath larn'd our
        letters,
    For tee, tou cud figure and write;
I mind[29] what a monstrous hard task and a lickin
    Tou gat when tou fit wi' Tom Wheyte;
Wherever yen ranges, the chops and the changes
    Oft mek a tear gush frae my e'e.

MATTHEW.

Then, Gabey, thou minds when we brak Dinah'
    worchet—
    Stown apples bairns aw think are sweet—
Deuce tek this bad 'bacco! de'il bin, it 'll draw nin,
    Yen mud as weel smuik a wet peat!—
What, yonder's Rob Donaldson got a lang letter,
    And some say it talks of a peace;
But that 'll nit happen i' thy time or my time,
    Widout we can get a new lease.
Here, lass! bring some yell in, drinkin's nae failin,
    Let's moisten our clay ere we dee.

GABRIEL.

Ay, Matt! what they buried auld Glaister last
    Monday—
    Peer Jwosep! we went to ae schuil!—
He married deef Marget, the Gammelsby beauty,
    A silly proud cat-witted fuil:
Ae son pruiv'd a taistrel, and brak up at Lunnon,
    But Jwosep he gat aw to pay;
Anudder, they said, turn'd out nit quite owre honest,
    Sae gat off to Botany Bay.—
O, man! this frost pinches, and kills fwok by inches,
    It's e'en meade a cripple o' me!

MATTHEW.

Ay, Gabey! it's lang sin thou married Ann Lawson;
 Tou minds when we off like the win
Frae kurk to the yellow-house?—What, I was weel
  mounted,
 And left them aw twea mile behin.
Then there was Young Gabey, our weyfe was his
  goddy,
 A brave murry cursnin we had;
We kent nought o' tea, or sec puzzen i' thar days,
 But drank tweyce-brew'd yell till hawf mad:
There was Kitt and Ned Neilson, and Dan and Wat
  Wilson,
 They've aw geane and left thee and me.

GABRIEL.

There's ae thing, guid Matthew, I've lang thought of
  axin,
 And that tou mun grant if tou can;
When I's stiff and cauld, see me decently coffin'd,
 And laid down aseyde my weyfe Ann.
My peer granson Jwosep, he thrives and he grows up,
 O luik till him when I's low laid!
Mind he gaes to the kurk, and sticks weel till his
  larnin,
 And get him a bit of a trade;
The neybors will bless thee, it wunnet distress thee,
 And happy auld Gabriel can dee.

MATTHEW.

Keep up thy heart, Gabey! nae guid comes o' grievin;
 Aye laugh at the warl, if thou'd thrive;
I've buried three weyves, and mun e'en hav anudder,
 I's quite young and rash—*eighty-five;*
Then sec a hard drinker, a wrustler, a feghter,
 A cocker I've been i' my time;
And as for a darrak, in barn or in meadow,
 Whea match'd me, when just i' my prime?
I ne'er thought o' whinin, or gowlin or pinin—
 We're wise when we chearfu' can be.

Nay but, neyber Matthew, when ninety lang winters
 Ha'e bent you, and powder'd the pow,
We grane i' the nuik, wi' few friens or acquaintance,
 And just fin we cannot tell how :
For me, I's sair fash'd wi' a cough and the gravel,
 And ae single tuith i' my head ;
Then, sin my peer bairn they tuik off for a sowdger,
 I've wish'd I were nobbet weel dead ;—
The house uncle ga'e me the squire e'en ta'en frae me:
 There's nought but the warkhouse fur me !

MATTHEW.

My fadder, God rust him! wi' pinchin and pleenin,
 Screap'd up aw the gear he cud get ;
I've been a sad deevil, and spent gowd i' gowpens,
 But still ha'e a hantel left yet:
Come gi'es thy hand, Gabey![30] tou's welcome as may be,
 My purse and my ambrie to share ;
We'll talk of auld times,—eat, drink, and be merry :
 Thy granson sall get what we spare :—
Then leet thy pipe, Gabey ! tou's welcome as may be,
 They's ne'er mek a beggar o' thee !

———

UNCLE WULLY.

Tune—" Woo'd and married an a'."

' It's a comical warl this we live in,'
 Says Calep, and Calep says reet ;
For Matty, that's got aw the money,
 Has e'en geane and wedded deyl'd Peat
He's nobbet a heather-feac'd maz'lin,
 And disn't ken whisky frae yell ;
But her, weel brong up and a scholar,
 Has just meade a fuil o' hersel !
De'il bin but she'd little to de,
To tek sec a hawflin as he,
That nowther kens A, B, nor C !—
Nay, what sec a pair can ne'er 'gree!
Ile ne'er hes a teale widout laitin,

And hardleys can grease his awn clogs;
He marry a decent man's dowter!
    He's fitter to lig amang hogs!
At the clock for an hour he'll keep glymin,
    But de'il e'er the time he can tell;
And my niece, for that ae word husband,
    Has e'en geane and ruin'd hersel.
                                De'il bin, &c.

Her fadder, God keep him! my billy,
    Aye thought her the flow'r o' them aw;
And said on his deeth-bed, ' O, Wully!
    ' Luik till her, man, when I lig low!'
I meade her beath reader and writer—
    Nin bang'd her, the maister can tell;—
But, speyte o' beath larnin and manners,
    She's e'en meade a guff of hersel.
                                De'il bin, &c.

When lasses get past aw advisin,
    Our's then turns a piteous case;
A cwoat or sark yen may shep them,
    But aw cannot gi'e them God's grace:
For me, I'll e'en deet my hands on her,
    And this aw our neybors I'll tell;
She's meade a bad bed, let her lig on't,
    And think how she's ruin'd hersel.
De'il bin but she'd little to de,
To tek sec a mazlin as he,
That nowther kens A, B, nor C!—
Nay, what sec a pair can ne'er 'gree!

GUID STRANG YELL.

Our Ellek likes fat bacon weel,[31]
    And haver-bannock pleases Dick;
A cowd-lword meks lal Wully fain,
    And cabbish aye turns Philip sick;
Our deame's for gurdle-keake and tea,
    And Betty's aw for thick pez-keale;

Let ilk yen fancy what they wull,
    Still my delight is guid strang yell.

I ne'er had muckle, ne'er kent want,
    Ne'er wrang'd a neybor, frien, or kin ;
My weyfe and bairns 'buin aw I prize—
    There's music i' their varra din :
I labour suin, I labour late,
    And chearfu' eat my humble meal ;
My weage can feed and clead us aw,
    And whiles affords me guid strang yell.

What's aw the warl widout content ?
    Wi' that and health man can't be peer ;
We suin slip off frae friens and foes,
    Then whea but fuils wad feight for gear :
'Bout kings and consuls gowks may fratch ;
    For me I scworn to vex mysel,
But laugh at courts and owre-grown knaves,
    When I've a hush o' guid strang yell.

BURGH RACES.

O, Wully ! had tou nobbet been at Burgh races ![32]
    It seem'd, lad, as if aw the warl were met ;
Some went to be seen, others off for divarsion,
    And monie went there a lock money to bet :
The cup was aw siller, and letter'd reet neycely,
    A feyne naig they've put on't, forby my lword's
        neame ;
It hods nar a quart, for monie drank out on't,
    And open'd their gills till they cu'd'nt creep heame.

There was, ' How fens te, Tommy ?'—' What, Jwosep !
    I's gaily ?[33]
    ' Wey, is there ought unket i' your country seyde ?
' Here, lanlword ! a noggin !'—' Whea rides the Col-
    lector ?'
' What Meason' auld meer can bang aw far and wide !'

There wur snaps, yell, nuts, ginger-bread, shwort-
   keakes, and brandy,
   And tents full o' ham, beef, and nowble veal pye ;
There was *Greenup* wi' a reet & true list o' the horses,
   The neames o' the awners and reyders forby.

Er they saddl'd, the gamlers peep'd sair at the horses;
   Sec scrudgin, the fwok were just ready to brust ;
Wi' swearin and bettin they meade a sad hay-bay :
   ' I'll lig six to four !'—' Done ! cum down wi' the
   dust !'
' What think ye o' Lawson ?'—' The field for a guinea !'
   ' I'll mention the winner ! dare onie yen lay ?'
Jwohn Blaylock' reed handkitcher wav'd at the diss-
   nens ;
   At startin, he cried, ' Yen, twee, three, put away !'

They went off like leetnin—the auld meer's a topper—
   She flew like an arrow, and shew'd tem her tail ;
They hugg'd, whupp'd, and spurr'd, but cud niver
   yence touch her—
   The winners they rear'd, & the lwosers turn'd pale ;
Peer Lawson gat dissen'd, and sae sud the tudders,
   Furst heat was a chase, and the neist a tek-in ;
Then some drank their winnins ;—but, wofu' disaster,
   It rain'd, and the lasses gat wet to the skin.

Like pez in a pot, neist at Sandsfield they caper'd, —
   The lads did the lasses sae kittle and hug ;
Young Crosset, i' fettle, had got bran new pumps on,
   And brong fisher Jemmy a clink i' the lug ;
The lasses they belder'd out, ' Man thysel, Jemmy !'34
   His comrades they poud off his cwoat and his sark ;
They fit, lugg'd, and lurry'd, aw owre blood and batter,
   The landlword com in, & cried, ' Shem o' sec wark !'

There wur smugglers, excisemen, horse-cowpers, and
   parsons,
   Sat higglety-pigglety, aw fare a-like ;
And mowdy-warp Jacky—ay, man, it was funny !—
   He meade them aw laugh when he stuck in a creyke.

There were lasses frae Wigton, & Worton, & Banton—
  Some o' them gat sweethearts, while others gat neane;
And bairns yet unbworn 'll oft hear o' Burgh races,
  For ne'er mun we see see a meetin agean.

BIDDY.

Tune—"*Since love is the plan.*"

'Twas frost and thro' leet, wid a greymin o' snaw,
When I went to see Biddy, the flow'r o' them aw;
To meet was agreed on at Seymy' deyke nuik,
Where I saunter'd wi' monie a seegh and lang luik,
But poud up my spirits and off till her heame,
For when fwok mean reet, wey, what need they think
    sheame!

I peep'd through the window to see what was duin;[35]
Her fadder sat whusslin, and greasin his shoon;
Her mudder sat darnin, and smuikin the while;
And Biddy was spinnin, the neet to beguile;
Her thread it aye brak, she seem'd sad as cud be,
And yen sat aside her, a stranger to me.

She turn'd her head frae him, and niver yence spak;
He struive for a kiss, then she up in a crack,
And suin i' the faul, wi' great pleasure we met,
But that happy moment we ne'er can forget:
To be mine she promis'd agean and agean,
And the priest, if God spare us, will suin mek us yen.

DINAH DUFTON.

Tune—"*Good night, and joy be wi' you a'.*"

Peer Dinah Dufton's e'en wi' bairn,[36]
    Oh, but I's unco sworry for't!
A bonnier or a teydier lass,
    No niver yet fell i' the durt:
Auld Tim, her fadder, turn'd her out
    At mid neet, tho' 'twas frost and snaw;

She owre the geate,—what cud she de ?—
  And sobb'd and gowl'd, and telt us aw.

My fadder shuik his head at furst,
  But spak and acted like a man ;
' Dinah !' says he, ' tou sannot want,
  Sae keep thy heart up, if tou can ;
I've lads and lasses o' my awn,
  And nin can tell what they may de :
To turn thee out ! peer luckless bairn !
  Thy fadder e'en mun hardened be !"

God niver meade a heartier lass,
  For she wad sing for iver mair ;
Yet, when peer fwok were in distress,
  To hear on't, Oh ! it hurt her sair !
This luive, they say, hides monie fau'ts ;
  Peer thing ! the warl she little knew !
But if she'd been by me advis'd,
  She waddent hed see cause to rue.

At Rosley Fair she chanc'd to leet
  O' mangrel Wull, that wicked tuil ;
He'd larn'd to hannel weel his feet,
  And kept a bit o' dancin schuil :
A fortune-teller neist he brib'd,
  To say the match was meade abuin ;
But when he'd brong his ends about,
  He nobbet laugh'd and left her suin.

Now Dinah's apron's grown quite shwort ;
  Dull, downcast, outcry o' the lave !
Aw day she whinges in our loft,
  And wishes she were in her grave :
But mangrel Wull, that wicked tuil,
  My fadder says sall lig in jail ;
And he that ruins onie lass,
  De'll tek the man that wad him bail.

NED CARNAUGHAN.

TUNE—" *The Miller of Dee.*"

My mudder was teakin her nuin's rest,
　My fadder was out at the hay,
When Ned Carnaughan com buncin in,
　And luik'd as he'd gotten a flay :
' O, Sib !' says he, ' I's duin wi' te ;—
　' Nay, what, thou blushes and staires !—
' I seed the last neet wi' bow-hough'd Peat,
　' And de'il tek them that cares !'

Says I to Ned, to Ned says I,
　' What's aw this fuss about?
' I's seer he's a reet lish country lad,
　' And tou's just a parfet lout :
' But whea were liggin i' Barney's croft,
　' And lakin like twea hares?
' And whea kiss'd Suke frae lug to lug?
　' Wey, deil tek them that cares !'

Says Ned, says he ' the thimmel gi'e me [37]
　' I brong thee frae Branton fair,
' And gi'e back the broach and true-love knot,
　' And lock o' my awn reed hair ;
' And pay me the tuppence I wan frae thee
　Ae neet at pops and pairs ;
' Then e'en tek on wi' whea thou likes—
　' The de'il tek them that cares !'

The broach and thimmel I flang at his frace,
　The true-love knot i' the fire ;
Says I, ' tou's nobbet a hawflin bworn—
　' Fash me nae mair, I desire ;—
' Here, tek thy tuppence, a reape to buy,
　' And gi'e thysel nae mair airs ;
' But hing as hee as Gilderoy—
　' The de'il tek them that cares !'

1

THE COCKER O' CODBECK.

Tune—" *Patrick's day i' th' morning.*"

There was ill gusty Jemmy, the cocker o' Codbeck,[38]
    He follow'd blin Leethet' lass years twee or three;
She laid in o' twins, and was e'en broken-hearted,
    For Jemmy had left her—and, neist, what did he,
But ran owre to Hesket, and wedded anudder;
    Suin peer Greacy Leethet was laid in her grave;
The last words she spak were, " O God, forgi'e Jemmy!
I may rue the day when he stuil my heart frae me!
  Tho' I's gawn to leave you, my innocents save!"
      Her twea bairns she kiss'd,
      And then sunk into rest.
  O but sec like fellows sud suffer!

I ne'er can forget, when the corpse cross'd the lonnin,
    Amang auld and young there was nit a dry e'e;
Aw whop'd she was happy—but, O man! her fadder
    When they cover'd the coffin, we thought he wad dee!
He cried, " I've nae comfort sin I've lost my Greacy!
  O that down aseyde her my head I could lay!"
For Jemmy, de'il bin him! he's kent nout but crosses,
He's shunn'd by the lads, and he's hiss'd by the lasses,
    And Greacy's ghost haunts him by neet and by day;
      Nae neybor luiks near him,
      The bairns they aw fear him;
  And may sec like fellows still suffer!

CANNY CUMMERLAND.

Tune—" *The humours of Glen.*"

'Twas ae neet last week, wid our wark efter supper,
    We went owre the geate cousin Isbel to see;
There were Sibby frae Curthet, and lal Betty Byers,
    Deef Bebby, forby Bella Bunton and me;
We'd scarce begun spinnin, when Sib a sang lilted,
    She'd brong her frae Carel by their sarvent man;
'Twas aw about Cummerlan fwok and feyne pleaces,
    And, if I can think on't, ye's hear how it ran.

Yer buik'd-larn'd wise gentry, that's seen monie counties,
   May preach and palaver, and brag as they will
O' mountains, lakes, valleys, woods, watters, & meadows,
   But canny auld Cummerlan caps them aw still :[59]
It's true we've nae palaces sheynin amang us,
   Nor marble tall towers to catch the weak eye ;
But we've monie feyne castles, where fit our brave
     fadders,
   When Cummerlan cud onie county defy.

Furst Graystock we'll nwotish, the seat o' girt Norfolk,
   A neame still to freemen and Englishmen dear ;
Ye Cummerland fwok, may your sons & your gransons
   Sec rare honest statesmen for iver revere :
Corruption's a sink that 'll puzzen the country,
   And lead us to slav'ry, to me it seems plain ; .
But he that has courage to stem the black torrent,
   True Britons sud pray for, agean and agean.

Whea that hes climb'd Skiddaw, hes seen sec a prospec,
   Where fells frown owre fells, and in majesty vie ?
Whea that hes seen Keswick, can count hawf its beauties,
   May e'en try to count hawf the stars i' the sky :
There's Ullswater, Bassenthwaite, Westwater, Derwent,
   That thousands on thousands ha'e travell'd to view ;
The langer they gaze, still the mair they may wonder,
   And aye, as they wonder, may fin summet new.

We've Corby,[10] for rocks, caves, & walks sae delightfu',
   That Eden a paradise loudly proclaims ;
O that sec like places hed aye sec like awners,
   Then mud monie girt fwok be proud o' their neames!
We've Netherby tui, the grand pride o' the border,
   And haws out o' number nae county can bang ;
Wi' rivers romantic as Tay, Tweed, or Yarrow,
   And green woodbine bowers weel wordy a sang.

We help yen anudder ; we welcome the stranger ;
   Ourselves and our country we'll iver defend ;

We pay bits o' taxes as weel as we're yable,
　　And pray like true Britons, the war had an end :
Then, Cummerlan lads, and ye lish rwosy lasses,
　　If some caw ye clownish, ye needn't think sheame;
Be merry and wise, enjoy innocent pleasures,
　　And aye seek for health and contentment at heame.

JEFF AND JOB.

Tune—"*Fye, gae rub her o'er wi' strae !*"

JEFF.

Come, Job, let's talk o' weel-kent places,
　　When young tearin chaps were we :
Now nin nar us but fremm'd feaces—
　　Few to seyde wi' thee and me !—
Years are geane by twee and twonty,
　　Sin I kent thy curly pow—
Aye the furst at wark and spwortin,
　　Were Jeff Heyne and Jwosep Howe.

JOB.

Ay, Jeff ! we've lang kent yen anudder ;
　　Monie a time when chaps were crouse,
And meade a brulliment and bodder,
　　Jeff and Job ha'e clear'd the house ;
Nin leyke thee cud fling the geavelick ;[41]
　　Nin leyke me lak'd at fit-baw ;
Wi' pennysteans tou was a darter—
　　I at trippet bang'd tem aw.

JEFF.

Then, Job, I mind at your kurn-supper,[42]
　　When I first saw Elcy Greame,
I cuddent eat—my heart it flutter'd—
　　Lang Tom Leytle watch'd us heame :
We were young, and beath i' fettle—
　　He wad feight—we e'en set tui ;
In the clarty seugh I sent him—
　　Elcy skirl'd, what cud she dui ?

JOB.

And, Jeff, when met at Cursmas cairdins,[43]
　Few durst lake wi' thee and me ;
When we'd hack'd the lads aw roun us,
　Off to the lasses' bed went we ;
The ass-buird sarrat as a teable,
　Legs anunder t' claes were laid ;
Forby laughin, kissin, jwokin,
　Monie a harmless prank we play'd.

JEFF.

Now, Job, we pay for youthfu' follies—
　Aw our happy days are geane ;
Tou's turn'd grousome, bare, and dozen'd,
　I's just worn to skin and beane.
But maister's comin in a flurry—
　Sarvents aye sud meynd their wark ;
I mun off to deetin havver—
　Fares-te-weel till efter dark !

TIB AND HER MAISTER.

I's tir'd wi' liggin aye my leane ;
　This day seems fair and clear ;
Seek th' auld grey yad, clap on the pad,
　She's duin nae wark te year :
Furst, Tib, get me my best lin sark,
　My wig, and new-greas'd shoon ;
My three-nuik'd hat and mittens white—
　I'll hev a young wefe suin ![14]
　　A young weyfe for me, Tib,
　　　A young weyfe for me ;
　　She'll scart my back whene'er it yuks,
　　　Sae married I mun be !

' Wey, maister ! you're hawf blin and deef—
　' The rain comes pouring down ;—
' Your best lin sark wants beath the laps,
　' Your three-nuik'd hat the crown ;

‘ The rattens eat your clouted shoon ;
   ‘ The ryad's unshod and leame ;
‘ You're bent wi' yeage leyke onie bow,
   ‘ Sae sit content at heame.
     ‘ A young weyfe for ye, man !
      ‘ A young weyfe for ye !
     ‘ They'll rank ye wi' the horned nowt
      ‘ Until the day ye dee !'

O, Tib, thou aye talks leyke a fuil !
   I's fail'd, but nit sae auld ;
A young weyfe keeps yen warm i' bed,
   When neets are lang and cauld :
I've brass far mair than I can count,
   And sheep, and naigs, and kye ;
A house luiks howe widout a weyfe— .
   My luck I'll e'en gae try.
     A young weyfe for me, Tib,
      A young weyfe for me ;
     I yet can lift twee pecks o' wots,
      Tho' turn'd o' eighty-three.

‘ Weel, maister, ye maun ha'e your way,
   ‘ And sin ye'll wedded be,
‘ I's lish and young, and stout and strang,
   ‘ Sae what think ye o' me ?
‘ I'll keep ye teydey, warm, and clean,
   ‘ To wrang ye I wad scworn.'
Tib, gi'es the hand—a bargain be't—
   We'll off to kurk to-mworn !
     A young weyfe for me, Tib,
      Tou was meade for me ;
     We'll kiss and coddle aw the neet,
      And aye we'll happy be !

JWOHNY AND MARY.

TUNE—" *Come under my plaidie.*"

Young Mary was canny and bonny as onie lass,
Jwohny was lusty and weel to be seen ;

Young Mary was aye the best dancer at marry neets,
    Jwohny had won monie a belt on the green :
Lang, lang they were sweethearts, and nwotish'd by
    neybors ;
    Th' auld fwok they talk'd, and oft bragg'd o' the
    twee,
For Jwohny thought nin i' the warl like young Màry,
    And Mary thought Jwohny aw she wish'd to see.

A wee swope guid yell is a peer body's comfort,[45]
    But wo be to him that oft drinks till blin fou !
Young Jwohny ae day off wi' bigg to the market,
    And drink wi' some neybors, he little thought how.
His auld fadder watch'd till the black hour o' midneet ;
    Widout his deer Jwohny the naig gallop'd heame :
They sought, and they fan him that mwornin i' Eden,
    Amang the green busses that nod owre the stream.

Auld Gibby he gowls, and aye talks of his Jwohny,
    And sits by his greave, and oft meks a sad meane ;
Peer Mary, the flow'r of aw flow'rs i' the parish,
    Ne'er hods up her head, now her Jwohny is geane.
The dangerous yell-house kills monie brave fellows,[46]
    To get heame quite swober can ne'er be thought
    wrang ;
Nae guid comes o' drinkin.—Ye lads aw around me,
    At fair, or at market, aye think o' my sang !

THE CLAY DAUBIN.

Tune—" Andrew Carr."

We went owre to Deavie' Clay Daubin,[47]
    And faith a rare caper we had,
Wi' eatin, and drinkin, and dancin,
    And rwoarin, and singin leyke mad ;
Wi' crackin, and jwokin, and braggin,
    And fratchin, and feightin and aw ;
Sec glorious fun and divarsion
    Was ne'er seen in castle or haw.

Sing hey for a snug clay biggin,
     And lasses that leyke a bit spwort ;
Wi' friens and plenty to gi'e them,
     We'll laugh at King Gworge & his cwort.

The waws wer aw finish'd er darknin ;
     Now, greypes, shouls, and barrows thrown by,
Auld Deavie spak up wid a hursle —
     " Od rabbit it ! lads, ye'll be dry ;
See, deame, if we've got a swope whusky[48] —
     I's sworry the rum bottle's duin—
We'll starken our keytes, I'll uphod us—
     Come, Adams, rasp up a lal tune !"

When Bill kittl'd up " Chips and Shavins,"
     Auld Philip poud out Matty Meer,
Then nattl'd his heels like a youngen,
     And caper'd about the clay fleer ;
He deeted his gob, and he buss'd her,
     As lish as a lad o' sixteen ;
Cries Wull, " Od dy ! fadder's i' fettle !
     His marrow 'll niver be seen !"

Reet sair did we miss Jemmy Coupland—
     Bad crops, silly man, meade him feale ;
Last Sunday forenuin, efter sarvice,
     I' th' kurk-garth, the clark caw'd his seale. [49]
Peer Jemmy ! of aw his bit oddments
     A shettle the bealies ha'e ta'en,
And now he's reet fain of a darrak,
     For pan, dish, or spuin, he hes neane.

Wi' scons, leather-hungry,* and whusky,
     Auld Aggy cried, " Meake way for me !
Ye men fwok, eat, drink, and be murry,
     Wheyle we i' the bower git tea."
The whillymer eat teugh and teasty,
     Aw cramm'd fou o' grey pez and seeds ;

* This is a ludicrous name given to a poor sort of cheese made of
skimmed milk, and made use of by some of the peasants of Cumberland as a part of their meals.   It is also sometimes called Whillymer, and sometimes Rosley Cheshire.

They row'd it up teane agean tudder—
  Naè dainties the hungry man needs.

Now in com the women fwok buncing—
  Widout tem there's niver nee fun ;
Wi' whusky aw weeted their wizzens,
  But suin a sad hay-bay begun ;
For Jock, the young laird, was new wedded,
  His auld sweetheart Jenny luik'd wae ;
While some were aw titterin and flyrin,
  The lads rubb'd her her down[50] wi' pez strae.

Rob Lowson tuik part wi' peer Jenny,
  And brong snift'ring Gwordie a cluff ;
I' th' scuffle they leam'd Lowson' mudder,
  And fain they'd ha'e stripp'd into buff :
Neist Peter caw'd Gibby a rebel,
  And aw rwoar'd out, that was wheyte wrang ;
Cried Deavie, ' Sheak hans, and nae mair on't—
  ' I's sing ye a bit of a sang.'

He lilted " The King and the Tinker,"
  And Wully strack up " Robin Hood ;"
Dick Mingins tried " Hooly and Fairly,"
  And Martha " The Babs o' the Wood :"
They push'd round a glass like a noggin,
  And bottom'd the greybeard complete ;
Then crack'd till the muin glowr'd amang them,
  And wish'd yen anudder guid neet.

THE FELLOWS ROUND TORKIN.*

TUNE—" The Yorkshire Concert."

We're aw feyne fellows round Torkin ;
  We're aw guid fellows weel met ;
We're aw wet fellows round Torkin,
  Sae faikins we mun hev a sweat :
Let's drink to the lasses about us,
  'Till Day's braid glare bids us start ;

A wood covered hill, near Crofton Hall, in Cumberland,

We'll sup till the saller be empty—
    Come, Dicky, lad, boddom the quart.
I'll gi'e ye says Dick, durty Dinah,
    That's ay big wi' bairn fwok suppose ;
She sticks out her lip like a pentes,
    To kep what may drop frae her nwose :
Like a hay-stack she hoists up ae shoulder,
    And scarts, for she's nit varra soun :
Wi' legs thick as mill-posts, and greasy,
    The deevil cud nit ding her down !

We're aw odd fellows round Torkin ;
    We're aw larn'd fellows weel met ;
We're aw rich fellows round Torkin,
    Sae faikins we mun hev a sweat :
Let's drink to the lasses about us,
    'Till day's braid glare bids us part ;
We'll sup till the saller be empty—
    Come, Matthew, lad, boddom the quart.

I'll gi'e ye says Matt, midden Marget,
    That squints wi' the left-handed e'e ;
When at other fellows she's gleymin,
    I's freeten'd she's luikin at me :
She smells far stranger than carrion,
    Her cheeks are as dark as hung beef,
Her breasts are as flat as a back-buird ;
    'Mang sluts she's aye counted the chief !

We're aw wise fellows round Torkin ;
    We're aw neyce fellows weel met ;
We're aw sad fellows round Torkin,
    Sae faikins we mun hev a swet :
Let's drink to the lasses about us,
    'Till Day's braid glare bids us part ;
We'll sup 'till the saller be empty—
    Come, Gwordy, lad, boddom the quart.

I'll gi'e ye, says Gworge, geapin Grizzy,
    Wi' girt feet and marrowless legs ;

Her red neb wad set fire to brumstone;
  Her e'en are as big as duck eggs:
She's shep'd like a sweyne i' the middle,
  Her skin freckl'd aw like a gleid;
Her mouth's weyde as onie town yubben,
  We're freeten'd she'll swally her head?

We're aw strang fellows round Torkin;
  We're aw lish fellows weel met;
We're aw top fellows round Torkin,
  Sae faikins we mun hev a sweat:
Let's drink to the lasses about us,
  'Till day's braid glare bids us start;
We'll sup till the saller be empty—
  Come, Wully, lad, boddom the quart.

I'll gi'e ye, says Wull, winkin Winny,
  That measures exact three feet eight,
But wi' roun-shoulder'd Ruth, or tall Tibby,
  She'll scart, and she'll girn, and she'll feght:
She's cruik'd as an S— wid a hip out,
  Her feet flat and braid, as big fluiks;
Her feace is as lang as a fiddle,
  And aw spatter'd owre wi' reed plouks!

We're aw young fellows round Torkin;
  We're aw teeght fellows weel met;
We're aw brave fellows round Torkin,
  Sae faikins we mun hev a sweat:
Let's drink to the lasses about us,
  'Till day's braid glare bids us part;
We'll sup till the saller be empty—
  Come, Mwosy, lad, boddom the quart.

I'll gi'e ye, says Mwose, mantin Matty,
  That lisps thro' her black rotten teeth;
You can't catch five words in ten minutes:
  If gowlin, she'd flay yen to death:
Her feace like auld Nick's nutmig grater,
  And yellow neck bitten wi' fleas;
She's troubl'd wi win ay at meale teymes,
  And belshes to give hersel ease.

We're aw cute fellows round Torkin ;
　We're aw sharp fellows weel met ;
We're aw rare fellows round Torkin,
　Sae faikins we mun hev a sweat :
Let's drink to the lasses about us,
　'Till day's braid glare bids us part ;
We'll sup 'till the saller be empty—
　Come, Nathan, lad, boddom the quart.

I'll gi'e you says Natt, noisy Nanny,
　That chows shag 'bacco for fun ;
She cocks her belly when walkin,
　And ay luiks down to the grun :
She talks beath sleepin and wakin,
　And crowks like a tead when she speaks ;
On her nwose en the hair grows like stibble,
　And gravey drops run owre her cheeks !

We're aw teugh fellows roun Torkin ;
　We're aw rash fellows weel met ;
We're aw queer fellows round Torkin,
　Sae faikins we mun hev a sweat :
Let's drink to the lang, leame, and lazy,
　Deef, dum, black, brown, bleer-e'ed, and blin,
May they suin get weel weddet, and beddet,
　If lads they can onie where fin !

THE DALSTON PLAYER-FWOK.

TUNE—" *Derry Down.*"

Come, stur the fire, Shadrich ! and harken to me ;
I went up to Dawston their player-fwok to see,
And paid my cruik'd tizzy, and gat a front seat ;
Thrang as three in a bed, they were wedg'd in that neet.
　　　　　Derry Down, &c.

Furst, the ban on their hoyboys and pipes did sae cruin,
Tho' they blew oft and sair, it ay seem'd the seame tune.
Aw was famish confusion—but when they began,
Lack-a-day ! the Fair Penitent pruiv'd but a man !
　　　　　Derry Down, &c.

When they chink'd a lal bell, there was yen summet spak,
But he hung down his head, and he held up his back ;
The picture caw'd Garrick abuin the stage stood,
I thought it yence laugh'd, and i' faith weel it mud !
Derry Down, &c.

Like a hawf white-wash'd sweep, yen *Orashi*† bunc'd in,
And he tweyn'd leyke an edder, and cock'd up his chin ;
In his yallow plush breeks, and lang black rusty sword,
Wid his square gob weyde open—thought I, what a
   Lword !
Derry Down, &c.

He was drucken, (that's certain ;) he cudde :t get on ;
Loavins ! cried an auld woman ; what, that's Rutson'
   Jwohn !
Mess, but he's a darter !—A topper ! says I,
Was he but in a meedow, he'd freeten the kye.
Derry Down, &c.

In bonny flower'd weastcwoat, and full-bottom'd wig,
Auld *Siholto* he squeek'd leyke a stuck guinea pig ;
Then his dowter he fratch'd, and her sweetheart forby,
O man, it was movin, and meade the bairns cry.
Derry Down, &c.

Yen whisper'd me softly—That's Clogger Jwohn Bell.
Says I, leyke eneugh, of that man I've heard tell.
Now a tweesome talk'd loud, but nit varra discreet,
For they promis'd twea whores‡ afore nuin they wad
   meet.
Derry Down, &c.

Frae tae fit to tudder, *Lothari* he hopp'd,
Aw leyke clock-wark ; his words tui how neycely he
   chopp'd !
Peer body ! he waddent lig whiet when dead,
Sae they e'en lugg'd him out by the heels and the head.
Derry Down, &c.

† The manner in which they pronounced the different names.

‡ Two hours

K

There was yen wid a weast thick as onie barl kurn,
He poud up his pettikits, then gev a gurn ;
And he luik'd as to say, Now what think ye o' me ?
A lal lass spak the truth—it was shocken to see !
           Derry Down, &c.

Next a cliver lish chap, wid his feyne reed leed cheeks,
Blew his nwose wi' his fingers, & hotch'd up his breeks ;
Then he tuik a fresh chow, and the auld'n threw out,
And said, Dui be whiet—what's aw this about ?
           Derry Down, &c.

The schuilmaister, gager, and twee or three mair,
Hed seen Mister Punch play his pranks at a fair ;
Efter far-larned threepin, at last, at the Bell,
'Twas agreed, nit ev'n Punch cud thur heroes excel.
           Derry Down, &c.

Sec struttin and wheynin may please dwoatin fuils,
Or rough-headed callans just sent off to schuils :
But hadst thou e'er dreamt o' sec actin, dear ROWE,
For sarten thou ne'er wad ha'e written at aw.
           Derry Down, &c.

Ye wise men o' Dawston stick chwose to your wark,
Sit at heame wi' your weyves & your bairns efter dark ;
To be caw'd kings and heroes is pleasin indeed,—
But before you turn player-fwok, furst larn to read !
           Derry Down, &c.

OUR JWOHNNY.

TUNE—" Lillibulero."

Our Jwohnny's just turn'd till a parfet atomy,
    Nowther works, eats, drinks, or sleeps as he sud ;
He seeghs in a nuik, and fins faut wid his poddish,
    And luiks like a deyl'd body, spoil'd for aw gud.
He reaves in his sleep, and reads buiks o' luive letters,
    As turn efter dark, nae, he'll nit dui at aw !
But ae neet, last week, I determin'd to watch him,
    And suin, wi' his sweetheart our Jwohnny I saw.

I cowr'd my ways down, ahint our young eshes,
  And by went the tweesome,—he seem'd nit the seame ;
They laugh'd, kiss'd and cutter'd—nought had past
      atween them ;
  I gat what I wanted, and sae crap off heame :
Our lanlword lass, Letty, his heart hes in keepin,
  To be seer she's a sarvant, but weel to be seen ;
She's lish, young and bonny, and honest as onie,
  In hard workin poverty I see nought that's mean !

The fadder o' Jwohnny was my fellow-sarvant ;
  God rest him ! his marrow I's ne'er to see mair !
Auld Matthew hed gear, and follow'd me weekly,
  And cut me a lock of his gray grizzled hair.
Had I wedded Matthew, I'd now been a leady,
  But foorscwore and twenty can never agree :
Our Jwohnny may e'en try his luck, and get wedded,
  And they sal ha'e baith stock and crop when I dee.

KING ROGER.

TUNE—" *Hallow Fair*."

'Twas but tudder neet, efter darknin,
  We sat owre a bleezing turf fire ;
Our deame she was sturrin a cow-drink,
  Our Betty milk'd kye in the byre :
" Ay, fadder !" cried out our lal Roger,
  I wish I wer nobbet a king !"
" Wey, what wad te dui ? (says I,) Roger,
  Suppwose tou cud tek thy full swing ?"

" Furst, you sud be lword judge, and bishop ;
  My mudder sud hev a gold crutch :
I'd build for the peer fwok feyne houses,
  And gi'e them—aye, ever sae much !
Our Betty sud wed Charley Miggins,
  And wear her stamp'd gown ev'ry day ;
Sec dancin we'd hev in the cock-loft,
  Bill Adams the fiddle sud play.

" A posset I'd hev to my breakfast,
　　And sup wid a breet siller spuin ;
For dinner I'd hev a fat crowdy,
　　And strang tea at mid efternuin :
I'd wear neyce wheyte cottinet stockins,
　　And new gambaleery clean shoes,
Wi' jimp lively black fustin briches,
　　And ev'ry feyne thing I cud choose.

" I'd hev monie thousands o' shippen,
　　To sail the weyde warl aw about ;
I'd say to my soldiers, Gang owre seas,
　　And kill the French dogs, out and out !
On our lang-tail'd naig I'd be mounted,
　　My footmen in silver and green ;
And when I'd seen aw foreign countries,
　　I'd mek Aggy Glaister my queen.

" Our meedow sud be a girt worchet,
　　And grow nought at aw but big plums ;
A schuilhouse we'd build——As for maister,
　　We'd e'en hing him up by the thums.
Joss Feddon sud be my head huntsman,
　　We'd keep seeven couple o' dogs,
And kill aw the hares i' the kingdom ;
　　My mudder sud wear weel-greas'd clogs.

" Then Cursmass sud last, ay for ever !
　　And Sundays we'd ha'e tweyce a-week ;
The muin sud show leet aw the winter ;
　　Our cat and our cwoley sud speak :
The peer fwok sud live widout workin,
　　And feed on plum-puddin and beef ;
Then aw wad be happy, for sarten,
　　There nowther cud be rwogue or thief !"

Now thus ran on leytle king Roger,
　　But suin aw his happiness fled ;
A spark frae the fire brunt his knockle,
　　And off he crap whingin to bed :

Thus fares it wi' beath young and auld fwok,
 Frae king to the beggar we see ;
Just cross us i' th' midst o' our greatness,
 And peer wretched creatures are we !

KITT CRAFFET.

Tune—" *Come under my plaidie.* "

Isaac Crosset, o' Chawk, a feyne heed-sten hes cutten,
 And just setten't up owr anent the kurk^en ;
A chubby-feac'd angel o' top on't they've putten,
 And varses, as gud as e'er com frae a pen :
It's for auld Kit Craffet, our wordy wise neyber,
 God rest him ! a better man ne'er wore a head ;
He's nit left his fellow thro' aw the heale county,
 And monie peer fwok are in want, now he's dead.

I mind when at schuil, a reet top scholar was he ;
 Of lakin or rampin nae nwotion had he,
But nar the auld thworn he wad sit and keep mwosin,
 And caw'd it a sin just to kill a peer flee :
A penny he never let rest in his pocket,
 But gev't to the furst beggar body he met ;
Then at kurk he cud follow the priest thro' the sarvice,
 And as for a trible he never was bet.

Tho' he wan seeven belts lang afwore he was twenty,
 And in Scealeby meedow oft took off the baw,
Yet he kent aw the beyble, algebra, Josephus,
 And capp'd the priest, maister, exciseman and aw.
He cud talk about battles, balloons, burning mountains,
 And wars, till baith young & auld trimmel'd for fear,
Then he'd tell how they us'd the " peer West Indie
  neegers,"
 And stamp wid his fit, aye, and drop monie a tear.

When he red about parliments, pleaces, and changes,
 He flang by the paper, and cried, " Silly stuff !
The *Outs* wad be *in*, and the *Ins* rob their country,
 They're nit aw together worth ae pinch o' snuff !

His creed was—Be statesmen but just, Britons loyal,
  And lang as our shippen reyde maisters at sea,
We'll laugh at the puffin o' vain Bonnyparty,
  As suin may he conquer the deevil as we.

Then when onie neybor was fash'd by the turnies,
  Oh, it meade him happy if he cud be bail !
Twea-thurds of his income he gev away yearly,
  And actually tuik peer Tom Linton frae jail.
He was yence cross'd in luive by a guid-for-nought
      hussy,
  But if onie lass by her sweetheart was wrang'd,
He wad give her guid counsel, and lecture the fellow,
  And oft did he wish aw sec skeybels were hang'd.

He cud mek pills and plaisters as weel as our doctor,
  And cure cholic, aga, and jaunice forby ;
As for grease, or the glanders, red watter, or fellen,
  Nin o' them was leyke him, amang naigs or kye :
What, he talk'd to the bishop about agriculture,
  And yence went to Plymouth to see the grand fleet;
As for the brave sailors trail'd off by the press-gangs,
  " Od die them !" he said, " that can never be reet !"

He ne'er was a drinker, a swearer, a feghter,
  A cocker, a gamler, a fop, or a fuil ;
But left this sad warl just at threescwore and seeven,
  I' the clay house his granfader built wi' the schuil.
Oh ! monie a saut tear will be shed ev'ry Sunday,
  In reading the varses they've stuck on his steane ;
'Till watters run up bank, and trees they grow down
      bank,
  We never can luik on his marrow agean !

***

ELIZABETH' BURTH-DAY.

Tune—" Lillibulero."

JENNY.

" Ay, Wulliam ! neist Monday's Elizabeth' burth day!
  She is a neyce lass, tho' she were nin o' mine.

We mun ax the Miss Dowsons, & aul Brodie' young
    fwok :
I wish I'd but seav'd a swop geuseberry wine.
She'll be sebenteen ; what, she's got thro' her larnin ;
    She dances as 1 did, when furst I kent thee.
As for Tom, her cruik'd billy, he stumps leyke a
    cwoach-horse ;
    We'll ne'er mek a man on him, aw we can dee."

WULLIAM.

" Hut, Jenny ! hod tongue o' thee ! praise nae sec
    varment,
    She won't men a sark, but reads novels, proud brat !
She dance ! What she turns in her taes, thou peer
    gonny,
    Caw her Bet, 'twas the neame her auld granny
    ay gat.
No, Tommy for my money ! he reads his beyble,
    And hes sec a lovinly squint wid his een ;
He sheps as leyke me, as ae bean's leyke anudder ;
    She snurls up her neb, just a shem to be seen !"

JENNY.

" Shaf, Wully ! that's fashion—tou kens nout about it;
    She's stryt as a resh, and as red as a rwose,
She's sharp as a needle, and luiks leyke a leady ;
    Thou talks, man—a lass cannot meake her awn
    nwose !
She's dilicate meade, and nit fit for the country ;
    For Tom, he's knock-knee'd, wi' twea girt ass-
    buird feet ;
God help them he sheps like ! they've little to brag
    on ;
    Tho' our's, I've oft thought, he was nit varra reet."

WULLIAM.

" O, Jen ! thou's run mad wi' thy gossips and trum-
    pery :—
    Our lal bit o' lan we maun sell, I declare ;

H 3

I yence thought thee an angel,—thou's turn'd just a
    deevil,
  Has fash'd me reet lang, and oft vexes me sair :
This fashion and feasting brings monie to ruin,
  A duir o' my house they shall nit come within ;
As for Bet, if she dunnet gang off till a sarvice,
  When I's dead and geane she shall nit hev a pin."

JENNY.

" Stop, Wull! whee was't brong thee that fortune?
    peer gomas !
  Just thurteen gud yacres as lig to the sun ;
When I tuik up wi' thee, I'd lost peer Gwordy
    Glossip,
  I've rue'd sin that hour to the kurk when we run :
Were thou cauld and coffin'd, I'd suin get a better ;
  Sae creep off to bed, nit a word let us hear !
They shall come, if God spare us, far mair than I
    mention'd—
  Elizabeth' burth-day but comes yence a-year !

BORROWDALE JWONNY.
Tune—" I am a young fellow."

I's Borrowdale Jwonny, just cumt up to Lunnon,
  Nay, girn nit at me, for fear I laugh at you ;
I've seen knaves donn'd i' silks, and guid men gang in
    tatters,
  The truth we sud tell, and gi'e auld Nick his due.
Nan Watt pruiv'd wi' bairn—what, they caw'd me
    the fadder ;
  Thinks I, *shekum filthy!* be off in a treyce !
Nine Carel bank nwotes mudder slipt i' my pocket,
  And fadder neist ga'e me reet holesome adveyce.

Says he, Keep fra'et lasses! and ne'er luik ahint thee ;
  We're deep as the best o' them, fadder, says I.
They pack'd up ae sark, Sunday weastcwoat, twee
    neckcloths,
  Wot bannock, cauld dumplin, and top stannin pie :

I mounted black filly, bade God bless the auld fwok,
  Cries fadder, Tou's larn'd, Jwohn, and hes nought
    to fear ;
Caw and see cousin Jacep! he's got aw the money ;
  He'll get thee sum guverment pleace, to be seer !

I stopp'd on the fell, tuik a lang luik at Skiddaw,
  And neist at the schuil-house amang the esh trees;
Last thing, saw the smuik rising up frae our chimley,
  And fan aw quite queer, wid a heart ill at ease :
But summet within me, cried, Pou up thy spirits!
  There's luck, says auld Lizzy, in feacin the sun ;
Tou's young, lish, and clever, may wed a feyne leady,
  And come heame a Nabob—aye, sure as a gun !

Knowing manners, what, I doff'd my hat to aw strangers
  Wid a spur on my heel, a yek siplin in han,
It tuik me nine days and six hours comin up-bank,
  At the *Whorns*—aye,'twas *Highget,* a chap bad mestan:
Says he, How's aw friends in the north, honest Johnny?
  Odswunters ! I says, what, ye divvent ken me !
I paid twee wheyte shillins, and fain was to see him,
  Nit thinkin on't road onie 'quaintance to see.

Neist thing, what big kurks, gilded cwoaches, hee houses,
  And fwok runnin thro' other leyke Carel Fair ;
I ax'd a smart chap where to fin cousin Jacep,
  Says he, Clown, go look ! Friend, says I, tell me
    where ?
Fadder' letter to Jacep had got nae *subscription,*
  Sae, when I was glowrin and siz'lin about,
A wheyte-feac'd young lass, aw dress'd out like a leady,
  Cried, Pray, Sir, step in ! but I wish'd I'd kept out.

She poud at a bell, leyke our kurk-bell it sounded,
  In com sarvent lass, and she worder'd some weyne ;
Says I, I's nit dry, sae, pray, Madam, excuse me ;
  Nay, what she insisted I sud stop and deyne.
She meade varra free—'twas a shem and a byzen !
  I thowt her in luive wi' my *parson,* for sure ;

And promis'd to caw agean :—as for black filly,
  (Wad onie believ't!) she was stown frae the duir!

Od dang't! war than that—when I greap'd my breek-
    pocket,
  I fan fadder' watch, and the nwotes were aw gaen;
It was neet, and I luik'd lang and sair for kent feaces,
  But Borrowdale fwok I cud niver see neane.
I slept on the flags, just ahint the kurk-corner,
  A chap wid a girt stick and lantern com by,
He caw'd me peace-breaker—says I, thou's a lear—
  In a pleace leyke a saller they fworc'd me to lie.

Nae caff bed or blankets for silly pilgarlic;
  De'l a wink cud I sleep, nay, nor yet see a steyme;
Neist day I was ta'en to the Narration Offish,
  When a man in a wig said, I'd duin a sad creyme.
Then ane ax'd my neame, and he pat on his speckets,
  Says I, Jwohny Cruckdeyke—I's Borrowdale bworn;
Whea think ye it pruiv'd but my awn cousin Jacep,
  He seav'd me fraet gallows, aye that varra mworn.

He spak to my Lword, some hard words, quite out-
    landish,
  Then caw'd for his cwoach, and away we ruid heame;
He ax'd varra kind efter fadder and mudder,
  I said they were bravely, and neist saw his deame:
She's aw puff and pouder; as for cousin Jacep,
  He's got owre much gear to teake nwotish o' me;
But if onie amang ye sud want a lish sarvent,
  Just bid me a weage—I'll upod ye, we's 'gree.

LANG SEYNE.

Tune—" *Tak your auld cloak about ye.*"

The last new shun our Betty gat,
  They pinch her feet, the deil may care!
What, she mud ha'e them leady like,
  Tho' she hes cworns for evermair:

Nae black gairn stockins will she wear,
    They mun be wheyte, and cotton feyne!
This meks me think of other times,
    The happy days o' auld lang seyne!

Our dowter, tui, a palace† bought,
    A guid red clwoak she cannot wear;
And stays, she says, spoils leady's sheps—
    Oh! it wad mek a parson swear.
Nit ae han's turn o' wark she'll dui,
    She'll nowther milk or sarrat sweyne—
The country's puzzen'd round wi' preyde,
    For lasses work'd reet hard lang seyne.

We've three guid rooms in our clay house,
    Just big eneugh for sec as we;
They'd hev a parlour built wi' bricks,
    I mud submit—what cud I dee?
The sattle neist was thrown aseyde,
    It meeght ha'e sarra'd me and mine;
My mudder thought it mens'd a house—
    But we think shem o' auld lang seyne!

We us'd to ga to bed at dark,
    And ruse agean at four or five;
The mworn's the only time for wark,
    If fwok are hilthy, and would thrive:
Now we get up,—nay, God kens when!
    And nuin's owre suin for us to deyne;
I's hungry or the pot's hawf boil'd,
    And wish for times like auld lang seyne.

Deuce tek the fuil-invented tea!
    For tweyce a-day we that mun hev:
Then taxes get sae monstrous hee,
    The deil a plack yen now can seave!
There's been nae luck throughout the lan,
    Sin fwok mud like their betters sheyne;
French fashions mek us parfet fuils;
    We're caff and san to auld lang seyne!

         † Pelisse.

THE AULD BEGGAR.

I met the auld man, wid his starv'd grey cur near him,
   The blast owre the mountain blew cauld i' the vale;
Nae beame to receive him, few strange fwok to hear him,
   And thin wer his patch'd duds, he mickle did ail:
A tear dimmed his e'e, his feace furrowed by sorrow,
Seemed to say, he frae whope nit ae comfort cud borrow,
   And sad was the beggarman's teale.

" Behold," he cried, seeghing, " the spwort of false
   fortune !
The peer wretched outcast, the beggar you see,
Yence boasted o' wealth, but the warl is uncertain,
   And friens o' my youth smeyle nae langer on me :
I's the last o' the flock, my weyfe Ann for Heaven
   left me,
Of my only lad, Tim, accurst war neist bereft me ;
   My yage's suppwort lang was he !

Yence in the proud city, I smeyl'd amang plenty.
   Frae east and frae west, monie a vessel then bore
To me the rich cargo, to me the feyne dainty,
   And the peer hungry bodies still shar'd of my store ;
A storm sunk my shippen, by false friens surrounded,
The laugh o' the girt fwok,—this meade me confounded,
   Ilk prospec for ever was o'er !

I creep owre the mountains, but meast in the vallies,
   And wi' my fond dog share a crust at the duir ;
I shun the girt fwok, and ilk house leyke a palace,
   For sweetest to me is the meyte frae the puir :
At neet, when on strae wi' my faithfu' dog lyin,
I thank Him that meade me, for what I's enjoying ;
   His promise I whope to secure."

THE BUCK OF KINGWATTER.†

Tune—" The Breckans of Brampton."

When I was single, I rid a feyne naig,
   And was caw'd the Buck o' Kingwatter ;

† The river King, near Gilsland.

Now the cwoat o' my back has got but ae sleeve,
　And my breeks are aw in a tatter.
Sing, Oh, the lasses! the lazy lasses!
　Keep frae the lasses o' Branton!
I ne'er wou'd hae married, that day I married,
　But I was young, feulish, and wanton.

I courted a lass—an angel I thought—
　She's turn'd out the picture of evil;
She geapes, yen may count ev'ry tuith in her head,
　And shouts, fit to freeten the deevil.
　　　　　Sing, Oh, the lasses, &c.

To-day she slipt out, some 'bacco to buy,
　And bade me mind rock the cradle;
I cowp'd owr asleep, but suin she com in,
　And brak aw my head wi' the ladle.
　　　　　Sing, Oh, the lasess, &c.

I ne'er had a heart to hannel a gun,
　Or I'd run away, and leave her.
She pretends to win purns, but that's aw fun,
　They say she's owr kind wi' the weaver.
　　　　　Sing, Oh, the lasses, &c.

I dinnerless gang ae hawf o' the week;
　If we get a bit meat on a Sunday,
She cuts me nae mair than wad physic a sneype;
　Then we've tatey and point ev'ry Monday.
　　　　　Sing, Oh, the lasses, &c.

Tho' weary o' life, with this gud-for-nought wife,
　I wish I cud get sec anudder;
And then I cud gi'e the deevil the tane,
　For taking away the tudder!

Sing, Oh, the lasses! the lazy lasses!
　Beware o' the lasses o' Branton!
I ne'er wou'd hae married, that day I married,
　But I was young, feulish, and wanton.

　　　　　F

MARGET O' THE MILL.

TUNE—"*Tom Starboard.*"

Her fadder's whope, her mudder's preyde,
 Was black-ey'd Marget o' the Mill,
And summer day, or winter neet,
 Was happy, chearfu', busy still ;
And Ralph, her fadder, oft declar'd,
 His darlin forty punds shou'd have
The day a husband tuik her han,
 And mair, if lang he skeap'd the greave.

The lily and the deyke-rwose beath,
 Were mix'd in Marget's bonny feace ;
Her form mud win the cauldest heart,
 And her's was Nature's modest greace ;—
Her luik drew monie a neybor laird,
 Her e'en luive's piercin arrows fir'd ;
But nae rich laird cud gain the han
 O' this fair flow'r, by aw admir'd.

Oh, luckless hour ! at town ae day,
 Yen in a soldier's dress she saw ;
He stule her heart—and frae that hour,
 May Marget date a leyfe of woe ;—
For now she shuns aw roun the mill,
 Nae langer to her bosom dear ;
And faded is her bonny feace,
 And dim her e'e wi' monie a tear.

Peer Marget ! yence a fadder's preyde,
 Is now widout a fadder left ;
Deserted, aw day lang she moans,
 Luive's victim, of ilk whope bereft !
Ye lasses, aw seducers shun,
 And think o' Marget o' the Mill ;
She, crazy, daunders wid her bairn,
 A prey to luive and sorrow still.

MADAM JANE.

TUNE—"*I will ha'e a Wife.*"

Money meks us bonny,
   Money meks us glad.;
Be she auld or ugly,
   Money brings a lad.
When I'd neer a penny,
   Deil a lad hed I—
Pointin ay at Jenny,
   Laughin, they flew by.

Money causes flatt'ry,
   Money meks us vain.;
Money changes aw things—
   Now I'm *Madam Jane*.
Sin Auld Robby left me
   Houses, fields, nit few,
Lads thrang round i' clusters—
   I'm a beauty now!

Money meks us merry,
   Money meks us bra';
Money gets us sweethearts—
   That's the best of a'!
I ha'e fat and slender,
   I ha'e short and tall;
I ha'e rake and miser—
   I despise them all!

Money they're aw seeking,
   Money they's get neane;
Money sends them sneaking
   Efter *Madam Jane*.
There's ane puir and bashfu',
   I ha'e i' my e'e;
He's get han and siller,
   Gin he fancies me.

   Money meks us bonny, &c.

YOUNG SUSY.

TUNE—"*Dainty Davie.*"

Young Susy is a bonny lass,
A cauny lass, a teydey lass,
A mettled lass, a hearty lass,
    As onie yen can see;
A clean-heel'd lass, a well-spok lass,
A buik-larn'd lass, a kurk-gawn lass,
I watena how it com to pass,
    She's meade a fuil o' me.

I's tir'd o' workin, plowin, sowin,
Deeting, deykin, threshin, mowin;
Seeghin, greanin, never knowin
    What I's gawn to de.

I met her—aye, 'twas this day week!
Od die! thowt I, I'll try to speak;
But tried in vain the teale to seek,
    For sec a lass is she!
Her jet black hair hawf hides her brow,
Her een just thirl yen thro' and thro'—
But, Oh! her cheeks and cherry mou
    Are far owre sweet to see!
      I's tir'd o' workin, &c.

Oh, cou'd I put her in a sang!
To hear her praise the heale day lang,
She mud consent to kurk to gang;
    There's puirer fwok than me!
But I can nowther rhyme nor rave,
Luive meks yen sec a coward slave;
I'd better far sleep i' my grave—
    But, oh! that munnet be!

I's tir'd o' working, plowing, sowing,
Deetin, deykin, threshin, mowin;
Seeghin, greanin, never knowin
    What I's gawn to de.

THE REDBREAST.

Tune—"*Hallow Fair.*"

Come into my cabin, red Robin!
　Threyce welcome, lal warbler, to me!
Now Skiddaw hes got his wheyte cap on,
　Agean I'll gi' shelter to thee.
Just hop thy ways into my pantry,
　And feast on my peer humble fare;
I never was fash'd wid a dainty,
　But meyne, man or burd sal ay share.

Now four years are by-geane, red Robin,
　Sin furst thou com singin to me;
But, O how I's chang'd, little Robin,
　Sin furst I bade welcome to thee!
I then had a bonny bit lassie,
　Away wid anudder she's geane;
My friends wad oft caw at my cabin,
　Now dowie I seegh aw my leane.

Oh, where is thy sweetheart, red Robin?
　Ga' bring her frae house-top, or tree;
I'll bid her be true to sweet Robin,
　For false was a lassie to me.
You'll share ev'ry crum i' my cabin,
　We'll sing the cauld winter away;
I wunnet deceive ye, peer burdies!
　Let mortals use me as they may.

THREESCWORE AND NINETEEN.

Aye, aye, I's feeble grown,
　And feckless—weel I may!
I's threescwore and nineteen,
　Aye, just this varra day!
I ha'e na teeth, my meat to chew,
　But little sarras me!
The best thing I eat or drink,
　Is just a cup o' tea!

K 3

Aye, aye, the bairns mak gam,
 And pleague me suin and late;
Men fwok I like i' my heart,
 But bairns and lasses hate!
This gown o' mine's lang i' the weast,
 Aul-fashion'd i' the sleeve;
It meks me luik like fourscwore,
 I varily believe!

Aye, aye, what I's deef,
 My hearin's quite geane;
I's fash'd wi' that sad cough aw neet,
 But little I complain.
I smuik a bit, and cough a bit,
 And then I try to spin;
And then I daddle to the duir,
 And then I daddle in.

Aye, aye, I wonder much,
 How women can get men;
I've tried for threesowore years and mair,
 But never could get yen.
Deil tek the cat—what is she at?
 Lie quiet on the chair:
I thowt it e'en was Daniel Strang,
 Comin up the stair!

Aye, aye, I've bed and box,
 And kist, and clock, and wheel,
And tub, and rock, and stuil, and pan,
 And chair, and dish, and reel;
And luiking-glass, and chammer-pot,
 And bottles for smaw beer;
Mouse-trap, sawt-box, kettle, and——
 That's Danny sure I hear!

Aye, aye, he's young enough,
 But, oh! a reet neyce man;
And I wad ne'er be caul in bed,
 Cud I but marry Dan.

Deuce tek that cough! that weary cough—
   It never let's me be;
I's kilt wi' that and gravel beath—
   Oh, Daniel, come to me!

SILLY ANDREW.

Tune—"*Wandering Willie.*"

O how can I get a bit weyfe? says lang Andrew,
  Shadric, come tell me, lad, what I mun dee;
     Tou kens I's just twenty,
     Ha'e houses, lans plenty,
     A partner I want—ay—
  But nin'll ha'e me!

'Twas furst blue-e'ed Betty that meade my mouth
    watter,
  She darn'd my auld stockins, my crivet and aw;
     Last harvest. when sheerin,
     Wi' jeybin and jeerin,
     She fworc'd me to swearin—
  Bett ne'er mair I saw.

Neist reed-heeded Hannah to me seem'd an angel,
  And com to our house monie a neet wid her wark;
     I yence ax'd to set her,
     She said she kent better:
     Whea thinks te can get her?
  E'en daft Symie Clark.

Then smaw-weasted Winny meade gowns for our
    Jenny;
  Andrew, man, stick tull her! mudder oft said;
     She hes feyne sense and money
     Young, lish, smart and bonny,
     Is a match, aye for onie.
  But she's for black Ned.

Then how can I get a bit weyfe? tell me, Shadric.
  Tou mun be reet happy, they're aw fond o' thee.

I've followed Nan, Tibby,
Sall, Mall, Fan, and Sibby,
Ett, Luke, Doll, and Debby;
But nin'll ha'e me.

AULD ROBBY MILLER.

TUNE—" *Gin I had a wee House.*"

Oh, cud I but see the blithe days I ha'e seen,
When I was a lish laughin lass o' sixteen;
Then lads lap around, and said nin was leyke me,
Now they're aw fled away, and I's turn'd thurty-three.
A single leyfe's but a comfortless leyfe,
It sounds unco sweet to be caw'd a weyfe;
To get a bit body I've tried aw I can—
Waes me for the lassie that can't get a man.

When day-leet's aw geane, and I sit down to spin,
I wish some young fellow wou'd only step in;
At the market I saunter, and dress at the fair,
But nae lad at peer Keaty a luik will e'er spare.
A single leyfe's but a weary dull leyfe,
It sounds unco sweet to be caw'd a weyfe;
In vain a peer lassie may try ilka plan,
Caw her rich, and I'll venture she'll suin get a man.

There's auld Robby Miller, wi' his siller pow,
Bent double, and canna creep up the hill now;
Tho' steane-deef and tuithless, and bleer-e'ed and aw,
He hes gear, and I's thinking to gi'e him a caw.
A single leyfe's a heart-breakin leyfe,
It sounds unco sweet to be caw'd a weyfe;
I'll keame his lank locks, and dui what I can—
There's monie a young lassie wad tek an auld man.

He lives aw his leane; but he's surely to bleame,
When a wanter leyke me may be had sae near heame:
Wer we weddet to-morrow, he'd nit be lang here,
Then I'd buy a man to my mind wid his gear.

A single leyfe's a sorrowfu' leyfe,
It sounds unco sweet to be caw'd a weyfe;
I'll off to auld Robby,—aye, that's the best plan,
And coax him, and wed him, the canny auld man.

———

NANNY PEAL.

Eyes there are that never weep,
    Hearts there are that never feel;
God keep them that can dui baith,
    And sec was yence sweet Nanny Peal.
Tom Feddon was a sailor lad,
    A better never sail'd saut see;
The dangerous rocks reet weel he knew,
    The captain's favourite was he.

When out, and cronies drank or sang,
    Or danc'd the jig, or leetsome reel,
Peer Tom wad sit him on the yard,
    And fondly think o' Nanny Peal.
For, oh she was a hearty lass,
    A sweeter feace nin e'er did see;
And Luive lurk'd in her twee breet een,
    And Innocence itsel was she.

Oft, i' the kurk, the neybor lads
    At her a bashfu' luik wad steal;
Oft, at the markets, stare and point,
    And whisper—"See! that's Nanny Peal."
But Tom was aw her heart's deleyte;
    And, efter voyages twee or three,
(In which he wad feyne presents bring,)
    Baith fondly whop'd they'd married be.

And now this teyde they quit the pwort;
    Tom wid a kiss his faith did seal;
They cry'd, they seegh'd, whop'd suin to meet—
    'Twas hard to part wi' Nanny Peal!
The sea was cawm, the sky was clear,
    The ship she watch'd while eye cud see;

" The voyage is short !" she tremblin said,
   " God sen him seafe and suin to me!"

Afwore her peer auld mudder's duir,
   She sung, and thowt, and turn'd her wheel ;
But when that neet the storm com on,
   Changed was the heart of Nanny Peal.
And sad was she the next lang day ;
   The third day warse—still warse grew she ;
Alas ! the fourth day brought the news,
   Baith ship and men were lost at sea !

She heard, she fainted on the fluir ;
   Much did her peer auld mudder feel ;
The neybors roun, baith auld and young,
   Dropt monie a tear for Nanny Peal.
Sin' that, she wanders aw day lang,
   And gazes weyldly on the sea ;
She's spent, peer thing, to skin and beane,
   And ragged, wretched now is she.

Oft reydin on the wheyte-topp'd waves,
   She sees her Tom towerts her steal ;
And then she laughs, and caws aloud,
   " O come, O come to Nanny Peal !"
God keep thee, helpless, luckless lass !
   On earth thou munnet happy be ;
But leyfe is wearin fast away—
   Thou suin in Heaven peer Tom wilt see.

———

ANDREW'S YOUNGEST DOWTER.

TUNE by the Author.

Where Irthin* rows to Eden's streams,
   Thro' meedows sweetly stealin,
Owerhung by crags, hawf hid by furs,
   There stans a cwozey dwellin ;
And there's a lass wi' witchin feace,
   Her luik gi'es pain or pleasure,

† A river in the neighbourhood of Brampton.

A rwose-bud hid frae pryin een,
  The lad's deleyte and treasure;
For when I saw her aw her leane,
  I mair than mortal thowt her,
And stuid amaz'd, and silent gaz'd
  On Andrew's youngest dowter.

Her luik a captive meade my heart,
  How matchless seem'd ilk feature!
The sun, in aw his yearly course,
  Sheynes on nae fairer creature;
I watch'd her thro' the daisied howmes,
  And pray'd for her returnin;
Then track'd her foot-marks through the wood,
  My smitten heart aw burnin;—
Luive led me on; but when, at last,
  In fancy meyne I thowt her,
I saw her awn dear happy lad
  Meet Andrew's youngest dowter.

Sing sweet, ye wild birds i' the glens,
  Where'er young Lizzy wanders;
Ye streams of Irthin, please her ears
  Aw day wi' soft meanders;
And thou, the lad ay neist her heart,
  Caress this bonny blossom—
Oh, never may the thworn o' care
  Gi'e pain to see a bosom!
Had I been king o' this weyde warl,
  And kingdoms cud ha'e bought her,
I'd freely parted wi' them aw,
  For Andrew's youngest dowter!

SOLDIER YEDDY.

TUNE—" The widow can bake."

Peer Yeddy was brought up a fadderless bairn,
His jacket blue duffle, his stockins cworse gairn;
His mother—sad greaceless—liv'd near Talkin Tarn,
  But ne'er did a turn for her Yeddy.

Weel shep'd, and fair feac'd, wid a bonny blue e'e,
Honest-hearted, ay merry, still teydy was he ;
But nae larnin had gotten, nor kent A B C;—
     There's owre monie like silly Yeddy.

Suin tir'd o' the cwoal-pit, and drivin a car,
Won by fedders, cockades, and the fuil'ries o' war,
He wad see feyne fwok, and grand pleaces afar—
     The bad warl was aw new to lal Yeddy.

How temptin the liquor, and bonny bank nwote !
How temptin the pouder, sash, gun, and red cwoat !
Then the Frenchmen, die bin them ! we'll kill the
     whole twote !
     These, these were his thoughts, honest Yeddy.

Awhile wi' his cronies he'll smuik, laugh, and sing,
Tell of wonders, and brag of his country and king,
And swagger, and larn of new oaths a sad string—
     These little avail simple Yeddy.

For suin he may sing to another-guess tune,
His billet a bad yen, his kelter aw duin ;
And faint at his post, by the pale winter muin,
     Nae comfort awaits luckless Yeddy.

When Time steals his colour, & turns his pow grey'
May he tell merry stories, nor yence rue the day,
When he wander'd, peer lad, frae the fell seyde away ;
     This, this is my wish for young Yeddy.

Of lads see as him may we ne'er be in want,
And a brave soldier's pocket of brass ne'er be scant ;
Nit the brags o' proud Frenchmen auld England can
     daunt,
     While we've plenty like young soldier Yeddy.

THE DAWTIE.

Tune—" *I'm o'er young to marry yet.*"

JENNY.

Though weel I like ye Jwohnny lad,
     I cannot, munnet marry yet !

My peer auld mudder's unco bad,
  Sae we a wheyle mun tarry yet;
For ease or comfort she has neane—
Leyfe's just a lang, lang neet o' pain;
I munnet leave her aw her leane,
  And wunnet, wunnet marry yet.

JWOHNNY.

O Jenny, dunnet brek this heart,
  And say we munnet marry yet;
Thou cannot act a jillet's part—
  Why sud we tarry, tarry yet?
Think, lass, of aw the pains I feel;
I've leyk'd thee lang, nin kens how weel!
For thee I'd feace the varra deil—
  O say not we maun tarry yet.

JENNY.

A weddet leyfe's oft dearly bowt;
  I cannot, munnet marry yet:
Ye ha'e but little—I ha'e nought,
  Sae, we a wheyle mun tarry yet.
My heart's yer awn, ye needna fear,
But let us wait anudder year,
And luive, and toil, and screape up gear—
  We munnet, munnet marry yet.

'Twas but yestreen, my mudder said,
  O, dawtie, dunnet marry yet;
I'll suin lig i' my last cauld bed;
  Tou's aw my comfort—tarry yet.
Whene'er I steal out o' her seet,
She seeghs, and sobs, and nought gangs reet—
Whisht!—that's her feeble voice;—Guid neet!
  We munnet, munnet marry yet.

L

THE CODBECK WEDDING.

TUNE—"*Andrew Carr.*"

True is my song, though lowly be the strain.

They sing of a wedding at Worton,
 Where aw was feight, fratchin, and fun;
Feegh! sec a yen we've hed at Codbeck,
 As niver was under the sun:
The breydegruim was weaver Joe Bewley,
 He com frae about Lowthet Green;
The breyde, Jwohnie Dalton' lish dowter,
 And Betty was weel to be seen.

Sec patchin and weshin, and bleachin,
 And starchin, and darnin auld duds;
Some lasses thought lang to the weddin—
 Unax'd, others sat i' the suds.
There were tweescwore and seebem invited,
 God speed tem, 'gean Cursenmass-day;
Dobson' lads, tui, what they mun come hidder—
 I think they were better away.

Furst thing oggle Willy, the fiddler,
 Caw'd in, wi' auld Jonathan Strang;
Neist stiff and stout, lang, leame, and lazy,
 Frae aw parts com in wi' a bang;—
Frae Brocklebank, Fuilduirs, and Newlands,
 Frae Hesket, Burkheads, and the Height,
Frae Warnell, Starnmire, Nether Welton,
 And awt' way frae Eytonfield. *

Furst auld Jwohnny Dawton we'll nwotish,
 And Mary, his cannie douse deame;
Son Wully, and Mally, his sister;
 Goffet' weyfe, Muckle Nanny by neame;
Wully Sinclair, Smith Leytle, Jwohn Aitchin,
 Tom Ridley, Joe Sim, Peter Weir,

* Names of Cumberland villages.

Gworge Goffet, Jwohn Bell, Miller Dyer,
    Joe Head, and Ned Bulman were there.

We'd hay-cruiks, and hentails, and hanniels,
    And nattlers that fuddle for nought;
Wi' skeape-greaces, skeybels, and scruffins,
    Wi' maffs better fed far than taught;
We'd lads that wad eat for a weager,
    Or feight, ay, till bluid to the knees;
Fell-seyders, and Sowerby riff-raff,
    That deil a bum-bealie dare seize.

The breyde hung her head, and luik'd sheepish,
    The breydegruim as wheyte as a clout;
The bairns aw gleym'd thro' the kurk windows,
    The parson was varra devout:
The ring was lost out of her pocket,
    The breyde meade a bonny te-dee;
Cries Goffet' weyfe, 'Mine's meade o' pinchback,
    And, la ye! it fits till a tee.'

Now buckl'd, wi' fiddlers afwore them,
    They gev Michael Crosby a caw;
Up spak canny Bewley the breydegruim,
    ' Get slocken'd, lads, fadder pays aw.'
We drank till aw seem'd blue about us,
    We're aye murry deevils, tho' peer;
Michael's weyfe says, ' Widout onie leein,
    A duck mud ha'e swam on the fleer.'

Now, aw 'bacco'd owre, and hawf-drucken,
    The men fwok wad needs kiss the breyde;
Joe Head, that's aye reckon'd best spokesman,
    Whop'd guid wad the couple beteyde.
Says Michael, ' I's reet glad to see you,
    Suppwosin I gat ne'er a plack.'
Cries t' weyfe, ' That'll nowther pay brewer,
    Nor get bits o' sarks to yen's back.'

The breyde wad dance *Coddle me Cuddie*;
    A threesome then caper'd Scotch reels;

Peter Weir cleek'd up auld Mary Ca'ton,
   Leyke a cock round a hen neist he steals;
Jwohn Bell yelp'd out ' Sowerby Lassies;'
   Young Jwosep, a lang country dance,
He'd got his new pumps Smithson meade him,
   And fain wad show how he cud prance.

To march round the town, and keep swober,
   The women fwok thowt was but reet;
' Be wise, dui, for yence,' says Jwohn Dyer;
   The breydegruim mud reyde shouder heet;—
The youngermak lurried ahint them,
   Till efter them Bell meade a brek;
Tom Ridley was aw baiz'd wi' drinkin,
   And plung'd off the steps i' the beck.

To Huless's now off they sizelled,
   And there gat far mair than eneugh;
Miller Hodgson suin brunt the punch ladle,
   And full'd every glass wid his leuf;
He thought he was teakin his mouter,
   And deil a bit conscience bes he;
They preym'd him wi' stiff punch and jollup,
   'Till Sally Scott thowt he wad dee.

Joe Sim rwoard out, ' Bin, we've duin wonders;
   Our Mally's turn'd howe i' the weame.'
Wi' three strings atween them, the fiddlers
   Strack up, and they reel'd towerts heame;
Meyner Leytle wad now hoist a standert—
   Peer man! he cud nit daddle far,
But stuck in a pant buin the middle,
   And yen tuik him heame in a car.

For dinner, we'd stew'd geuse and haggis,
   Cow'd-leady, and het bakin pie,
Boil'd fluiks, tatey-hash, beastin puddin,
   Saut salmon, and cabbish; forby.
Pork, pancakes, black puddins, sheep trotters,
   And custert, and mustert, and veal,

Grey-pez keale, and lang apple dumplins—
  I wish every yen far'd as weel.

The breyde geavin aw roun about her,
  Cries, ' Wuns ! we forgat butter sops.'
The breydegruim fan nae teyme for talkin,
  But wi' staonin pie greas'd his chops.
We'd loppar'd milk, skimm'd milk, & kurn'd milk,
  Well watter, smaw beer, aw at yence ;
' Shaff ! bring yell in piggins,' roars Dalton,
  ' Deil tek them e'er cares for expence.'

Now aw cut and cleek'd frae their neighbors,
  .'Twas even down thump, pull and haul ;
Joe Head gat a geuse aw together,
  And off he crap into the faul ;
Muckle Nanny cried ' Shem o' sec weastry !'
  The ladle she brak o'er ill Bell ;
Tom Dalton sat thrang in a corner,
  And eat nar the weight of his sel.

A hillibuloo was now started,
  'Twas, ' Rannigal, whee cares for tee ?'
' Stop, Tommy—whe's weyfe was i' the carrass ?
  Tou'd ne'er been a man, but for me !'
' Od dang thee !'—' To jail I cud send thee,
  Peer scraffles !'—' Thy lan grows nae gurse.'
' Ne'er ak ! its my awn, and its paid for ;
  But whea was't stuil aald Tim Jwohn' purse ?'

Ned Bulman wad feight wi' Gworge Goffet—
  Peer Gwordy he nobbet stript thin,
And luik'd leyke a cock out o' fedder,
  But suin gat a weel-bleaken'd skin ;
Neist, Sanderson fratch'd wid a hay-stack,
  And Deavison fuight wi' the whins ;
Smith Leytle fell out wi' the cobbles,
  And peel'd aw the bark of his shins.

The hay-bay was now somewhat seyded,
  And young fwok the music men miss'd,

They'd drucken leyke fiddlers in common,
  And fawn owre ayont an aul kist;
Some mair fwok that neet were a-missin,
  Than Wully, and Jonathan Strang—
But decency whispers, 'What matter!
  Tou munnet put them in the sang.'

Auld Dalton thowt he was at Carel,
  Says he, 'Jacob! see what's to pay;
Come, wosler! heaste—get out the horses,
  We'll e'en teake the rwoad, and away.'
He cwop'd off his stuil, leyke a san bag,
  Tom Ridley beel'd out, 'Deil may care!'
For a quart o' het yell, and a stick in't,
  Dick Simson 'll tell ye far mair.

Come, bumper the Cummerlan lasses,
  Their marrows can seldom be seen;
And he that won't feight to defend them,
  I wish he may ne'er want black e'en.
May our murry-neets, clay-daubins, races,
  And weddins, aye finish wi' glee;
And when ought's amang us worth nwotish,
  Lang may I be present to see.

THE BEGGAR AND KATIE.

Tune—"*O'er the muir amang the heather.*"

KEATIE.

Whee's rap rappin at the duir,
Now when our aul fwok are sleepin?
  Thou'll git nowt here if thou's puir—
Owre the hills thou'd best be creepin!
  When sec flaysome fuils we see,
Decent fwok may start and shudder;
  I'll nit move the duir to thee—
Vagrant-leyke, thou's nowt but bodder!

BEGGAR.

Oh! gude lassie, let me in!
I've nae money, meat, or cleedin—

Starv't wi' this caul angry win;
Aul an helpless—Deeth ay dreedin!
Let me lig in barn and byre;
Ae brown crust will pruive a dainty;—
Dui, sweet lass! what I desire,
If thou whop'st for peace and plenty!

KEATIE.

Beggars yen may weel despise—
To the sweyne-hull hie an swat thee,
Rap nae mair if thou be wise—
Here's a dog wad fain be at thee:
Sec leyke hawf-wits, far and weyde,
Beggin breed, and meal, and money,
Some may help to show their preyde—
I'll ne'er lift mey han to onie!

BEGGAR.

Move the duir to sec as me;
Lift thy han to fwok when starvin;
Meynd, er lang, thou peer may be;
Pity beggars, when desarvin.
Nobbet lissen to the storm,
Think how monie now mun suffer!
Let me in thur limbs to warm,
And wi' preyde, due thanks I'll offer!

KEATIE.

I've a sweetheart; sud he caw,
Monstrous vex'd I'd be to see him;
He helps beggars, yen and aw,
Leyke a fuil; nae guid 'twill de him!
He hes gear; I'll ne'er be peer—
Say nowt mair, or Snap sal beyte thee;
Noisy sumph! what, our fwok hear
Thy crazy voice—Be off! od wheyte thee!

BEGGAR.

Keate, it's teyme to change mey voice—
Heartless wretch, they weel may caw thee;

Fain I meade thee ay mey choice,
Sin the hour when furst I saw thee:
Lang thy sweetheart I hae been;
Thowt thee gude, an lish, an cliver—
Ne'er will I wi' thee be seen,
Come what will!—Fareweel for ever!

THE HAPPY COUPLE.

Tune—"*Ettrick Banks.*"

Come, Mary, let's up Eden seyde,
An chat the ebemin hours away;
Tho' hard we toil, leyke millions mair,
Industrious fwok sud ay be gay;—
Far frae the slanderous noisy town,
It's sweet the murmerin streams to hear,
An share the joys o' peace an luive,
Wheyle some buy plishure far owre dear.

Just mark that peer bit freetent hare,
Now neet draws on, frae heame she'll steal;
The weyld burds sweet, in deyke or wood,
Now bid the sinkin sun fareweel;
They joyfu sing the sang ov thenks,
On rock, on meedow, bush, or tree;
Nor try their partners to deceive—
O, that ilk mortal sae wad be!

That savage hawk, owre hill an glen,
Seeks some weak warbler to destroy;
True emblem o' the tyrant, man,
To crush the peer oft gies him joy:
The burds rejoice, an hae their toil,
Unshelter'd, blithe the blasts they bedye;
Wheyle oft, wi' plenty, man compleens,
Snug, seated by his awn fire-seyde.

Our sons come runnin, Dick an Ned,
Twee feyner niver went to schuil;

I'd suiner see them coffin'd low,
　　Than owther turn a fop or foil.
The maister says Dick's fit for kurk ;
　　And Ned in law peer fwok may seave :
What, judge and bishop they may sit,
　　When thee an me lig i' the greave.

Aa, Mary ! nowt e'er hurts mey meynd,
　　But when I cross the kurk-garth gang,
I think I see our aul fwok still,
　　For nowther wad dui onie wrang !
A helpless orphan tou was left,
　　An fadder, mudder, scarce e'er saw ;
Beath lost at sea——Nay, dunnet cry ;
　　A better warl let's whop they know.

Sweet bloom'd aw roun, that summer mworn,
　　I carv'd our neames, now pleas'd we see ;
Leyke us the tree was in its preyme,
　　But now it withers, sae mun we !
Sworn foes to streyfe, the joys of leyfe
　　We've shar'd sin furst I meade thee meyne ;
Reet cheerfu still, we'll bear ilk ill,
　　But come what will, let's ne'er repeyne !

THE AUL HOLLOW TREE.

TUNE—" Come under my plaidie."

When beame I ay wander, and see the sun settin,
　　Queyte free frae hard labour an care, till the mworn,
My thoughts turn to yen that nin roun e'er saw frettin,
　　A bonnier, a better, nay, ne'er yet was bworn.
Tho' I's a peer sarvent, an money's wheyle's scanty,
　　An maister's tarn'd temper some daily wad dree ;
　　　　At ebemin, tho' weary,
　　　　My heart's ay queyte cheery,
When Peggy I meet nar the aul hollow tree.

When twee bits o' bairns, theer we offen sat laikin,
　　An wheyles wer fworc'd in by weyl win or the rain ;

Now luikin owre picters, new seevy caps meakin,
  Or sharin an apple, that ay meade us fain.
We'd lissen the blackburd, lark, throssle, or lennet,
  And hares playin nar us, in summer we'd see ;
        Lambs merry wad wander,
        Its brenches anunder ;
But few now will nwotish an aul hollow tree.

How happy the days, when our teens we've just enter'd,
  And luive gies a glance frae the lass we haud dear ;
But, O, when yen's driven frae the heart's dearest
      treasure,
  In fancy, we'll gaze on her oft wid a tear :
Content hails the mwornin, and joy the day clwoses,
  When evenin to lovers true comfort can gie ;
        When nature's seen smeylin,
        An dull cares begueylin,
An teyme's spent in peace nar the aul hollow tree.

Mey cruikt cankert maister, queyte greedy, hawf crazy,
  Oft cowshens his niece aw peer fellows to shun ;
An Peggy, wi' smeyles, ne'er an uncle yence crosses,
  Nor e'er can by wealth, preyde, or flattery be won.
I've wheyles thowt o' leavin the snarlin aul body,
  To hunt out some other, wheas heart's fou o' glee ;
        Luive whispers, " O, bear aw !
        Ay cheer aw, nor fear aw ;
Just think o' past teymes nar the aul hellow tree."

At dances she's courted by chaps thrang about her,
  But ne'er yence was seen to gie onie a frown ;
To win her wi' feynery, the squire oft hes sowt her,
  An sent owre a silk shawl an gran sattin gown ;
She'd laugh at the thowt, an the seame hour return them,
  Then bid him nit whope a squire's mistress she'd be ;
        Far titter than weer them,
        She'd burn them or tear them,—
At neet I hard aw nar the aul hollow tree.

Whene'er the sky's cawm, and the muin wheyte as siller,
  And partridges caw the lost partners to meet,

We steal out thegither, and leave the crabb'd uncle—
He snwores on the sattle, ay neet efter neet ;
Wi' yage he's bent double, an row'd up in trouble,
But dreams nit sweet Peggy her heart hes gien me ;
Till kindred may loss him,
We'll ne'er wish to cross him,
But spen hours o' luive at the aul hollow tree.

When laid i' the greave, nar his decent deame Jenny,
Of aw neybors roun him, but few will repeyne ;
Sud mey favourite, Peggy, be left nit ae penny,
Ere threyce the muin changes I whop she'll be meyne.
. If peer, or if wealthy, ay merry when healthy,
We'll pray that aw countries for ever may 'gree ;
We'll comfort ilk other,
But brethren ne'er bother,
An think o' days geane nar the aul hollow tree.

What trees er leyke mortals—yeks strang, an weyde
spreedin,
Wake willows to every leeght breeze will ay bow ;
Girt cedars, leyke breers that men cattle keep treedin,
Are nourisht aleyke, yen an aw, the warl thro' ;
On yerth, seame as bairns, for a wheyle they're seen
creepin,
Oft robb'd of a brench—pity sae it sud be !
Some grow up thegither,
In youth monie wither—
A teype o' frail man is the aul hollow tree !

NOTES.

NOTE 1.—*I got aw the news far and nar.*—Amidst the laborious duties which his condition of life imposes upon him, a Cumbrian peasant finds leisure and opportunities for collecting and disseminating village-news. His intelligence is gathered in different quarters, but generally at the mill, while his batch of corn is grinding; or at the smithy, while his clogs are receiving their customary load of iron. When he has completed his collection, be travels with all the expedition of a courier, from village to village, from house to house, gratifying every inquisitive mind, and attracting every vacant ear. He is the "historian of his native plain," and gives an accurate relation of a wrestling or a boxing match, discriminating the respective merits of the combatants, and pointing out the causes that led to victory or defeat. If his own actions be the subject of his conversation, he becomes more than usually eloquent, elevating his tone and diction agreeably to the precept of Salust : "*dictis exæquanda sunt facta,*" great actions demand a correspondent grandeur of style. To discover the extent of his political knowledge to the public, he assembles a group of his neighbours round his evening fire, or, after the fatigues of the day are finished, goes to the ale-house,

"Where village statesmen talk with looks profound,
"And news much older than their ale go round."—*Goldsmith.*

NOTE 2.—*De'il bin!*—A common mode of swearing among the Cumberland clowns. It is certainly a testimony of the refined manners, if not of the improved morals of the age, that oaths are banished from all polite circles, and are only to be found among the dregs of the commonalty.

NOTE 3.—*I was sebenteen last Collop-Monday.*—The
first Monday before Lent is provincially called *Collop-
Monday*, and the first Tuesday *Pancake-Tuesday*; because
on these two days collops and pancakes form the chief
repast of the country people—a custom derived from
our ancestors, who gave full indulgence to their appe-
tites a day or two before the arrival of that long and
meagre season, the Quadragesimal Fast.

NOTE 4.—*The Impatient Lassie.*—The passion of
love, restrained by forms and ceremonies in the higher
classes of society, breaks out in all its vehemence in the
breast of a simple, uneducated country peasant. In
him it is an instinct of nature, unchecked by delicacy,
and unrefined by sentiment. As if ashamed to ac-
knowledge its dominion, he visits the object of his
affections under the shades of night, and always on
a Saturday, that the effects of the night's vigils might
be done away by the holiday of the succeeding day.
His fair one waits for him with all the impatient ardour of love, chides the loitering moments; and, should
he not reach her habitation at the appointed hour, suffers all the anguish of foreboding fears :—Some dis-
astrous accident has befallen him—some coolness in his
passion has taken place—some rival, with more beauty
or more address, has supplanted her in his affections.
Apprehensions like these continue to agitate her bosom,
till a tap at the window or door announces the arrival
of her suitor.

NOTE 5.—*Sit down and I'll count owre my sweethearts.*—To have a great variety of sweethearts, is, in
the opinion of a simple country girl, a virtual acknow-
ledgment of the predominating force of her charms;
and she seldom discovers her error, till she finds herself neglected by every man whose esteem would be
valuable, and whose addresses would do her honour.
Of so delicate a nature is female reputation, that the
conduct of a young woman ought not only to be free

from guilt, but also free from suspicion; and surely
her chastity may be disputed, who, without any regard
to their character, conduct, and views, indiscriminately
admits of the visits of various suitors.

NOTE 6.—*To the pockel-whole, &c.*—In this ballad
poor *Snip* bears testimony to the effects of love by his
blunders; and he who laughs at his imbecility, and
can behold the charms of a lovely woman without
emotion, must be something *less*, or something *more*,
than man :—

> " For who can boast he never felt the fires,
> The trembling throbbings of the young desires,
> When he beheld the breathing roses glow,
> And the soft heavings of the living snow ;
> The waving ringles of the auburn hair,
> And all the rapt'rous graces of the fair?
> Ah! what defence, if fix'd on him he spy
> The languid sweetness of the steadfast eye !"—*Lusiad.*

The charms of the fair have indeed in all ages tri-
umphed over the human breast. The piety of David
and the wisdom of Solomon gave way when opposed
to their force ; and Julius Cæsar, the conqueror of the
world, forgot his fame and his victories in the arms of
an Egyptian beauty. Even the mighty Hercules threw
down his club with which he had achieved so many
arduous enterprises, and became a humble suitor at
the feet of an imperious fair one.

NOTE 7.—*'Twas last Leady Fair, &c.*—This fair
is held on Lady-day at Wigton ; and, like other Cum-
rian fairs, passes away amidst mirth, music, & dancing.

NOTE 8.—*Wi' Laird Hodgson, &c.*—In Cumber-
land the appellation of *laird* is applied to the proprietors of landed property, and to their eldest sons. Their
oldest daughters are styled *ladies.*

NOTE 9.—*For that was the pleace my grandfadder
was bworn in.*—A predilection for the place of our nativity is a patriotic prejudice, that does honour to our
feelings, and shows a heart formed for receiving the

best impressions. It displays itself in early life, and does not diminish with years, with absence, with travel, or with distance. A Cumbrian mountaineer feels its influence, when, amidst the rudest scenes of nature, he contentedly sits down in his paternal cottage, takes his homely fare, sings his artless song, or joins in the rustic dance.

NOTE 10.—*Tom Linton.*—A man of licentious opinions and dissolute morals is considered, by his companions in guilt, as a liberal thinker, and as a man of spirit and gallantry; but, to the virtuous and wiser part of the world, he appears as a timid and illiberal-minded wretch, callous to every honourable feeling, and as contracted in his understanding as he is depraved in his heart. It may seem strange that such a description of men exist in a kingdom peculiarly distinguished by the excellency of its constitution, its laws, and its religion. But if, among the great and illustrious characters which our country has produced, there may be found some who disgrace her, who can help it? The soil, that gives growth and vigour to the majestic oak, frequently nourishes the loathsome reptile.

NOTE 11.—*The happy family.*—The numerous instances of domestic felicity, which we meet with among the lower classes of society, and the dissatisfaction and inquietude which so often prevail among the higher ranks, will convince us, that to acquire riches and distinction, is not to acquire contentment and happiness. With health, industry, and virtue, happy in his domestic relations, in his kindred, in his friends, with limited wishes, and all his thoughts at home, the poor man enjoys comforts which wealth cannot purchase, or rank confer. Every remove from his humble, unambitious situation, would probably be so many removes from innocency and peace. Poverty, indeed, however supported by virtue, has its peculiar distresses; but what are its distresses to the pangs felt by guilty affluence? On the innocent and uncorrupted heart gleams of comfort are continually darting through the darkest shades of human life.

NOTE 12.—*Now monie a wife will weep for joy.*—Peace brings so many blessings, and puts a period to so many calamities, that it can hardly be purchased by too great sacrifices. What pleasing sensations does it afford to a feeling and patriotic heart to hear the carol of joy and contentment in every village; to see domestic happiness restored to an afflicted family, by the return of a husband, a father, or a favourite son; to behold the spirit of trade, commerce, and agriculture revive, and receive new energies; and to see wealth, plenty, and happiness diffused through the nation by a hundred different channels! If such be the effects of peace, who can behold without a tear those guilty laurels which have been obtained in unjust wars, amidst scenes of blood and devastation,—amidst the widow's tears and the orphan's cries!

NOTE 13.—*I think o' my playmates, &c.*—We always look back with pleasure on our early years, because at that period every object that surrounds us appears in gay and pleasing colours; our hearts are light, our affections warm, our hopes eager, and our pursuits ardent. In whatever part of the world we reside, we always feel a passionate desire to return to the spot where we passed the hours of our early life; to see again the companions of our childhood; to retrace the scenes of our juvenile frolics; to re-visit the green where we have sported, the shades under which we have reposed, and the banks where we often loitered. A modern poet, in describing the scenes where his early youth was passed, breaks out in the genuine language of poetry and of nature:

> " Ah, happy hills! ah, pleasing shade!
> " Ah, fields belov'd in vain!
> " Where once my careless childhood stray'd,
> " A stranger yet to pain!

M 3

" I feel the gales that from you blow
" A momentary bliss bestow,
" As, waving fresh their gladsome wing,
" My weary soul they seem to sooth,
" And, redolent of joy and youth,
" To breathe a second spring."—GRAY.

These tender feelings, which exist in a more or less degree in every bosom, afford a melancholy attestation, that the more we advance in life the more are our years loaden with sorrow, with care, and with discontent!

NOTE 14.—*That farmers are happier, &c.*—The poets, in their descriptions of human felicity, generally draw their images from pastoral life, because they suppose where there is simplicity there is also innocence and happiness. But when we search in rural life for the original from which they draw their beautiful pictures, we search for what is not always to be found. We often see there vice in all its grossness, and the tranquillity of life destroyed by the agitation of the passions. With the ploughman's song and the shepherd's lute we sometimes hear the murmurs of complaint, and the voice of discontent.—In every situation the degree of happiness and misery will be found in proportion to the prevalence of virtue and vice.

NOTE 15.—*Oh this weary, weary warl!*—Such will be the exclamation of every one who has lived to that period of life when the powers of sensation are blunted, when worldly objects no longer attack the heart, and when those amusements which gave rapture to youth can no longer please. Weighed down with infirmities and sorrow, and standing on the stage of life as a friendless, forlorn, insulated individual, the burden of an old man's song must ever be, " Oh this weary, weary world!"

NOTE 16.—*Lal Stephen.*—The hero of this ballad seems to have been, from his multifarious accomplishments, the Creighton of his village. Though diminu-

tive in stature, yet his agility and prowess, his superior
skill in rural occupations, and expertness at gymnastic
exercises, highly exalted him in the eyes of his countrywomen, and gave him a reputation that was not soon
to decay ; and a clown is as proud of his rustic honours
as a warrior is of his laurels, or a poet is of his bays.

NOTE 17.—*To set me out a mile o' geate.*—Sometimes a girl shows her affection to her lover by accom-
panying him a part of the road on his return home ;
and the enamoured rustic usually repays this mark of
regard by an increased love in his next visit to her.

NOTE 18.—*At Carel I stuid wi' a strae i' my mouth.*
In Cumberland, servants who are employed in husbandry are seldom engaged for a longer term than half
a year. On the customary days of hiring, they proceed to the nearest town, and, that their intentions
might be known, stand in the marke-place with a
sprig or straw in their mouths.

NOTE 19.—*Them ill reed-cwoated fellows, &c.*—In
every profession there are men who disgrace it. We
cannot condemn in too severe terms those sergeants of
recruiting parties who inlist their countrymen, when
excess of drinking has deprived them of all reason and
reflection. To recruit our army, it is not necessary
to have recourse to unjustifiable arts. There will never be wanting volunteers to fill its ranks, as long as
we know the value of that constitution which secures
to us our civil and religious liberties.

NOTE 20.—*Matthew Macree.*—This noted rustic
seems to have reached the pinnacle of village fame.
He had recommended himself to the notice of the fair,
like the knight errants in the times of chivalry, by the
variety of his accomplishments. He excelled at run-
ning, wrestling, leaping and boxing. His Stentorian
voice and sonorous sounds gained him the reputation

of a singer and a scholar. And let no person despise
Matthew Macree. He attained as much distinction
as satisfied his ambition; and what greater gratifi-
cation do they receive who fill the world with their
names?

NOTE 21.—*I can't for the life o' me get her to work.*
—When love makes an attack upon us, he never grants
us a truce till he has subdued the heart. He pursues
us to our occupations, to our amusements, to our clo-
sets, to our chambers. The whole mind is engrossed
by the object of our affections, and nothing gives us
pleasure but what has an immediate or indirect relation to it; while with the possession or loss of it we
connect our happiness or misery.

NOTE 22.—*How monie a scwove this angry nect.*—
The comforts that are found in a cottage often more
than counterbalance the toils and hardships attending
a life of poverty. Happy in the society of his wife
and family, blest with a healthy and vigorous constitution, industrious, temperate and innocent, what is
there in the nature of things that can improve his
condition?—When he becomes dissatisfied, it is when
he suffers his thoughts and imagination to roam
among scenes of grandeur—among luxuries and ex-
pensive pleasures—among the pompous pursuits and
amusements of the great—all of which are but so
many different modifications of splendid misery.

NOTE 23.—*At town, kurk, market, &c.*—A beautiful country girl makes a swain feel the force of her
charms wherever she beholds him: even " Sunday
shines no sabbath-day to him." At his very devotion
she points against him the artillery of her eye. In
short, she attacks him in every place, and, what is still
more cruel, when she has subdued his heart, often
plays with his passion, refusing her hand to the man
whose affections she has gained. She ought, however,

to observe, that a conqueror's glory is his lenity, and that her behaviour to her captives ought to be humane, if not generous; and not like that of a heathen victor, who dragged them at the wheels of his triumphant chariot.

NOTE 24.—*But as for Jwohnie, &c.*—In every Cumbrian village there is generally a rustic politician, who has established his political reputation among his countrymen by volubly discoursing on the state of the nation. At his leisure hours, he assembles a group of his neighbours round his fire-side, reads to them a provincial newspaper, comments upon every paragraph, reviews every transaction, points out all the errors of the ministry, and concludes by laying down a system of politics, which, in his opinion, would put the good things of life more within the reach of him and his countrymen, and enable them to dine and breakfast upon roast-beef and plum-pudding, instead of *cow'd lword* and oatmeal pottage.

NOTE 25.—*Our Parson says we bang'd them still.*— Nothing tends more to inspire valour than a knowledge of the achievements of our ancestors. A British soldier does not calculate the number of his enemies when he recalls to mind the battles of Crecy, Poictiers, and Agincourt. The study of history, particularly that of our own country, should therefore form an important part in the system of education. It will be the means of making us better patriots and better men; for he must be lost to every honourable feeling, whose loyalty and patriotism do not kindle at the names of a Falkland and a Montrose.

NOTE 26.—*The witch-weyfe begg'd in our backseyde.* In Cumberland, the word "backside" implies that space of ground which lies immediately behind the house; but, in its common acceptation, it conveys an idea *less refined,* and is particnlarly apt, in the mouth of a rustic, to wound the delicate ear of a fine lady, unacquainted with its provincial signification.

" A plain Cumberland farmer, being called to London on some law-business, took the opportunity to visit his landlord, whose residence was in Spring-Garden ; but not finding him at home, he entered into a chat with his daughter, a fashionable fine lady, who very civilly shewed him all the house, and was highly diverted with his remarks on every thing he saw.   In the course of his survey honest HODGE, casually resting his hand upon a certain *be-corked* part of her dress, exclaimed with much simplicity, while he popped his head out of the window,—' *The leevin surs, Miss ! what a muckle* BACKSIDE *you ha'e gotten !   It cannot seerly be aw your awn ?* i. e.   Wonderful, Miss !   what a spacious *backside* you have gotten !   It cannot surely be all your own ?   To this *plain* question a blush was the only answer which the lady returned.

NOTE 27.—*Whea was't that brak our landword garth ?*—To pillage a garden or an orchard is generally considered as a venial fault in a school-boy, and even praise is bestowed on the spirit with which the enterprize is executed.   But certainly every tendency to vice cannot be too soon corrected, as a disposition to virtue cannot be too soon formed.

NOTE 28.—*My Gwordie's whussle weel I ken.*—A life of severe labour does not depress the spirits of a peasant.   On his return to his cottage, after the toils of the day are over, he makes the woods and valleys vocal with his song, and " *the maid of his heart*" is generally the theme of his praise ; happy if his notes catch her ear, and happier still if they be heard with partiality, and incline her to meet with equal ardour the passion that dictated them.

NOTE 29.—*I mind what, &c.*—The pleasures which e aged enjoy are mostly supplied by memory.—

Amidst their increasing infirmities, they dwell with
peculiar delight on the days of their youth,—on those
happy hours when every object seemed gilded in the
brightest colours—when the heart was light, and all
around them joy and festivity. They are fond of re-
counting their juvenile frolics, exploits, and adventures ; and, when they are the narrators of their own
actions, a partiality for the subject generally leads to a
minuteness of detail that would weary every ear, except that of garrulous old age.

NOTE 30.—*Come, gie's thy hand Gabey.*—Modern
friendships are for the most part rather nominal than
real ; they profess much, but mean nothing. Their
language never comes from the heart. It is formal
and ceremonious, breaks out in fulsome compliments
and extravagant panegyric, and applies nearly the same
set of phrases to the genius and to the dunce, to the
wise and the foolish, to the virtuous, to the vicious.

NOTE 31.—*Our Ellek leykes fat bacon weel.*—There
is nothing fastidious in the appetite of a Cumbrian
rustic. His repast at noon generally consists of a
crowdy, a *cow'd-lword*, and a piece of bacon. If the
bacon be boiled, he sups the broth ; if fried, he pours
the melted fat among his pototoes. A *cow'd-lword* is
a cant name for a kind of pudding composed of oatmeal, tallow, suet, and hog's-lard ; which, to a rustic
palate, is always a luxurious dish. A *crowdy* is composed of oatmeal and the marrow of beef or mutton
bones, and is the introductory dish that takes off something from the keenness of a ploughman's appetite.—
When potatoes solely constitute the dinner, the mess
is more than usually large. After boiling some time,
they are beaten and mashed by a club-headed wooden
instrument, called a *tatoe-chopper*, and the whole mass
placed upon a platter. In the centre of this fuming
pile is a cavity filled with melted butter, or the fat of
bacon, into which every one at table merges his spoon

or knife loaden with potatoes.—The breakfast and supper generally consist of thick pottage, a kind of food made of oatmeal and water, and boiled till it become a viscous mass. The general bread of the peasantry is composed of barley fermented with dough, and baked in an oven. In the parts bordering on Scotland a sort of barley and oat-cakes, called *scons* and *hannocks*, are used.

NOTE 32.—*O, Wully! had tou nobbet been at Burgh Races!*—Some villages in Cumberland have their annual horse races. The prize is commonly a saddle or a bridle, and the horses that run for it are the property of the neighbouring *lairds* and farmers, and, without any previous discipline, are brought from the plough or cart to the course. When the race is finished, the country lads proceed with their sweethearts to the village ale-house, where they dance, sing, and drink, and talk over the adventures of the day. The races celebrated in this ballad took place on the 3rd of May, 1804, at Brough, or Burgh, a village in the neighbourhood of Carlisle, where our warlike Edward died on an expedition that was to decide the fate of Scotland. The prize was a silver cup, given by Lord Lowther, which, besides its intrinsic value, 50l., conferred an honour on the winner, equal at least to the garland of wild olive, worn by the victors at the Olympic games.

NOTE 33.—*There's ' How fens te, Tommy,' &c.*—When an honest Cumbrian rustic meets an acquaintance, he addresses himself to him by the warm interrogatory, " How fens te ?"—that is, How fares it with you in respect to health? If the person to whom the question is addressed be in a good state of health, the reply is, " I's gaily;" that is, I am in good health and spirits.

NOTE 34.—*Man thysel, Jemmy!*—Before the company depart from country horse-races, a stubborn contest with fists usually commences, in which the rustic warriors are animated by the praises of their sweethearts.—Sometimes a courageous rural dame takes an active part in the battle, and brings succour to her fainting lover by directing, with the vigour of an amazon, a few desperate blows against the nose of his antagonist.

35.—*I peep'd through the window, &c.*—The windows of many farm-houses in Cumberland are without shutters, and some of them without curtains ;—so, during a winter night, while the fire is cheerfully blazing, the whole family, and every part of the kitchen and furniture are revealed to the sight of every idle eves-dropper. The honest sweetheart, however, when he pays his nocturnal visit to his dulcinea, peeps through the glass with no other view than of gratifying his sight with the looks and motions of the fair object of his affections, happy if he find no rival participating in her smiles and conversation.

NOTE 36.—*Peer Dinah Dufton, &c.*—It must be an insensible heart that does not feel for those unfornate females who have been seduced from the paths of virtue and innocence, by the artifices of a set of men who are the disgrace of their country, and the pests of society.—The crime of seduction has spread general misery. It has even filled rural life (from which the poets of all ages have drawn their finest images of felicity) with complaint, disease, and wretchedness ; and if such be its effects, he is no friend to his country who does not wish that some effectual check were put to it.

NOTE 37.—*Says Ned, says he, the thimmel gi'e me.*—A village swain endeavours to ingratiate himself into the favour of his sweetheart by making her such presents as are within the reach of his humble circumstances, such as handkerchiefs, ribbons, gloves, thimbles, beads, &c. In all ranks of life, the cold virtue of savingness gives way to the warmth of love.

NOTE 38.—*There was ill gusty Jemmy, the Cocker o' Codbeck.*—A cocker is a character that a humane

N

mind will always contemplate with disgust. The diversion which he is fond of can only gratify a heart lost to virtue and divested of feeling, or attract an understanding feeble, and barren of ideas. When we see the profligate and squalid crowds that attend a country cock-fight, we cannot but feel for the honour of human nature, and regret that a practice, which has such a direct tendency to brutalize the heart, should be suffered to prevail in a country which can boast of the mildest government and the purest religion.

NOTE 39.—*But canny aul Cummerlan, &c.*—The traveller, whose object is amusement, and not the acquisition of money, may gratify his passion by a tour through Cumberland. Scenes of picturesque beauty will everywhere present themselves to his eye. Keswick, where mountains, rocks, precipices, and cataracts are contrasted with peaceful vales and placid lakes, has been justly called " *The Elysium of the North;*" for if Elysium is to be found upon earth, it must surely be in that happy vale, which Nature has so peculiarly distinguished by her bounties, and surrounded with such rich and magnificent scenery; and where may be found a race of men leading happy and peaceful lives, strangers to the follies, and unagitated by the passions, that fill the rest of the world with crimes and misery.

NOTE 40.—*We've Corby, &c.*—Corby Castle, by far the most delightful situation in Cumberland, (perhaps in the north,) stands on the banks of Eden, four miles from Carlisle. Its hanging woods of various hues, hoarse murmuring streams, stupendous rocks, echoing cells, and extensive walks, have so often been the traveller's theme, that any attempt at minute description might justly be deemed vanity in our author.

The present owner, HENRY HOWARD, Esq. has long been adding beauties to a place, where Nature seems to say—
  Behold me, man, in all my wild attire!

And while he, from every manly, patriotic, and virtuous principle, enjoys the confidence of the highest circles, his amiable lady is the idol of the tenantry and neighbouring villagers :—

Softening the pangs of sickness, want, and sorrow,
While thousands ruin seek in lewd excess,
And rob the wretched, Heav'n has plac'd beneath them.—R.A.

NOTE 41.—*Nin leyke thee curl fling the gavelick.*—
The brawny rustics of Cumberland are fond of athletic exercises. They sometimes make a trial of their strength by pitching the gavelick, or lever, and sometimes by lifting huge stones, almost equal in size and weight to that with which the might Hector forced the Grecian fortifications :—

" A pond'rous stone bold Hector heav'd to throw,
Pointed above, and rough and gross below :
Not two strong men th' enormous weight could raise,
Such men as live in these degen'rate days."—ILIAD.

NOTE 42.—*Then, Job, I mind at your kurn-supper.*
When a Cumbrian farmer has cut down his corn, he makes an entertainment, to which he invites the reapers and a few of his neighbours. This entertainment is called a *kurn* or *churn;* because a quantity of cream, slightly churned, was originally the only dish which constituted it. In the progress of modern luxury, other dishes have been added to this rural feast, and a rustic epicure may now riot amidst a profusion of pies, plum-puddings, and dumplings.

NOTE 43.—*And, Jeff, when met at Cursmass cairdins.*—In Cumberland, a succession of diversions, feasts, and merriments, distinguishes the holidays of Christmas. Of the different festive meetings which take place at that season, card-playing constitutes a considerable portion of the amusement ; and the cottage that can supply a stool, ashes-board, and a rush-light, has sufficient accommodations for a rustic card-player.

NOTE 44.—*I'll hev a young weyfe suin.*—A man, with his bosom inflamed with love, while his head is

crowned with the hoar of age, exhibits as strange a
phenomenon as the mountain that contains fire in its
bowels, while its summit is crowned with snow; and
when he leads a young woman to the altar, he is always subject to the ridicule of the world. But if it
be true, what the author of the " Valetudinarian's
Bath Guide" advances, that the breath of young girls
has a salubrious effect on the constitution of old men,
his marriage, at so late a period of life, ought to be rather adduced as an instance of mature wisdom than
of doating folly.

NOTE 45.—*A wee swope guid yell is a peer body's
comfort.*—A poor man's comforts and amusements are
confined within narrow limits; but, as narrow as they
are, there are those who would wish to contract them.
They would not only take from his dance and *merry
night,* but also his pot of ale at the village ale-houses,
where, after the labour of the day, he sometimes re-
laxes himself among companions of similar manners,
pursuits, and habits of life; and an indulgence certainly innocent, provided it be not carried to an excess
ruinous to himself and family. His life is a life of
labour, and often of distress. If he sometimes steal
from care and toil to the place " where nut-brown
draughts inspire," who can blame?

NOTE 46.—*The dang'rous yell-house kills monie brave
fellows.*—Moderate cups administer comfort to the heart,
open its springs, and keep up the spirit of social intercourse; but numerous are the evils which flow from
intemperate drinking. How many promising youths,
who, by their talents and genius, were capable of sus-
taining the dignity of the human character, has this
baleful habit sunk into insignificance and contempt, or
hurried to an untimely grave! How many bosoms,
formed for virtue and happiness, has it filled with guilt
and misery!—In the time of King Edgar, the vice of
drunkenness so much prevailed, that he endeavoured

to check it by limiting the number of ale-houses, and
ordered nails or pins to be fixed, at stated distances,
in the drinking cups and horns, by which marks the
drinkers were to regulate their draughts, or suffer
punishment. What effect these regulations produced '
at that time I do not know ; but I'm afraid that pins
and penalties would be feeble barriers against the vigorous draughts of a modern toper.

NOTE 47.—*We went owre to Deavie' clay-daubin.*—
In the eastern and northern parts of Cumberland, the
walls of houses are in general composed of clay, and
in their erection take seldom more than the space of a
day. When a young rustic marries, the highest ambition of his heart is to be the master of an humble
clay-built cottage, that might afford shelter to him and
his family. As soon as he has selected a proper site,
which usually borders on some moor that affords turf
and peat for fuel, he signifies his intentions to his
neighbours, who, on the appointed day, punctually
muster on the spot where the intended building is to
be raised, each individual bringing a spade and one
day's provisions along with them.—That every thing
might be done in order, and without confusion, a particular piece of work is assigned to each labourer.
Some dig the clay, some fetch it in wheelbarrows,
some water it and mix it with straw, and some heave
it upon the walls. The rustic girls, (a great many of
whom attend on the occasion,) fetch the water, with
which the clay is softened, from some neighbouring
ditch or pond. When the walls are raised to their
proper height, the company have plenty to eat and
to drink ; after which the lads and the lasses, with
faces incrusted with clay and dirt, take a dance upon
the clay-floor of the newly-erected cottage.

NOTE 48.—*See, deame, if we've got a swope whusky.*
Whisky, diluted with water, is the common beverage
of the rustic inhabitants of the north of Cumberland ;

and though their rum bottle may sometimes be exhausted, they seldom fail to be pretty well stocked (notwithstanding the vigilance of the exciseman) with contraband whisky.

NOTE 49.—*I' th' kurk-garth the clark caw'd his seale.*—" The kurk-garth, or church-yard, on a Sunday morning, (observes an ingenious friend,) is to the country people of Cumberland what the Exchange is to the merchants of London, and answers all the purposes of business or amusement, from whence general information is to be sent round the parish.—The *kurk fwoke*, or congregation, therefore, usually stop about the church-door, after the service is done, to hear these notices which are mostly given by the parish clerk, elevated upon a *thruff*, or flat tombstone, sometimes from a written paper, and sometimes taken verbally from the mouth of the party concerned. This latter mode, in the tone and dialect of an old formal psalm-singer, produces often a very curious effect, as is exemplified in the following notice, actually delivered a few years ago at the door of Stanwix church, near Carlisle :

Clerk.—Hea-a-z-yes ! This is to give nwotice, that there is to be, on Wednesday neist, at—(When ?)

Man.—Twelve.

Clerk.—Twelve of the clock precisely—(Whar ?)

Man.—Linstock.

Clerk.—At Linstock, near Rickarby, a sale of—— (What ?)

Man.—Esh for car-stangs.

Clerk.—A sale of esh wood, for car-stangs ; and if any body wants to ken aught mair about it, they mun apply to—(Wheay ?)

Man.—Thomas Dobson.

Clerk.—Thomas Dobson, clerk of Stanwix ; that is, Mister.—(Any thing mair ?)

Man.—Nay, that's aw.

Clerk.—Wa then, God save the King !—(How fend ye, Mister Ritson ? how fend ye ?)"

" This manner of making a public proclamation through the medium of a prompter, is by no means modern ; it occurs exactly in the second scene of the third act of ' The New Inn,' by Ben Johnson."

NOTE 50.—*The lads rubb'd her down wi' pez-strae.*— A Cumbrian girl, when her lover proves unfaithful to her, is, by way of consolation, rubbed with pease-straw by the neighbouring lads ; and when a Cumbrian youth loses his sweetheart, by her marriage with a rival, the same sort of comfort is administered to him by the lasses of the village.

GLOSSARY.

A

Abed, in bed
Abuin, above
Ae, one
Advisin, advising
Afwore, before
A-fit, on foot
Agean, against
Ahint, behind
A-horse, on horseback
Ail, to be indisposed
Aikton, a village near Wigton
Ajy, awry
Alang, along
Allyblaster, allabaster
Amang, among
Ambrie, pantry
Anent, opposite
Anunder't, under it
Anudder, another
Aroun, around
Ass-buird, ashes-board; a box in which ashes are carried
'At, contraction of that
Atomy, skeleton
Atween, between
Auld, old
Aunty, aunt

Aw, all
Awn, own
Ax, to ask
Ay! expression of wonder
Ayont, beyond

B

'Bacco, tobacco
Bairns, children
Bandylan, a female of bad character
Bang, to beat; an action of haste, as, " he com in wi' a bang"
Baith, both .
Bane, bone
Bailies, bailiffs
Bannocks, bread made of oatmeal, thicker than common cakes
Backseyde, the yard behind a house
Bashfu', bashful
Batter, dirt
Bawk, a cross beam
Behint, behind
Bein, being
Bet, a wager; beat
Bettermer, better
Beyde, to endure, to stay

Belder, to bellow, vocife-
  rate
Belsh, to emit wind from
  the stomach
Biggin, building
Bit, a small piece
Billy, brother
Bizen, (see shem)
Bleaken'd, blacken'd
Blate, bashful
Bleer-e'ed, blear-ey'd
Bleets, blights
Bleckell, Blackwell, a vil-
  lage near Carlisle
Blin, blind
Bluid, blood
Bluim, bloom
Blaw, blow
Blusteration, the noise of
  a braggart
Boggle, hobgoblin
Bout, a turn; action
Bodder, bother
Bowt, bought
Bonnie, pretty
Bow-hough'd, having
  crooked houghs
Brack, broke
Brag, boast
Braid, broad
Bran new, quite new
Brat, a coarse apron
Bray, to beat
Bravely, in a good state
  of health
Breer, briar
Breet, bright
Brees'd, bruis'd

Breeks, breeches
Breyde, bride
Brig, bridge
Brong, brought
Brunt, burnt
Brulliment, broil
Brast, burst
Buin, above
Buits, boots
Bumm'd, struck; beat
Bunc'd, an action of haste,
  as, "he bunc'd in amang
  us"
Buck up, to subscribe
Butter-shag, a slice of
  bread spread with butter
Butter-sops, wheat or oaten
  bread, soaked in melted
  butter and sugar
Bworn, born
Bwor'd, bor'd
Bygeane, bygone; past
Byre, cow-house

C

Cabbish, cabbage
Caff, Chaff
Cairds, cards
Carel, Carlisle
Canny, decent looking,
  well-made
Capper, one who excels
Car, cart
Carras, a shade, or cart-
  house, wherein carts are
  kept
Cat-witted, silly and con-
  ceited

Ceyder, cider

Chap, a general term for man, used either in a manner of respect or contempt

Chawk, chalk

Cheyde, chide

Chiel, a young fellow

Chimley, chimney

Chops, mouth

Claes, clothes

Clashes, tale-bearers

Clarty, miry

Claver, to climb

Cloggs, a sort of shoes, the upper part of strong hide leather, and the soles of birch or alder, plaited with iron

Cleed, to clothe

Cleek, to catch as with a hook

Click-clack, the noise that the pendulum of a clock makes in its vibrations

Clink, a blow

Clipt dinment, a thin, mean-looking fellow

Clipt and heel'd, properly dressed, like a cock prepared to fight

Cliver, clever

Cluff, a blow

Co', come or came

Cockin, cock-fighting

Cocker, a feeder or fighter of cocks

Com, came

Corp, corpse

Cow'd-lword, a pudding made of oatmeal and suet

Cowp, to exchange

Cowt, colt

Crack, to chat, to challenge to boast, or do any thing quickly, as, " I's dui't in a crack"

Crackets, crickets

Crammel, to perform any thing awkwardly

Crap, crept

Creyke, creek

Cronie, an old acquaintance

Croft, a field behind the house

Crouse, lofty, haughty

Cruds, curds

Cruin, to bellow, to hum a tune

Cud, could

Cudy Wulson, Cuthbert Wilson

Cuil, cool

Cummerlan, Cumberland

Cunn'd, counted

Curley pow, curled head

Cursinin, christening

Cursty, Christopher

Cursmas, Christmas

Curtchey'd, curtsey'd

Cutty, short

Cutten, cut down

Cutter'd, whispered

Cwoach, coach

Cwoals, coals
Cwoat, coat
Cwoley, a farmer's or shepherd's dog
Cwose-house, corse-house

D

Daddle, hand
Daft, half-wise, sometimes wanton
Daggy, drizzly
Dander, to hobble
Darrak, a day's labour
Dapper, neatly dressed
Darter, active in performing a thing
Dawstoners, inhabitants of Dalston, a village near Carlisle
De, do
Deame, dame
Deavie, David
Ded, or deddy, father
Dee, to die
Deeins, doings
Deef, deaf
De'il bin, devil take
Deet, died ; to clean
Deeth, death
Deetin, winnowing corn
Deyl'd, mop'd, spiritless
Deyke, hedge
Diddle, to hum a tune
Dis, does
Dispert, desperate
Dissnins, a distance in horse-racing, the eighth part of a mile

Divvent, do not
Doff, to undress
Don, to dress
Donnet, an ill-disposed woman
Downo, cannot, i.e. when one has the power, but wants the will to do any thing
Dowter, daughter
Douse, jolly, or sonsy-looking ; according to others, solid, grave, and prudent
Dozen'd, spiritless and impotent
Dub, a small collection of stagnant water
Dubbler, a wooden platter
Dui, do
Duir, door
Duin, done
Dud, did
Duds, coarse clothes
Dunch, to strike with the elbows
Dunnet, do not
Dung owre, knocked over
Durdem, broil, hubbub
Durtment, any thing useless
Dust, durdem, one of the many provincial names for money
Dwoated, doted

E

Ee, eye

Een, eyes
Efter, after
Eley, Alice
Eleeben, eleven
Ellek, Alexander
En, end
Eneugh, enough
Eshes, ash-trees

F

Fadder, father
Famish, famous
Fan, found, felt
Fash, trouble
Fares-te-weel, fares-thee-
 well
Fau't, fault
Faul, farm-yard
Faw, fall
Feace, face
Feale, fail
Feckless, feeble, wanting
 effect
Feight, fight
Fettle, order, condition
Feyne, fine
Fit, foot, fought
Fin, to find, to feel
Flacker'd, flutter'd
Flay, fright, to fright
Fleek, flitch
Flegmagaries, useless frip-
 peries of female dress
Fluir, or fleer, floor
Flyre, to laugh
Font, foolish
Forby, besides
Forret, forward

Fou, full
Fowt, a fondling
Frae, from
Frase, fray
Fratch, quarrel, to quarrel
Freeten'd, frightened
Freet, to grieve
Fremm'd, strange
Frostit, frosted
Frow, a worthless woman
Fuil, fool
Furbelows, useless silks,
 frills, or gauzes, of a
 female dress
Furst, first
Fuss, bustle
Fwoal, foal
Fworc'd, forc'd
Fwolk, folk
Fwurm, a form, a bench

G

Ga, to go
Gaen, gone
Gam, game
Gamlers, gamblers
Gammerstang, a tall awk-
 ward person, of bad gait
Gang, to go; a confede-
 rated company of infa-
 mous persons
Gar, to compel
Garth, orchard or garden
Gat, got
Gate, road or path
Gawn, going
Gayshen, a smock-faced,
 silly-looking person

o

Gear, wealth, money, the tackling of a cart or plough

Gev, gave

Git, get

Girn, grin

Girt, great

Gliff, glance

Glyme, to look obliquely, squint

Glowre, to stare

Glump'd, gloom'd

Gob, mouth

Gowd i' gowpens, gold in handfuls

Gowk, the cuckow; a thoughtless, ignorant fellow, who harps too long on a subject

Gowl, to weep

Graen, to groan

Graith'd, dressed, accoutered

Grandideer, grenadier

Grandy, grandmother

Granfadder, grandfather

Granson, grandson

Greace, grace

Greave, grave'

Greymin, a thin covering of snow

Grousome, grim

Greype, a three-pronged instrument for the purpose of cleaning cowhouses

Gulder, to speak amazingly loud, and with a dissonant voice

Gully, a large knife

Guff, a fool

Guid, good

Gurdle, the iron on which cakes are baked

Gwordie, George

H

Hack'd, won every thing

Ha'e, have

Hale, whole

Hallan, partition wall

Hantel, large quantity

Hankitcher, handkerchief

Hap, to cover

Hardleys, hardly

Hauld, hold, shelter

Havey-scavey, all in confusion

Hawflin, a fool

Haw, a hall

Hawf, half

Havver, oats

Hay-bay, hubbub

Heaste, haste

Hether-fac'd, rough-fac'd

Hee, high

Het, hot

Head-wark, head-ach

Helter, halter

Hed, had

Hes, has

Hev, have

Hirpled, limped

Hinmost, hindmost

Hing, hang

Hinney, honey
Hizzy, huzzy
Hod, hold
Hout ! pshaw !
Hotch, shake ; to shake
Howdey, a midwife
Hug, to squeeze
Hur, her
Hulk, a lazy, clumsy fellow
Hursle, to raise up the shoulders
Hunsup, scold ; quarrel

I

I', contraction of in
Ilk, or ilka, every
I's, contraction of I am
It 'll, contract, it will
Ither, other
Indie, East Indies
Iver, ever
Jaw, mouth
Jant, jaunt
Jen, or Jenny, Jane
Jeybe, jibe
Jobby, or Jwosep, Joseph
Jwoke, joke
John, or Jwohnie, John

K

Keale, broth
Ken-guid, the example by which we are to learn what is good
Keave, to give an awkward wavering motion to the body

Keek, to peep
Ken, to know
Kith, acquaintances
Kittle, to tickle
Knop, a large tub
Kurk, church
Kurk-garth, church-yard
Kurn, churn
Kye, cows

L

Lait, to seek
Laik, play ; to play
Laird, a farmer's eldest son, or one who already possesses laud
'Ill, contraction of will
Lal, little
Larnin, learning
Lanlword, landlord
Lant, a game at cards
Lanters, the players at lant
Lave, the rest
Lapstone, a shoemaker's stone, upon which he beats his leather
Latch, a wooden sneck, lifted sometimes with a cord, at other times with the finger
Lap, leapt
Leace, lace
Leady, lady
Leame, lame
Leate, late
Leane, alone
Leet, to meet with ; to alight

Leetsome, lightsome
Ledder, to beat
Lee, a lie
Leeve, live
Leather-te-patch, a plunging step in a Cumberland dance
Lig, to lie
Leethet'lass, Lewthwaite's lass
Lissen, to listen
Lish, active, genteel
Lonnin, a narrow lane leading from one village to another
Lock, a small quantity
Loff, offer
Loft, the upper apartment of a cottage
Lout, an awkward clown
Lowe, flame
Lowse, to untie
Lowp, a leap; to leap
Lug, pull; to pull
Lngs, ears
Luik, look; to look
Luim, loom
Luive, love
Lunnon, London
Lurry, to pull
Lwosers, losers
Lword, lord
Lythey, thick

M

Mair, more
Maister, master
Maist, most

Mak, make; to make
Mant, to stutter
Maks, sorts
Mangrel, mongrel
Man thysel, act with the spirit of a man
Mappen, may happen
Marget, Margaret
Marrow, equal; of the same sort
Mazle, to wander as stupified
Meade, made, made
Mess, indeed, truly
Meer, mare
Midden, dunghill
Mickle, large, much
Mid-thie, mid-thigh
Mid-neet, mid-night
Mittens, gloves
Moilin, pining
Mowdywarp, a mole
Monie, many
Mud, might
Muir, moor
Muin, moon
Mun, must
Muck, dung
Murry, merry
Munnet, must not
Mudder, mother
Mworn, morn

N

Nae or nee, no
Naigs, horses
Nar, near
Nattle, to strike slightly

Neef, fist
Neame, name
Neet, night
Neist, next
Ne'er ask, never mind
Neb, nose
New-fangled, new-fa-
  shioned
Neybor, neighbour
Neyce, nice
Nimmel, nimble
Nin, none
Nit, not
Niver, never
Nobbet, only
Nowt, cattle
Nowther, neither
Nuik, nook
Nwotish, or nwotice, no-
  tice

O

Oaners, owners
Oddments, articles of no
  great value
Odswings! a rustic oath
Offen, often
Onie, any
Onset, dwelling-house &
  out-buildings
On't, contraction of it
Or, ere
Open'd their gills, gap'd
  wide, and drank much
Ought, aught
Owre, over
Owther, either

P

Paddock rud, frog spawn
Pang'd, quite full
Parfet, perfect
Pat, put
Pate, head
Paut, to walk heavily
Paw mair, stir more; thus,
  "the cat will never paw
  mair," means, the cat
  will never stir more
Pech, to pant
Pee'd, one ey'd
Peer, poor
Pell-mell, quick
Peet, a fibrous moss used
  for fuel
Pennystones, stones in the
  form of quoits
Pez, pease
Piggen, a wooden dish
Pick, pitch
Pick'd the fwoal, foal'd
  before the natural time
Pleugh, plough
Pleace, place
Pleenin, complaining
Plack, a single piece of
  money
Plied, read his book
Potticary, apothecary
Poddish, pottage
Pops and pairs, a game at
  cards
Pow, to pull; the head
Prent, print
Prod, thrust
Pruive, prove

Puil, pool
Puzzen, poison
Punch, to strike with the feet
Pwoke, poke

R

Rattens, rats
Reape, rope
Rear, to rise; to rally
Reed, red
Reet, right
Reek, smoke
Reyder, rider
Rin, run
Royster'd, vociferated
Roughness, plenty; store
Row up, to devour
Ruddy, ready
Rust, rest; repose
Russlin, wrestling
Ruse, arose
Rwoar'd, roar'd
Rwose, rose

S

Sackless. — The original meaning of this word is innocent, guiltless; but it is now applied in the sense of feeble, useless, insignificant, incapable of exertion
Sae, so
Sair, sore
Sairy, poor
Sarvant, servant
Sal, shall

San, sand
Sampleth, sampler
Sark, shirt
Sarra, to serve
Sattle, a long seat
Sault, salt
Sceape-greace, a hair-brain'd, graceless fellow
Scalder'd, scalded
Scwores, scores
Sceap'd, escap'd
Scons, cakes made of barley meal
Scraffle, struggle
Schuil, school
Scotty kye, Scotch cows
Scribe of a pen, line by way of letter
Scrudge, squeeze
Seame, same
Seec, sick
Seape, soap
Sec, such
Seegh, sigh
Seer, sure
Sel, self
Seed, saw
Seeben, seven
Seevy, rushy
See't contract. see it
Seet, sight
Sen, or seyne, since
Seugh, ditch
Selt, sold
Seypers, those who drink to the last drop; immoderate drinkers
Seyde, side

Setterday, Saturday

Sha' not, shall not

Shearin, reaping

Shem and a bizen, a shame, and besides a sin ; the word bizen being apparently a corruption of " By a sin," i. e. besides a sin

Shoon, shoes

Shot, reckoning; freed from

Shuik, shook

Sheynin, shining

Shuffle, to scrape with the feet ; to evade

Shouder, shoulder

Shoul, shovel

Shottel, schedule

Shwort, short

Shwort-keakes, rich fruit cakes, which the Cumbrian peasants present to their sweethearts at fairs

Sinseyne, since that time

Skirl'd, scream'd

Sleas, aloes

Slape, slippery

Slink, slinge

Slea, sly

Slap, to beat

Smiddy, smithy

Smaw, small

Smuik, smoke

Smutty, obscene

Smudder, smother

Snaps, small round gingerbread cakes

Snowrin, snoring

Sneck, latch or catch of a gate or door

Snift'rin, sniffling

Sour-milk, butter-milk

Sonsy, lucky, generous

Sowdgers, soldiers

Souse, to plunge or immerge

Spak, spoke

Speyce, spice

Splet, split

Spot, a place of service

Spwort, sport

Spunky, sparkling

Spuin, spoon

Starken, to tighten

Steyle, stile

Steek, to shut

Strack, struck

Stule, stole

Stuil, stool

Stown, stolen

Stwory, story

Stuid, stood

Strae, straw

Stibble, stubble

Stan, stand

Streenin, straining

Strappin, tall

Stoun, a sudden and transient pain

Stoury, dusty

Stowter, to walk clumsily

Sticks, furniture

Struive, strove

Sud, should

Summet, something

Suin, soon
Sumph, blockhead
Sworry, sorry
Swapp'd, exchang'd
Swope, a sup
Swat, sit down
Sweyne, swine

T .

Ta'en, taken
Taistrel, scoundrel
Tane, the one
Tarn'd, ill-natur'd
Tearan, tearing; a "tearan fellow is a rough, hot-headed person, who drives every thing before him, regardless of danger and of consequences
Te, thee; to te-dui, to do
Teable, table
Teaylear, taylor
Telt, told
Teale, tale
Teaking, taking
Tease, to importune, to pester
Teyney, small
Tek, take
Tem, them
Teyme, time
Teydey, neat
Teugh, tough
Teasty, tasteful
Teydins, tidings
Thar or thur, these
Thoum, thumb

Throsale, a thrush
Thworn, thorn
Thurteen, thirteen
Thowt, thought
Thick, friendly
Theek'd, thatch'd
Thrang, throng
Threep, to argue; to aver
Threed, thread
Thropple, windpipe
Thie, thigh
Thimmel, thimble
Tig, to strike gently
Titty, sister
To't, to the
Tou's, thou art
Tou'll, thou wilt
Toddle, to walk unstably, as children
Top, or topper, of a good quality
To-mworn, to morrow
Trippet, a small piece of wood obtusely pointed with which rustics amuse themselves
Trimmel, tremble
Trouncin, beating
Trig, tight
Trinkums, useless finery
Tudder, the other
Tui, too
Tuik, took.
Tuith-wark, tooth-ache
Tummel'd, tumbl'd
Tuppence, two-pence
Twea, or twee, two
Twonty, twenty

U

Unket, strange, particular news

Unco, very

Uphod, uphold

V

Varra, very

Varmen, or varment, vermin

Vap'rin, vapouring

W

Wad, would

Waddn't, contract. would not

Wae, sorry

Wa, dang it! a mode of swearing

Waffler, waverer

Wale, choice

Wan, to win

Wanters, persons who want wives or husbands

War, worse; were

Wark, work

War-day, every day in the week, except Sunday

Warl, world

Watter, water

Waw, wall.

Weage, wage

Wee, diminutive

Wey! expression of assent; why

Weyfe, wife

Weyte, blame

Webster, or wobster, weaver

Whack, thwack

Whaker, Quaker

Whart, quart

Wheyte, quite

Whye, a heifer

Whope, hope

Whornpeype, hornpipe

Whurry, wherry

Whisht! hush!

Whinge, to weep

Wheezlin, drawing the breath with difficulty

Whinin, whining

Whitten, Whitehaven

Whore, where

Whif, a blast

Whietly, quietly

Whilk, which

Wussle, or wursle, to wrestle

Whuzzin, whizzing

Whissenday, Whit-Sunday

Whoal, hole

Whey-feac'd, smock-fac'd

Wi', or wid, with

Wide-gobb, wide-mouth

Win, wind

Windy, noisy

Winnings, money won

Worchet, orchard

Wordy, worthy

Worton, Orton, name of a village

Wots, oats

Wrang, wrong

Wull, will
Wulling willing
Wully, or Wulliam, William
Wunnet, contract. will not
Wum, to dwell

Y

Yad, a mare
Yable, able

Yeage, age
Yallow, yellow
Yat, a gate
Yek, oak
Yell, ale
Yen, one
Yer, your
Ye's, ye shall
Youngermer, younger persons

M. AND J. JOLLIE, PRINTERS.